Great Britain Board of Trade

Reports on the Volume and Effects of Recent Immigration

from eastern Europe into the United Kingdom

Great Britain Board of Trade

Reports on the Volume and Effects of Recent Immigration
from eastern Europe into the United Kingdom

ISBN/EAN: 9783337169848

Printed in Europe, USA, Canada, Australia, Japan

Cover: Foto ©Suzi / pixelio.de

More available books at **www.hansebooks.com**

REPORTS

ON THE

VOLUME AND EFFECTS OF RECENT

IMMIGRATION

FROM EASTERN EUROPE

INTO THE UNITED KINGDOM.

Presented to both Houses of Parliament by Command of Her Majesty.

LONDON:
PRINTED FOR HER MAJESTY'S STATIONERY OFFICE,
BY EYRE AND SPOTTISWOODE,
PRINTERS TO THE QUEEN'S MOST EXCELLENT MAJESTY.

And to be purchased, either directly or through any Bookseller, from
EYRE AND SPOTTISWOODE, EAST HARDING STREET, FLEET STREET, E.C., and
32, ABINGDON STREET, WESTMINSTER, S.W.; or
JOHN MENZIES & Co., 12, HANOVER STREET, EDINBURGH, and
90, WEST NILE STREET, GLASGOW; or
HODGES, FIGGIS, & Co., LIMITED, 104, GRAFTON STREET, DUBLIN.

1894.

Price 1s.

GENERAL CONTENTS TABLE.

(For a more detailed contents table with regard to the Memorandum of
the Labour Department, *see* p. 25.)

To the SECRETARY OF THE BOARD OF TRADE.

SIR,

I HAVE the honour to submit to you the accompanying reports which have been prepared in accordance with your instructions by Mr. Willis of the Statistical Department, and by Mr. Llewellyn Smith, the Commissioner for Labour, on the subject of alien immigration.

The object of these reports is fully explained in each of them as far as their special purpose is concerned, but as they have been prepared in connection with other reports on the same subject, which have already been presented to Parliament, it may be useful to explain the connection between the different reports and the extent of the ground which they cover collectively.

The reports have been prepared in consequence of instructions issued about the commencement of the Parliamentary session of 1893, when there were various demands for information as to the progress of alien immigration into this country, and the facts and practice as to immigration in foreign countries, particularly in the United States. The reports already presented to Parliament are those of Mr. Schloss and Mr. Burnett, and relate specially to the latter subject, the facts as to the amount of immigration into the United States and the law and practice of that country in the matter being fully set out.* Mr. Schloss and Mr. Burnett, it will be recollected, visited the United States specially for the purpose of their inquiries, and their reports are now well known.

The accompanying reports deal specially with different aspects of the alien immigration question at home. The first, that of Mr. Willis, is a summary of the statistics of the immigration itself, with references to the various sources of information where fuller details are to be found. The annual reports on emigration and immigration during the last few years have supplied full information on the subject from time to time: but these reports deal with emigration from the United Kingdom as well as immigration into it, and it is believed that in any case a

_____ _____ ._ __ _

* See "Reports to the Board of Trade on Alien Immigration."—(C. 7113. 1893.)

well-digested summary of the various facts from the beginning, and not dealing specially with the figures of a particular year, will be convenient to those taking an interest in the subject. Having myself given a good deal of personal attention to these statistics, I desire to draw attention to the able manner in which Mr. Willis has brought the facts together in a few short pages, and shown how the figures from a great variety of sources—the returns obtained privately from shipping companies in the continental passenger trade, the alien lists, the returns of the Jewish charitable organisations, the police reports from different parts of the country, the consular reports from continental cities, and finally the censuses of 1881 and 1891—all corroborate each other.

The other report now presented, that from the Labour Department, contains the result of many inquiries which have been made, not only by the Commissioner for Labour personally but by other members of the staff of the Department, especially by Miss Collet, one of the Labour correspondents. These inquiries related to the destination and condition of the immigrants after they landed, and the social and economic effects of their aggregation in certain centres of population in this country. Two of the topics specially dealt with are the competition of the immigrants in the boot and shoe manufacturing industry, and their competition with female labour generally, these two special topics, however, being so treated as to throw light on the whole subject.

Comparing the information now presented with that laid before the House of Lords Committee on Sweating some years ago, and similar information laid before the House of Commons Committee on Alien Immigration about the same period, I believe I am fully justified in saying that the information now furnished will add greatly to the general knowledge of the subject, and, in fact, complete the data necessary for judging as to the character and extent of the immigration in question, and the nature of the measures of regulation or restriction, if any, which may eventually be considered expedient.

As to the conclusions respecting policy which the facts stated in the various reports may suggest, no opinion is of course expressed. The sole object has been to obtain a record of facts, continuing and extending the information given a few years ago to the Committees of Lords and Commons above referred to, so that the public and Parliament may be prepared for any further discussion that may take place. I trust it will be found that no small success has been achieved, commensurate with the efforts which have been made to obtain that success.

In submitting these reports I would also beg leave to add that for the latest facts it will still be necessary to refer to the monthly returns and annual report on emigration and immigration issued by the Department. The immigration continuing, the facts are being added to month by month. But the monthly returns and annual report, it is hoped, will themselves be made more useful by the full and connected explanations given in these special reports.

I have, &c.

(Signed) R. GIFFEN.

Commercial, Labour, and Statistical
  Departments, Board of Trade.
    May, 1894.

STATISTICAL REPORT.

To the Controller-General of the Commercial, Labour, and
Statistical Departments of the Board of Trade.

SIR,

THE following pages are intended as a kind of *compte
rendu* of the progress made with an inquiry, which has now
proceeded for some years, as to the movement of persons into
and out of the United Kingdom, so far as affecting the character
and magnitude of the foreign element in the population of these
isles. Much of the information collected has been published in
the annual reports on emigration and immigration laid before
Parliament in the last four years, but what is here proposed
is to give a summary account of the statistical material which is
now at the command of those investigating the subject of alien
immigration.

Origin and Objects of the Inquiry.

About the year 1886 public interest in the number of foreign
workers resident in this country became prominently manifested
as a result mainly of the attention devoted to the conditions of
labour in the East End of London. Statements were made to
the effect that a colony had sprung into existence here, and was
receiving continual accretions, of foreign labourers with a far
lower standard of comfort than English workmen had set up
for themselves, and content to accept low wages and long hours
of work as the price of finding a refuge in this country, and that
these repeated incursions of new arrivals, treading on the heels
of their predecessors before these had time to bring themselves
into line with their English fellow-workers, were responsible
largely for the evils set down to what was called " sweating."
Demands began to be made in the country and in Parliament
that the Government should restrict or control the immigration
of "destitute aliens." But this obviously could not be considered without a basis of well-ascertained facts capable of
numerical statement. The latest official statistics, however, were
those furnished by the census of 1881. These census figures,
analysed so as to show the nationalities, occupations, and distribution of foreigners resident in this country, were set out in
a series of tables published early in 1887 as an appendix to a
departmental memorandum explaining the absence of official
records of the number of passengers coming to the United
Kingdom from Europe. With this memorandum there was also
published a report by Mr. Burnett, Labour Correspondent of the
Board of Trade,—based on personal investigation in the East
End of London, and communications from trade officials in

A

other parts of the country,—on the dimension which the movement of foreign immigration appeared then to have attained. It was known that the immigrants in question were in the main Russian or Polish Jews, with perhaps, also, to a certain extent, Germans. But the census of 1881 showed less than 15,000 Russians and Poles as resident in the whole of England and Wales. Some years, however, had elapsed since that date, and there was evidence both from residents in the East End and from the reports of the Jewish Charitable Boards (to be referred to again below) that there had been, in the interval, a considerable inflow of persons of these nationalities.

Evidence to the same effect was given before two committees appointed in 1888, one (a Committee of the House of Lords) on "the Sweating System," and the other (a House of Commons Committee) on "Emigration and Immigration—Foreigners." This latter committee drew attention to the absence of official statistics on the subject of foreign arrivals in this country, and included the following among the recommendations appended to their report :—

(1.) "That measures should be adopted to secure a complete annual record of the number of alien steerage and deck passengers arriving and departing at the ports of the United Kingdom from and to ports in Europe, and that such annual record should be laid before Parliament."

(2.) "That measures should be adopted to provide for a record of the names, sexes, ages, occupations, nationalities, and destination of all alien steerage and deck passengers arriving at ports in the United Kingdom, and not in possession of through tickets to other countries."

Connexion of the Board of Trade with the Subject.

The department of Government to occupy itself with the consideration of these recommendations was naturally the Board of Trade, not only because the subject was one involving an important "labour" question, but also because the Board were already charged with the duty of collecting and reporting on statistics of the outward and inward flow of population between this country and places out of Europe. This duty was taken over by the Board from the Emigration Commissioners in 1873, with the administration of the Passengers Acts. The primary object of these Acts was to secure the safety and well-being of those passengers by sea known as "emigrants" in the ordinary sense of the word ; the furnishing, therefore, by the masters of vessels of lists of passengers—from which the emigration statistics are compiled—was incidental only to the machinery for carrying out these Acts, and the completeness of the lists was at first restricted by legal interpretations of the words "passenger" and "passenger ships" as used in the original Acts. In course of time, however, by alterations of law and practice, the lists were made to include all outward passengers to places " out,of Europe and not bordering on the Mediterranean Sea," and similar lists were also obtained for inward passengers arriving from the same countries. Obviously, then, there were here ready to hand important figures to supplement any that might be obtained as to movement between this country and Europe. Indeed, the latter figures could hardly be read to any useful meaning without the former. It was essential to know how many of the foreign arrivals from Europe in this country were merely passing through on their way to America, and the number of these foreign trans-migrants was included in the Emigration Returns.

Steps taken to obtain information.

But for ascertaining the numbers arriving and departing from and to European countries, there was no machinery available like that of the Passengers Acts, and the police information obtained in many countries through the passport system was wanting in England. As regards an exact account of the kind contemplated by the Committee of aliens leaving this country for Europe, it was found impossible to require this information from masters of ships without the enactment of a new law for the purpose. No such legislation has been in fact proposed, and there is do doubt that in view of the immense volume of passenger traffic with Europe, and the difficulties which would be occasioned by the short duration of the voyage, the carrying out of any legislation of the kind indicated would probably entail very considerable expense and vexatious interference with traffic. For the inward branch of the movement, however, recourse was had to an Act of 6 William IV. (c. 11), which provided, *inter alia*, that masters of all ships arriving " from foreign parts " should, under a penalty for non-compliance, hand in to the Customs authorities a written statement of the number of aliens (if any) on board, specifying their names, rank, occupation, and description. This Act had fallen into desuetude at most ports with the abandonment of the passport system, and at the time when the Committee on " Emigration and Immigration (Foreigners) " took evidence on the subject, it was found that the regular supply of nominal lists of incoming aliens as required by the Act was only enforced at the port of London, lists in partial compliance with the Act being also obtained at Hull, Hartlepool, and Leith. The Act itself, however, had never been repealed, and it was decided to bring it again into active operation so far as was necessary to obtain an account of the number of alien arrivals from Europe of the class with which the inquiry was concerned. Arrangements have accordingly been made, under which the alien lists referred to have been obtained since May 1890 from Aberdeen, Belfast, Bristol, Dover, Dublin, Folkestone, Glasgow, Goole, Grangemouth, Granton, Greenock, Grimsby, Harwich, Hull,

Kirkcaldy, Leith, Liverpool, London, Middlesborough, Newcastle, North Shields, South Shields, Sunderland, and West
Hartlepool, to which Southampton was added in November
1891, and Newhaven in September 1892, these ports, 26 in all,
of which 20 are on the east and south coasts, being all those
needing to be considered with reference to this immigration.

At Dover, Folkestone, Harwich, Southampton, and Newhaven,
where what may be called the "ferry-traffic" with the continent
is especially large, and obviously includes a very large proportion of persons of a quite different class from that contemplated in the inquiry, it has been thought sufficient that
alien lists should be furnished only for deck passengers and
those proceeding by rail as third-class passengers. At Hull,
West Hartlepool, Grimsby, and Leith large numbers of foreigners
are constantly arriving to at once proceed by rail across this
country and embark for America, and at these ports, therefore,
in respect of such alien immigrants as are actually in possession
of through tickets to other countries a return showing only the
total numbers of adults and children is accepted as sufficient,
detailed lists being, however, required of all alien arrivals not
holding such tickets.

In addition to other means by which care is taken to ensure
the accuracy of the lists furnished, it may be mentioned that
vessels—to a certain proportion of the total number arriving
each month at any port with aliens on board—are selected without warning and at irregular intervals for an actual count by
the Customs boarding officers, of the total number of alien passengers carried, and the result is compared with the alien list
previously prepared and handed in by the master, the latter
being required to explain any discrepancies discovered.

Further, with reference to aliens arriving at the port of
London from Hamburg, Bremen, and elsewhere, very full
particulars, apart from the alien lists, have been supplied for
the past three years by an examining officer of Customs, specially
assigned to the duty of inspecting and reporting on these arrivals. This officer, in his reports, details the information obtained
(generally with the assistance of an interpreter), on personal
visits to each ship on its arrival. Different features of the
movement have been from time to time specially dealt with, but
in general the reports have set out the total number of aliens on
board, distinguishing the number of men, women, and children,
and stating, so far as ascertainable, the number of Russian and
Polish Jews and members of other nationalities, frequently adding
also the names and occupations of the several alien passengers,
with the amount of money in their possession, and the addresses
to which they intend to proceed. The same officer has also,
at the request of the Board of Trade, been directed to visit, on
two or three occasions, the chief ports of arrival for foreign
immigrants on the east coast, and with the experience gained

in London has tested the accuracy of the returns of aliens furnished at these ports.

The result of these various checks and tests is to leave no doubt that the alien lists are substantially accurate.

It may be mentioned that the newspaper reports which have appeared from time to time—especially in the latter part of 1890 and in 1891 of the arrival of batches of Russian and Polish Jews in apparently destitute circumstances at Tilbury, St. Katharine's Dock, or elsewhere, have been investigated, and in no case have they been found to refer to immigrants who were not already included in the returns obtained by the Board of Trade under the arrangements which have been explained.

On the other hand, the alien lists no doubt include many persons who do not come within the scope of the inquiry, who are by no means "destitute," and are in fact ordinary travellers for business or pleasure. The corrections to be applied in this direction will be referred to subsequently.

The lack of any returns corresponding to the alien lists for foreign passengers outwards to the Continent has been stated above, and is very serious when it is desired to arrive at the balance of foreign immigrants who remain and become resident here. It has been sought, therefore, to throw light on the question by obtaining a numerical account of the total movement of passenger traffic outwards and inwards between this country and the Continent of Europe, and for this purpose returns of persons conveyed in each direction have been sought from and courteously furnished by the English railway companies carrying such passengers, by the Belgian Government (in respect of the Belgian State Mail Packets), and by the various shipping companies and private firms engaged in the traffic. It would not have been possible from these various sources to obtain complete returns of the nationality of passengers, but of the total number carried a practically complete account has been compiled which is of the greatest service.

Further, watch has been kept on the westward Jewish movement at its source and in its progress to Continental ports, and information has been obtained on the subject through the Foreign Office from H.M. Consuls at European ports, with especial reference to the existence and extent of any emigration to the United Kingdom of persons apparently destitute.

Finally, the reports of the Jewish Boards of Guardians and other charitable institutions have furnished another method of feeling the pulse of the current, while some information as to the means possessed by alien immigrants and their distribution throughout the country has been gained by inquiries made of the police in the chief towns of the kingdom.

These methods of inquiry, for which the Board of Trade are mainly responsible, constitute together the apparatus by which it has been sought, without applying to the Legislature for further powers of a more or less inquisitorial character, to keep a constant watch on the number of foreigners coming here from time to time from Europe. There is, however, much further valuable information on the subject as to a particular date—April 1891—available only within the past few months, in the tabulated results of the last census, to which reference will also be made subsequently.

Results of the Inquiry.

The means, then, now available for procuring continuous or periodical information having been explained with their limitations, it remains to review and interpret the results obtained.

1. Total balance of movement of Aliens inwards.

It will be convenient to take first the figures of the total movement of passengers into and from the United Kingdom. For intercourse with European countries we have the unofficial but practically complete figures obtained from the shipping companies and other passenger carriers, as described above, and for non-European countries we have the official returns made under the Passengers Acts. Combining these, we have a full account of the inward and outward movement to and from these shores, and are thus enabled to arrive at the balance of emigration or immigration resulting on the whole to this country. Without repeating the details given in the annual reports, we may here set out the totals for 1890-1-2-3, which are as under :—

—	1890.	1891.	1892.	1893.
Total number of passengers outwards from the United Kingdom :—				
To Europe - - - - -	392,925	418,003	405,998	395,362
„ other countries - -	315,980	334,543	321,397	307,633
Total outwards - - -	708,905	752,546	727,395	702,995
Total number of passengers inwards to the United Kingdom :—				
From Europe - - -	450,514	504,445	490,165	468,642
„ other countries - -	155,910	151,369	143,747	141,054
Total inwards - - -	606,424	655,814	633,912	609,696
Balance outwards -	102,481	96,732	93,483	93,299

Now it may be said that this balance outwards is made up, and more than made up, by the British and Irish who left the United Kingdom, the native emigration from this country in the years mentioned having reached numbers considerably in excess of the figures given above, and that this excess represents the contrary or inward balance of foreigners coming here to remain. And this is true to a certain extent. But it is important to observe that in considering this point it is not the *gross* but the *net* native emigration that must be taken into account; *e.g.*, in 1893, for every 100 persons of British and Irish origin who sailed for places out of Europe 49 came back, and those persons who go to and fro on business or pleasure must of course be omitted from the calculation of the number of natives permanently leaving this country. Referring again, then, to the annual reports we find the *net* number of emigrants (exclusive of foreigners) from this country to places out of Europe to have been 110,218 in 1890, 118,096 in 1891, 114,972 in 1892, and 109,090 in 1893.* If, then, we assume that the number of British and Irish going to the Continent is on the whole approximately balanced by the number returning from the Continent, we may deduct from these last figures the outward balances given in the above table, and treat the remainders as the *gross maxima* for the number of *aliens* who have come to this country to remain. These work out as under :—

1890 -	- 110,218 −	102,481 = 7,737
1891 -	- 118,096 −	96,732 = 21,364
1892 -	- 114,972 −	93,483 = 21,489
1893 -	- 109,090 −	93,299 = 15,791

From these gross figures an important deduction is at once to be made from the fact that the numbers used above for passengers brought from Europe include, and do not distinguish, foreign seamen who come to this country as passengers and ship again as crews, and who are thus counted inwards and not outwards. These are, however, shown separately in the Alien Lists from 1891 onwards, (though unfortunately we have not got complete figures for 1890), and numbered 9,797 in 1891, 10,349 in 1892, and 9,760 in 1893. Deducting these, we get as the balance of foreigners of all classes that arrived here, possibly for settlement, the numbers 11,567 in 1891, 11,140 in 1892, and 6,031 in 1893.

On the other hand, it is known that, contrary to the assumption temporarily made above, there is a small amount of British and Irish emigration viâ continental ports. The figures are given in the annual reports and were 1,405 in 1891, 1,113 in 1892, and 254 in 1893. Taking this movement into account, the foreign balance inwards would have to be correspondingly increased.

* These figures are inclusive of the (relatively small) number of passengers between this country and places out of Europe whose nationality was not distinguished in the passenger lists. If we assume that such persons may be distributed between native and foreign passengers to and from this country in the same proportion as those emigrants and immigrants whose nationality is given, the above figures for the *net* native emigration, and, by consequence, the number of foreign immigrants on balance subsequently deduced therefrom, would be diminished by 920 in 1891, 948 in 1892, and 807 in 1893.

Certain further corrections would no doubt need to be made for complete accuracy. Of one of these some measure has been given (see *note* on page 7) ; the rest are of small moment, and, operating in contrary directions, may be set against one another. On final balance therefore we may conclude, with approximate accuracy, that the whole foreign movement into the United Kingdom resulted in an addition to the alien population resident in this country of about 12,000 persons in 1891, of rather less than 11,500 in 1892, and of something under 6,000 in 1893.

2. *Alien Lists.*

The nature and contents of these lists have been fully explained above, and the most important numerical results collected from them will alone be here stated as briefly as possible, the full details being given in the tables appended to the annual reports. Complete figures for all the ports concerned and for the whole year are not available for 1890. In 1891 the number of aliens returned on the lists as passengers " *en route* to America and elsewhere" was 98,705, while those not so shown numbered 38,067 : in 1892 the corresponding numbers were 93,801, and 32,486 respectively ; while in 1893 the known trans-migrants were 79,518 in number, and the remainder 33,188.[*] Apart from the fact that many of those not holding through tickets yet re-book at once to places out of Europe, while others go on to America shortly by the assistance of friends or relief societies, it appears from these figures that the vast majority of those entered on the Alien Lists have taken their passages from home to America via England, and are therefore merely transient visitors to this country. These then form part of the foreign emigrants to non-European countries who are enumerated in the returns obtained under the Passengers Acts, and who numbered 112,275 in 1891, 107,351 in 1892, and 95,123 in 1893. They have been counted in the figures used above for the volume of outward movement and form no part, therefore, of the net inward balance with which we are dealing.

Turning, then, to the gross figures made up from the Alien Lists of those " not stated to hold through tickets to other countries," it is to be observed that these include the foreign seamen referred to above, who should, as already explained, be omitted for our present purpose. Making this deduction, the number of foreign arrivals shown in the Alien Lists who have to be here considered becomes 28,270 for 1891, 22,137 for 1892, and 23,599 in 1893.

---

[*] In these and subsequent figures from the Alien Lists of 1893, the number of immigrants recorded at Newhaven is omitted, as the corresponding figures for earlier years are not available. This omission is of small importance, as the route is not found to have been one adopted by the class of persons with which our inquiry is concerned.

The diminished numbers in 1892 formed the subject of comment in the annual emigration report for that year, and it was explained that passenger traffic by sea had shown a general diminution in consequence of the outbreak of cholera in Western Europe and the sanitary precautions thereupon adopted at the seaports. Similar restrictions operated also in 1893.

It is important to have the means of analysing still further the current of foreign immigration measured by these figures, and the most important questions that arise are : Of what nationalities are these immigrants ? From what ports in Europe do they embark ? To which of our ports do they come ? and the details given in the Alien·Lists enable answers to be given on these points.

The chief question, that as to nationalities, is best responded to by the following short table showing—

"The number of aliens, other than seamen, that arrived in the United Kingdom from European ports in 1891, 1892, and 1893, and were not stated to hold through tickets to other countries."

—	1891.	1892.	1893.
Russians and Poles - - -	12,607	7,538	7,721
Norwegians, Swedes, and Danes -	4,647	4,367	4,597
Germans - - - -	5,817	5,765	6,562
Dutch - - - - -	911	839	880
French - - - - -	1,453	910	977
Italians - - - -	734	783	641
Other nationalities - - -	2,104	1,935	2,221
Total - - -	28,270	22,137	23,599

Of these nationalities we know from the observation of our own Customs' Officers and the reports of Her Majesty's Consuls (*see below*), that the Scandinavian contingent and to a great extent the German, are made up of emigrants who go on to America. For the rest, other than Russians and Poles, the figures are small. The French too are notoriously a nation whose members leave home only to return again, and not to become permanent settlers abroad. This may be said, speaking generally, of the Dutch also, to judge from the small extent of their emigration out of Europe, the gross numbers for which (*i.e.*, without allowing for immigration) only amounted on the average for 1886–91 to 4,730 annually out of a population of over 4½ millions.

It is then the Russian and Polish element on which our attention may be concentrated. Of these immigrants, the majority have arrived at London, and, till the autumn of 1892, came for the most part from Hamburg, though since the disturbance of traffic then occasioned by the cholera outbreak, Bremen has

become the chief continental port of departure for this country.
For the port of London we have from the Alien Lists four
years' figures as to nationalities. In round numbers, 7,000
Russian and Polish Jews not having through tickets elsewhere
came to London in 1890, 9,700 in 1891, 5,600 in 1892, and
5,400 in 1893. Thus in 1891 (we have not got the complete
figures for 1890) of all the immigrants into the United Kingdom
of this description, London accounted for 77 per cent., in 1892
for 74 per cent., and in 1893 for 70 per cent., approximately
three-fourths, that is to say, in each year.

The remaining fourth was thus distributed :—

—	1891.	1892.	1893.
Arrived at Grimsby - - -	1,112	666	863
„ Hull - - -	504	499	933
„ Hartlepool, West - -	488	324	75
„ Tyne Ports - - -	104	48	43
„ Leith and Grangemouth -	164	113	109
„ Other Ports - - -	559	301	291

Of the total number of these Russians and Poles coming to
this country, all but 5 per cent. in 1891, and all but 7 per cent.
in 1892, came from Hamburg, and the immigrants of this nationality formed, in 1891, 76 per cent., and in 1892, 64 per cent., of
all the aliens (not being seamen and not known to be trans-
migrants) shown by the lists to have come here from Hamburg. In 1893, 41 per cent. of these Russians and Poles came
from Bremen, and only 37 per cent. from Hamburg. Of the
remainder 921, or 12 per cent., came from Amsterdam, Antwerp,
and Rotterdam.

Of the total number of 7,721 Russians and Poles (not known
to be trans-migrants) who arrived in this country in 1893, 4,164
were men, 2,023 women, and 1,534 children, i.e., in every 100
such immigrants there were 54 men, 26 women, and 20 children.
The corresponding per-centages in 1892 were 57, 26, and 17,
and in 1891 they were 55, 25, and 20. This proportion of children is much higher than for immigrants of other nationalities,
among whom they were found to bear a ratio of from 6 to 7 to
every 100.

These Russo-Polish immigrants are frequently classed as
" destitute." There is no doubt from the evidence of the consuls
who have visited them at the ports of embarkation, and of the
Custom House officers who see them on their arrival, that they
do in the main present a pitiable appearance on landing. There
is no complete official inspection attempted to discover the
means they possess. However, the officer of Customs previously
referred to as charged with the duty of personally visiting and
reporting on vessels arriving in the port of London with these

passengers, has obtained a considerable amount of information as to their means and intended destinations, with the result which may be stated as given in the Report issued in 1892 : " The immigrants have been found to include persons formerly " resident in London returning from visits to the Continent, " domestic servants coming to situations for which they had " already been engaged, as well as wives and families on their " way to join men already settled here : a considerable number " too were found to possess sums of money, rising in some in- " stances to 30l. and over "—these sums, it may be stated, being produced to the officer himself,—" which removed them from " the class of 'destitute' persons : further, some, though not in " possession of through tickets, intended to at once proceed to " America, South Africa, or Australia." It is however clear, so far as such examination has been possible, that in the great majority of cases the resources possessed on arrival are extremely scanty.

3. Jewish Boards of Guardians, &c.

Inquiries have not shown that these people have to any great extent become chargeable to our poor-law authorities, but it appears from the reports of Jewish charitable societies that these bodies extend assistance to a considerable number. Wherever possible this assistance takes the form of sending the applicants away from the United Kingdom, either on to America or back to their original homes. In this way the " London Jewish Board of Guardians " with the " Russo-Jewish Conjoint Committee," removed about 2,500 persons from London in each of the years 1892 and 1893, and more than 2,000 in 1891. This action, carried on as it is on so large a scale, considerably diminishes the numbers of the foreign Jewish colony. It must be explained however, that the persons so sent away were not all recent arrivals some having, in fact, been resident here for a considerable time, so that it is difficult to gauge the exact effect produced by these removals from this country between any given dates.

The statistics of the work done by the London Jewish Board of Guardians, with the Russo-Jewish Conjoint Committee—the chief of the charitable agencies here spoken of—are available for a considerable period, and may be referred to as throwing light upon the extent of destitution among these immigrants, who form the great majority of the applicants.

A summary view of the operations of the two bodies mentioned (taken together) is given in the following table, as to which it is to be noted that " new applications " are not confined to those made by new arrivals in this country, though these form the great majority of such applications.

Years.	Number of Applications for Relief (Cases).	Cases Relieved.	
		Total Number.	New Cases only.
1884 - - - - -	3,406	3,147	1,423
1885 - - - - -	3,692	3,514	1,656
1886 - - - - -	4,648	4,290	2,053
1887 - - - - -	3,536	3,434	1,296
1888 - - - - -	4,098	3,820	1,596
1889 - - - - -	3,657	3,309	1,209
1890 - - - - -	3,960	3,603	1,524
1891 - - - - -	5,340	4,912	2,458
1892 - - - - -	6,249	5,700	2,682
1893 - - - - -	6,587	6,083	2,869

Here the large figures of 1886 are balanced by the small number of 1887, and apart from this fluctuation the most noteworthy point is the considerable increase in 1891, maintained also in 1892 and 1893.

4. Statements of Police Authorities.

Since the end of 1890 inquiries have been annually addressed to the police authorities of the chief towns throughout the kingdom for information as to the existence of any colony of indigent foreign Jews in the towns under their supervision, and if any such existed, whether it had recently increased or not. The replies have disclosed the existence of such a colony in Leeds, Manchester, Liverpool, and Birmingham, though, except perhaps in Leeds, on a very small scale. The report from *Leeds* for 1891 stated that there appeared to have been an increase during the year of about 440 Russian and Polish Jews. For 1892 the report was to the effect that though the existence of cholera on the Continent had latterly checked the flow of this immigration, yet the total Jewish population of the town had apparently been added to within the year by about 1,500; it was further stated, "There is great poverty among them." At the beginning of the present year it was reported that a further influx of indigent Russian and Polish Jews took place in 1893. On the other hand the reports from *Manchester*, though referring to an increase in the number of persons of this class that arrived in 1891, state that such immigration fell off considerably in 1892 and again in 1893. From *Liverpool* it was reported at the beginning of this year that there were 19 families of destitute Russian and Polish Jews resident in the city. The reports furnished by the Chief Constable at *Birmingham* have contained statements of the number of alien Jews relieved by the Jewish Board in that town. These numbered 412 in 1891, 422 in 1892, and 459 in 1893. From Glasgow, Edinburgh, Newcastle-on-Tyne, Hull, Sheffield, Cardiff, Swansea, and Brighton reports have come as to the existence of immigration of the kind in question, but the numbers given of those who remain in these places are very small. The reports received each year from Bolton, Bradford, Bristol, Burton-on-Trent, Darlington, Derby, Hastings, Leicester, Merthyr Tydfil, Northampton, Nottingham, Oldham, Oxford, Plymouth, Portsmouth, Preston, Reading, South Shields, Stafford, Stockton, Sunderland, Wigan, and Wolverhampton were all to the effect that there are no destitute aliens, or very few, resident in these towns.

5. *Information derived from H.M. Consuls in Europe.*

Early in 1890, shortly after the inception of this inquiry, reports were obtained, through the Foreign Office, from H.M. consuls at European ports as to the existence of any emigration of destitute persons from within their districts likely to be directed to the United Kingdom, and similar reports have since been furnished annually. The reports from Copenhagen and from the Scandinavian ports state that the emigration thence to the United Kingdom is of persons who are by no means destitute, and who for the most part go to Hull, Leith, or London, on their way to the United States or Canada. The reports from other places in the north of Europe all speak of the westward stream of emigration from Russia as directed to Hamburg, or (latterly) Bremen. The reports from Hamburg refer to the fact that the bulk of intending emigrants arriving at that port take ship direct for America, while some cross to England to embark at Liverpool; some again, no doubt,—and these, it is said, appear to be in many cases fairly described as destitute,—take the shorter voyage to England with no immediate intention of proceeding beyond.

The statements received from other European ports are to the effect that no such emigration to the United Kingdom exists as that referred to, and this negative testimony is valuable as showing that no movement of this kind has gone on by any route which has escaped attention.

It is clear, then, that foreign immigration from Europe into this country is only part of a large movement of emigration westward from European countries, partly the ordinary efflux of the inhabitants of long-settled lands on their way to try their fortune in new countries, but partly also, of late years, made up of those escaping from the religious persecution to which they are subjected in their own homes.

Of this stream a branch takes its course *viâ* the United Kingdom, leaving here a certain residuum, principally of the Jewish refugees, unable at once to proceed further.

The fact that it is America which is the country affected to a greatly preponderating extent by this transference of population, will be made clear from the following figures, taken from the United States records, showing the number of Scandinavian,

Russian, Polish, German, and of Austrian and Hungarian immigrants into that country in each year from 1881 onwards:—

Years (ended 31st Dec.)	Norwegians, Swedes, and Danes.	Russians (other than Poles).	Poles.	Germans.	Austrians and Hungarians.
1881	91,810	8,513	6,283	249,572	28,193
1882	100,379	18,205	4,246	232,263	29,917
1883	63,638	15,014	2,151	184,389	30,236
1884	45,556	15,529	4,362	155,529	31,396
1885	39,070	16,951	3,101	107,908	25,637
1886	52,715	20,820	6,306	86,301	40,116
1887	78,863	25,815	4,360	111,324	39,087
1888	74,779	37,353	5,402	106,975	41,065
1889	51,048	33,487	4,806	95,965	42,170
1890	53,315	40,922	19,743	96,514	63,119
1891	62,935	73,271	31,301	123,438	70,711
1892	65,960	52,334	27,013	118,400	69,630
1893	60,197	51,497	6,122	89,603	65,878

The figures, it is to be noted, are not those of all inward
passengers, but refer only to those aliens who are believed by
the American authorities to have the intention of permanently
settling in the United States. Not only are they, taken as a
whole, far larger than those which we have reviewed of the
number of foreign immigrants who come to this country, but
this is true also of the nationalities with which our inquiry is
specially concerned. It is noteworthy that with a diminution
in German immigration, and while the Scandinavian element
is also either stationary or diminishing, there has been, in the
main a large increase among Russians, Poles, and Austrians and
Hungarians. The number of Russian and Polish immigrants,
which was under 15,000 in 1881, was over 100,000 in 1891.

Reference may here be made to the small number of foreign
emigrants from the United Kingdom to America who are
rejected by the United States' authorities as unfit settlers
according to their Immigration Laws, and who are therefore
brought back to this country. The total number of those so
dealt with on whatever grounds in the last six years, together
with the total number of foreign emigrants to the United States
from this country is as under:—

Years.	Foreign Emigrants from the United Kingdom.	
	Total going to the United States.	Number rejected by the United States' Authorities.
1888	95,390	15
1889	69,792	43
1890	81,109	18
1891	95,621	71
1892	85,182	111
1893	64,263	99
Total for the six Years (1888–1893)	491,357	357

It will be seen that the figures are extremely small in proportion to the total number of foreign emigrants who go from this country to the United States, and though there is some increase in recent years, yet in 1893 they were only ·15 per cent. of this total, while for the period 1888–93 the proportion was only ·07 per cent.

It remains to notice the information offered by the decennial census. This, though lying outside the continuous inquiry pursued by the Board of Trade, with which this memorandum has hitherto dealt, affords such a valuable means of periodically checking and supplementing (though at long intervals) the results otherwise obtained, that it is essential to the completeness of this statement to make use of the statistics as to the foreign population of the kingdom in April 1891 which have recently become available. A summary account will therefore be given of the chief facts disclosed by the census which are of interest in the inquiry with which we are concerned.

Census of 1891.

The total number of foreigners in the United Kingdom enumerated at the Census of 1891 was 219,523, as against 135,640 in 1881 and 113,979 in 1871. These are of course the gross figures of those present on the census day, including, therefore, seamen and a large number of other persons not residents but travelling in this country on business or pleasure.

It should be stated that, so far as regards England and Wales, which division of the United Kingdom accounts for more than nine-tenths of the number for 1891 given above, there are reasons for believing that the number of foreigners was somewhat understated at the enumeration of 1871 and of 1881, and overstated in 1891. Therefore to a certain extent, which, however, there are no means of measuring and allowing for, the rates of increase in the last decade, computed from these figures and stated below, are in excess of the truth.

The principal nationalities represented, and the numbers returned for the whole of the United Kingdom as belonging to these at the date of each census referred to, with the increase or decrease for each nationality, are shown in the following table, which also gives for comparison the total population of the United Kingdom :—

Number of Foreigners enumerated in the United Kingdom.*

Country of Birth.	1871.	1881.	1891.	Increase from 1871 to 1881.		Increase from 1881 to 1891.	
				Total.	Per Cent.	Total.	Per Cent.
France	19,618	16,194	22,475	– 3,424	– 17·5	6,281	38·8
German Empire	35,141	40,371	53,591	5,230	14·9	13,220	32·7
Holland	6,504	5,609	6,715	– 895	– 13·8	1,106	19·7
Italy	5,973	7,194	10,921	1,221	20·4	3,727	51·8
Norway, Sweden, and Denmark	8,978	9,671	16,542	693	7·7	6,871	71·0
Russia Russian Poland	9,974	15,271 { 25,736 21,959 }		5,297	53·1	32,424	212·3
United States	9,467	20,014	22,838	10,547	111·4	2,824	14·1
"America"	3,551	5,137	5,061	1,586	44·7	– 76	– 1·5
	99,206	119,461	185,838	20,255	20·4	66,377	55·6
Other Countries	14,773	16,179	33,685	1,406	9·5	17,506	108·2
Total Number of Foreigners	113,979	135,640	219,523	21,661	19·0	83,833	61·8
Total Population of the United Kingdom	31,484,661	34,884,848	37,732,922	3,400,187	10·8	2,848,074	8·2

* Not including the Isle of Man or the Channel Islands.

As already explained, the apparent increase in the number of foreigners between the Census of 1881 and that of 1891 is in excess of the real increase. As the figures stand we are shown an increase during the decade which in proportion to the numbers involved may perhaps be regarded as considerable, while in the case of certain nationalities the *ratio* of increase was undoubtedly very large.

But in comparison with the total population of this country the numbers are still quite insignificant, the above table showing for 1891 only 5·8 foreigners to every 1,000 inhabitants of the United Kingdom. It may be noted here, for comparison, that in the German Empire, according to the Census of 1890, foreigners numbered 8·8 per 1,000 of the population ; that in Austria proper, according to the census of the same year, they numbered 17·2 per 1,000 ; while in France the proportion (which has in that country been steadily rising at each successive census) was, in 1886, 29·7 per 1,000. In the United States of America the ratio is, of course, very high : in 1880 it was 143·2, and in 1890 had risen to 147·7 per 1,000.

It will be of interest to further analyse the census returns of foreigners in this country in 1891, and especially to localise them so far as possible.

The numbers shown as present in Scotland and Ireland are very inconsiderable. In Ireland there were altogether 12,900, or 2·7 in every 1,000 of the population, of whom 4,165 were returned as in Leinster, 3,367 in Munster, 4,127 in Ulster, and 1,241 in Connaught.

Of this total number 7,499 were stated to have been born in the United States or in "America," which probably also meant, in the majority of cases, the United States. Of the remaining 5,401, 1,232 were French, 940 Germans, 1,111 Russians, and 35 Poles. Compared with the census of 1881 this shows an increase of 103 French, 13 Germans, and 879 Russians and Poles; while in the total number of foreigners enumerated in Ireland there was an increase of 1,690.

In Scotland the total number of foreigners was 8,510, or 2·1 to every 1,000 of the population. Of those 2,052 were Germans, 1,977 natives of Norway, Sweden, or Denmark, 999 Russians, 476 Russian Poles, 749 Italians, and 446 French, while 660 were stated to have been born in the United States. Compared with the figures for 1881, these numbers show a slight diminution in the case of Germans and French, while Scandinavians had increased in the decade by 605, Russians and Russian Poles by 939, Italians by 421, and natives of the United States by 121. The increase in the total number enumerated was 2,111. In the parliamentary burghs of Edinburgh, Leith, and Glasgow were enumerated 4,253, or almost exactly one-half of the total number of foreigners in Scotland, and 673 more in Aberdeen, Dundee, and Greenock. The figures for each of these towns, showing separately the nationalities chiefly represented, are given below.

| Towns. | Foreigners present in 1891. | | | | | | | Total No. of Foreigners present in 1881. |
	French.	Germans.	Italians.	Russians and Russian Poles.	Scandinavians.	Americans (U. S.).	Total of all Nationalities.	
Aberdeen -	25	20	21	8	40	20	154	154
Dundee	29	66	23	11	46	50	283	248
Edinburgh	84	345	104	321	40	132	1,162	794
Glasgow -	90	480	348	696	214	161	2,208	1,553
Greenock -	13	67	13	31	77	—	226	105
Leith	5	166	20	150	371	6	883	1,308

The numbers appear to be too small to need comment.

O 82170.

In England and Wales the total number of foreigners enumerated at the Census of 1891 was 198,113, or ·68 per cent. of the population. In 1881 the number was 118,031, the apparent increase (subject to the reservation made above) being thus 80,082. The composition of this foreign element as to nationalities and sexes at each of these dates is shown in the following table :—

NUMBER OF FOREIGNERS in England and Wales according to the Census taken in each of the years 1881 and 1891.

Country of Birth.	1891.			1881.		
	Persons.	Males.	Females.	Persons.	Males.	Females.
Germany - -	50,599	30,386	20,213	37,301	23,714	13,587
Russia -	23,626	13,732	9,894	} 14,468	8,736	5,732
Russian Poland - -	21,448	11,817	9,631			
France - - - -	20,797	9,803	10,994	14,596	7,775	6,821
Norway, Sweden, and Denmark	14,004	11,662	2,342	7,917	6,708	1,209
Italy - - -	9,909	7,333	2,576	6,504	5,344	1,160
Switzerland - -	6,617	3,356	3,261	4,089	2,232	1,857
Holland - -	6,350	3,584	2,766	5,357	3,104	2,253
Belgium -	3,917	2,003	1,914	2,462	1,450	1,012
Austria - -	4,935	3,262	1,673	} 2,809	2,199	610
Hungary - - -	738	501	237			
United States of America -	19,740	9,726	10,014	17,767	9,226	8,541
Other Countries -	15,433	8,721	6,712	4,761	3,609	1,152
Total - -	198,113	115,886	82,227	118,031	74,097	43,934

It will be seen that to the increase of 80,000 from 1881 to 1891 Germans contributed 13,000, Russians and Russian Poles 30,600, and French and Scandinavians each 6,000. The French increase may be set against a decrease of 3,500 which took place between 1871 and 1881. The number of Scandinavians enumerated is largely made up of seamen, a fact which accounts for the great preponderance of males over females.

The important additions then to the foreign population were those of Germans, Russians, and Russian Poles. It will be observed that,—if we deduct Americans,—members of these nationalities formed, both in 1881 and in 1891, more than half the total number of foreigners in this country.

The manner in which the foreign element was distributed in various localities is shown in the following table, which gives for London and the provincial towns most affected the total number of foreigners and the number of Germans, Russians, and

Russian Poles, as enumerated at the Census of 1881 and that of 1891 :—

Towns.	Total Number of Foreigners.		Germans.		Russians.		Poles (Russian).	
	1891.	1881.	1891.	1881.	1891.	1881.	1891.	1881.
London	95,053	60,252	26,920	21,366	12,934	1,778	14,708	6,931
Liverpool	7,102	6,858	1,779	1,734	1,017	106	630	542
Manchester	8,941	2,805	1,321	691	3,379	126	1,701	762
Salford	1,222	489	227	103	229	9	177	9
Hull	2,742	2,251	906	1,006	310	128	316	217
Leeds	5,927	2,134	581	310	3,120	312	1,420	1,016
Birmingham	1,966	1,153	442	295	268	60	378	164
Cardiff	2,687	1,773	317	185	191	83	77	37
Newcastle-upon-Tyne	1,715	1,024	396	284	186	24	156	81
South Shields	1,118	719	334	168	33	55	12	13
Sunderland	1,293	683	410	260	187	35	64	46

Comparing this table with that last given, it will be seen that both in 1881 and in 1891 about half the foreigners enumerated in the whole of England and Wales were to be found in London. The increase during the decade was, however, proportionately less in the metropolis than in the provinces, the additional numbers being in London 58 per cent. of the foreign population of 1881, and in other parts of the country 78 per cent.

As to the towns, other than London, specified in this table, the only noteworthy increases are those shown for Manchester and Salford, and for Leeds, amounting in the former case to 6,859, and in the latter to 3,793. In both towns, Russians and Russian Poles are mainly accountable for the increase, to which they contributed 4,580 in Manchester and Salford, and 3,152 in Leeds. In the other towns mentioned, the 1891 figures are somewhat larger than those of 1881, but in none of them did the total addition to the foreign population reach 1,000. Most of them are ports, where a large proportion of the foreigners enumerated would be seamen. This is especially the case in regard to Scandinavians, who in 1891 numbered in Cardiff 815 (an increase of 524 over the figures of 1881), in Hull 713 (an increase of 233), in Newcastle-on-Tyne 506 (an increase of 238), in South Shields 744 (an increase of 387), and in Sunderland 301 (an increase of 166).

In London, the addition to the number of foreigners between 1881 and 1891 amounted (approximately) to 35,000, to which number, as appears from the table given above, Germans contributed 5,000, Russians 10,000, and natives of Russian Poland

8,000, while as regards other nationalities, the census showed that natives of France and of Austria-Hungary had each increased their numbers in London by about 2,000, Italians by 1,600, natives of Norway, Sweden, and Denmark (taken together) by 1,200, and Swiss by 1,000. It is then the number of Russians and Poles in London and their large augmentation (relatively), to which attention is mainly drawn by the figures here brought together. Of the 45,074 persons of these nationalities present in the whole of England and Wales in April 1891, 26,742, or 59 per cent., were found to be in London. And as the point has been raised that it is less the total number of these persons present in the whole country, than the density of their aggregation within certain limited areas that is of importance from a social, economic, and sanitary point of view, it will be of interest to give some figures bearing on their distribution within London.

The numbers (for Russians and Russian Poles, taken together) range from 17 in Chelsea to 13,538 in Whitechapel. The figures for the (registration) districts most concerned, are given in the following table, which includes also for comparison the numbers returned in 1881:—

Registration Districts.	Total Population.		Russians and Russian Poles.					
			1891.			1881.		
	1891.	1881.	Persons.	Males.	Females.	Persons.	Males.	Females.
Whitechapel	74,462	71,363	13,538	7,257	6,281	5,293	2,858	2,435
St. George-in-the-East	45,795	47,157	4,973	2,748	2,225	566	353	213
Mile End Old Town	107,592	105,613	3,440	1,868	1,572	893	522	371
Bethnal Green	129,132	126,961	970	542	428	254	156	98
Westminster	37,312	46,549	713	417	296	194	136	58
London City	38,320	51,405	480	281	199	165	269	196

In addition it may be noted that in Hackney there were enumerated at the last census 395 Russians and Russian Poles, in St. Pancras 225, and in Islington 214, while there were between 100 and 200 in each of the districts of Marylebone, Kensington, Holborn, Shoreditch, St. Giles, and Poplar. In none of the remaining 14 registration districts of London did the number of persons of these nationalities reach 100.

It will be seen that at the date of the census of 1891, there were in Whitechapel, St. George's in-the-East, and Mile End Old Town 21,951 Russians and Russian Poles, and that these districts consequently contained more than four-fifths of the total number of foreigners of these nationalities present in London. In 1881 the corresponding number was 6,752, the increase in the decade being therefore 15,199. It may be added that in the three districts named, Russians and Russian Poles formed 71 per cent. of the total number of foreigners enumerated in 1891, and that foreigners of all nationalities formed 13·6 per cent. of the total population.

Some particulars may be added of the *occupations* as described in the census returns, of the Russians and Russian Poles enumerated in England and Wales in April 1891.

Of the 13,732 male natives of Russia enumerated at the Census, 1,112 were under 10 years of age, while for 851 others no occupation was specified. Of the remaining 11,769, 3,836 were returned as tailors, 1,349 as shoemakers, 684 as cabinetmakers or upholsterers, 587 as seamen, 519 ´ as commercial travellers, 321 as costermongers, 314 as engaged in hat-making, and 313 as painters and glaziers.

Females of this nationality over 10 years of age whose occupation was described numbered 2,488, and of these 1,124 were stated to be occupied in tailoring, 193 as milliners and dressmakers, 173 in hat-making, and 221 as domestic servants.

As regards natives of Russian Poland, males numbered 11,817, of whom 898 were under 10 years of age, and 817 others did not specify their occupations. Of the remaining 10,102, 4,467 were shown as tailors, 1,166 as shoemakers, 397 as cabinetmakers and upholsterers, 227 as commercial travellers, 226 as costermongers, 220 as painters and glaziers, and 209 as hairdressers.

Of females born in Russian Poland, the occupation of 2,271 was specified, and of these 1,144 were engaged in " tailoring," 141 were milliners and dressmakers, and 211 domestic servants.

Taking together, then, the natives of Russia and Russian Poland, it appears from the Census figures that of the 23,539 males over 10 years of age present in England and Wales in April 1891, 8,303—i.e., more than a third—were engaged in some branch of the tailoring industry. while 2,268 women of these nationalities were also similarly occupied.

The other trades chiefly followed were boot and shoemaking, and cabinetmaking and upholstering, the former giving employment to 2,515 Russian and Russo-Polish males, and the latter to 1,081.

Conclusion.

It does not come within the scope of this paper to comment further on the figures here brought together, or to consider their bearing on economic or other problems. The aim has been to show what statistics are available for reference in regard to the subject of alien immigration, and at the same time to give such an account of the sources from which these statistics were derived as to allow of their proper interpretation.

It is to be regretted that the restricted period covered at present by the figures specially obtained at the instance of the Board of

Trade precludes the possibility of any useful attempt to check them in detail by the census figures, but it may be said that the latter give general confirmation to the conclusions expressed in the annual emigration reports, viz., that the number of alien immigrants for settlement in this country, though undoubtedly greater within the last few years, is still relatively small, compared with the population of the United Kingdom, and that London and, to some extent, Manchester and Leeds are the only places materially affected.

The figures obtained by the Department for 1891, 1892, and 1893, which may be used to supplement the census figures, have been already given in detail. The broad conclusions deducible are :—

(1.) The total number of aliens of all classes who arrived in this country and may be taken to have remained here amounted in 1891 to about 12,000, in 1892 to 11,500, and in 1893 to rather less than 6,000.

(2.) The total number of the class with which we are specially concerned who arrived in London without through tickets to other countries, less those subsequently sent away by charitable agencies, was in 1891 something over 7,000, in 1892 about 3,000, and in 1893 rather below this latter number.

These figures, then—setting off the early part of this year against that of 1891—have to be added to those of the census to arrive approximately at the numbers for the present time.

It will be necessary to await the completion of larger series of figures as to alien immigration from Europe than are now at our disposal before attempting to form any views as to possible regular sequences which may exist, of contraction or expansion of the movement. So far, moreover, as the figures relate to the Jewish refugee element, they are dependent upon accidental and arbitrary causes, for whose operation no law probably could be found. But it is clear that we are now in possession of means of knowing the exact extent of this movement, and no change of character, magnitude, or route can occur unobserved.

I have, &c.
(Signed)   J. G. WILLIS.

REPORT BY LABOUR DEPARTMENT.

To the CONTROLLER-GENERAL of the COMMERCIAL, LABOUR, and
STATISTICAL DEPARTMENTS of the BOARD of TRADE.

SIR,

THE following memorandum, prepared by the Labour Department, deals with certain aspects of alien immigration which have recently aroused considerable public interest, especially with the economic condition of a particular class of immigrants, and their effects upon some of the principal industries to which they resort.

The class of immigrants to which the memorandum relates are the Jews who, during recent years, have been arriving in this country in considerable numbers chiefly from Russia and Russian Poland. The unrestricted influx of these immigrants is held by some to be undesirable on the grounds (among others) that the competition of their labour in certain trades reduces the rate of wages and displaces British workpeople ; and, furthermore, that a large proportion of them are " paupers," becoming a burden, if not on the rates, at least upon public charity for support.

On the other hand, it has been replied that the immigrants have not seriously displaced British labourers or reduced their wages by competition, having engaged very largely in certain branches of particular trades into which native workpeople do not as a fact largely enter, and having thus created, or at least greatly increased a new branch of industry especially for export. It is also denied that their characteristics, as a community, can rightly be described as those of " paupers," and it is urged that while they seldom or never come upon the rates, the Jewish organisations by which they are assisted are not, so far as a great part of their operations are concerned, comparable to poor-law institutions. It is further alleged that the numbers of this class of immigrants arriving annually for permanent settlement in this country have been greatly exaggerated.

Of the questions raised in these arguments on both sides, the last-mentioned (viz., as to the numbers arriving in this country for settlement) has been determined within a very narrow margin of error in the statistical report prepared by Mr. Willis, which appears in another part of this volume. The following sections deal to some extent with the other two questions, viz., as to the industrial position occupied in this country by the Jewish immigrants and their effect upon British labour in certain trades : and as to their social condition especially as regards " pauperism " and dependence on charity for support.

The section dealing with the immigration of Jewish women and the effect of the competition of the immigrants generally on the position of women workers in the tailoring and kindred trades, has been prepared by Miss Collet, one of the labour correspondents of the Board of Trade. In the collection of the materials for the study of the boot and shoe trade, and the effects of foreign immigration thereon, which is given on p. 67, I have been largely aided by Mr. Drummond, one of the labour correspondents of the Board of Trade.

The Department has to return thanks for much kind assistance in its inquiries to the Chairman and officials of the Board of Customs; to Mr. R. E. Sprague-Oram, Her Majesty's Chief Inspector of Factories; Mr. J. B. Lakeman, Her Majesty's Superintendent Inspector of Workshops, and members of his staff; and to many representatives of employers' and workmen's organisations, Jewish institutions, and others whose names will be mentioned in the particular sections to which their co-operation referred.

I am, Sir,
Your obedient Servant,
H. LLEWELLYN SMITH.

25

CONTENTS OF MEMORANDUM BY LABOUR DEPARTMENT.

PART I.—GENERAL CHARACTER AND EFFECTS OF THE INFLUX.

Page.

(i.) Scope and Methods of Inquiry — 27
(ii.) Arrival and Distribution of Immigrants in London — 28
(iii.) Position of the Immigrants in East London — 35
  (a.) Concentration in Special Districts — 36
  (b.) Concentration in Special Trades — 39
(iv.) "Pauperism" and the Jewish Relief Organisations — 45
(v.) Sanitary Condition of the Immigrants — 56
(vi.) Condition as regards Crime — 60

PART II.—THE INDUSTRIAL POSITION OF THE IMMIGRANTS IN CERTAIN TRADES.

Section (a).—General Introduction — 63
Section (b).—Alien Immigration in relation to the Boot and Shoe Trade:—
  (i.) Present Position and Local Distribution of the Boot and Shoe Trade — 67
  (ii.) Recent Tendencies in the Boot and Shoe Trade — 68
  (iii.) Meaning of "Changes of Wages" and "Displacement of Labour" — 72
  (iv.) Character and Division of Processes — 74
  (v.) Recent Changes in the Organisation of the London Trade — 76
  (vi.) Wages and Methods of Remuneration — 81
  (vii.) Relation of Foreign Immigrants to Trade Disputes — 85
  (viii.) Magnitude of the Recent Revival of "Outwork" — 86
  (ix.) Alien Immigration in relation to other Branches of the Trade — 88
  (x.) Relation of Immigrants to growth of Foreign Trade — 90
  (xi.) General Summary — 91

PART III.—FOREIGN IMMIGRATION IN RELATION TO WOMEN'S LABOUR.

Section (a).—Introduction — 95
Section (b).—Results of Statistical Inquiry:—
  (i.) Position of Foreign Immigrant women on arrival in London — 99
  (ii.) Occupations of Married Jewesses — 102
Section (c).—Results of Trade Inquiry:—
  (i.) Tailoring trade in East London — 105
    „   „   West   „ — 115
    „   „   Leeds — 116
    „   „   Manchester — 123
    „   „   General Summary — 125
  (ii.) Cap-making in East London — 127
    „   „   Manchester — 128
    „   „   Summary — 129
  (iii.) Cigar-making in East London — 129
  (iv.) Waterproof garment-making in Manchester — 130
  (v.) Mantle-making — 130
  (vi.) General Summary — 131

PART IV.—CONCLUDING SUMMARY — 131

APPENDICES.

MEMORANDUM BY LABOUR DEPARTMENT.

PART I.—GENERAL CHARACTER AND EFFECTS OF THE INFLUX.

(i.)—Scope and Methods of Inquiry.

An effort is made in the following pages to present some picture of the actual process of immigration of Russian and Polish Jews to this country, of the social and economic conditions under which the immigrants live and work, and of the institutions by which in various ways they are assisted. The account is mainly confined to London where all the features of this kind of immigration can be studied on the largest scale, and where the problems connected therewith reach their acutest phrase. East London (with Hackney) contains 53 per cent. of the entire number of Russians and Poles living in England and Wales ; it is the greatest seat of the cheap boot and clothing trades and of the so-called " sweating system " and it is here that the operations of the great Jewish organisations can best be studied Manchester, Leeds, and other large provincial centres have also their colonies of foreign Jews, their " sweated " trades and their Jewish Boards of Guardians. So far however as the Labour Department is informed there are few special features in the immigration to those districts which cannot be studied in London and which it is necessary to treat in detail. On the other hand, there are obvious advantages in confining this part of the inquiry to a single centre so as to present a more vivid and consistent picture. In the succeeding sections a more detailed description is given of the position which the immigrants occupy in certain groups of trades, but, before such special study can be usefully made, it is necessary to obtain some idea of the general conditions of life, the forces at work and the recent changes and tendencies among the foreign Jewish colony in the heart of East London.

The materials for such a study are varied. Among official published documents may be mentioned the report of the Select Committee of the House of Commons on Immigration and Emigration which deals with the subject more or less completely up to the year 1889. The most important official publications of more recent date throwing light on the question, (in addition to the annual reports of the Board of Trade which are summarised in an earlier part of this volume), are the various volumes of the Census of 1891 which supply the statistical basis for any inquiry into the distribution of the immigrants by localities and trades. Among unpublished official documents of which use has been made may be mentioned the rough occupation sheets of the Census (kindly placed at the disposal of the Department by the Registrar General), and the reports made to the Board of Trade by a special officer of Customs, on the number and condition of the aliens arriving on each vessel bringing such passengers to the port of London. The reports of the Medical Officers of the London

County Council and of certain East London Districts throw light
on the sanitary condition of the workshops and dwellings
occupied by the immigrants.

Among unofficial publications supplying valuable information
with regard to certain aspects of the question are the reports of
the Jewish Board of Guardians, the Russo-Jewish Committee
and the Jews' Free Shelter. Reference should also be made to
the description of the "sweated" trades and of the Jewish community of East London contained in the volumes of Mr. Charles
Booth's " Life and Labour of the People,"* which deal with East
London.

Besides the use made of such documents as are indicated above,
a great part of the following account is based on special inquiry
on the spot. In the making of this inquiry I have been considerably aided by a personal acquaintance extending over six
years with many of the districts in which the immigrants chiefly
settle. I have particularly to thank the Chairman and officials of
the Jewish Board of Guardians and the Russian Conjoint Committee for giving me an opportunity of actually seeing the work
of those institutions in progress, and thanks for information and
assistance are also due to those connected with the Jewish
Shelter, the Free School, and other agencies, and to the medical
officers, clerks of guardians, and other individuals having special
knowledge of the districts affected.

(ii.)—Arrival and Distribution of Immigrants in London.

Vessels bringing aliens to London are boarded at Gravesend by an officer of Customs and a medical officer of the
Port Sanitary Authority. The latter passes the aliens in rapid
review and notes down any who appear filthy, and also those
who are unable to give a satisfactory address to which they are
going. These names are written down in two lists, No. 1 list
including those whose address is wanting or insufficient, No. 2
list including those who are specially filthy in appearance.
These two lists are handed by the doctor to the captain. At the
same time the Customs officer checks the accuracy of the alien
lists, calling over the names and obtaining, for the information of
the Board of Trade and Local Government Board, certain additional particulars with regard to each of the poorer class of
aliens not provided with a through ticket to other countries.
The vessel then enters Tilbury Dock or more often proceeds up
the river to one or other of the London docks. On arrival
in London all aliens not included in the two lists drawn
up at Gravesend by the medical officer are free to land at once.
The remainder are detained on board until the arrival of the

---

* " Life and Labour of the People," Vols. III. and IV., especially the chapters
relating to the Jewish Community, Immigration, Sweating, and the Tailoring, Bootmaking and Furniture Trades.

medical officer or his representative. At this point the authorised agent of the Free Jewish Shelter comes on board, and the aliens detained, whose address is wanting or insufficient, are handed over by the medical inspector to his charge.

A description of the work of the Free Jewish Shelter is given below. It is, however, necessary at this point to give some account of the origin and nature of the agreement entered into between the committee of the shelter and the Port Sanitary Authority under which the class of aliens specified above are, for the present, handed over to the charge of the shelter agent.

The power of detention of aliens exercised by the Port Sanitary Authority is entirely based on the regulations for the prevention of the introduction of cholera. In the case of persons likely to introduce cholera into the country it is customary to obtain the names and addresses, to forward these to the medical officers of health of the districts in question, and thus in times when cholera is prevalent to keep such persons, for a time, under close observation.

Formerly, however, a large proportion of the Russian and Polish Jews arriving in the Port of London had no addresses, and though now that the regulations are known this proportion has very largely decreased, a certain number still arrive with addresses that are insufficient or (in some cases) evidently false. There being no adequate means of detaining these immigrants until the addresses could be verified, the Port Sanitary Authority in May 1893 entered into an agreement with the Jews' Free Shelter in Leman Street to carry out the work of verification for them.

The authorities of the Shelter are notified by the Port Sanitary Authority (and also by arrangement with the railway companies) of the arrival of immigrants in the port. The agent accordingly meets vessels and trains and receives the detained aliens, all of whom are conducted to the Shelter. The understanding is that on arriving at the Shelter, all those with some kind of address are conducted to it by an agent of the Shelter, who should satisfy himself as to its correctness. As regards the remainder of the immigrants, viz., those who are on their way to other places, or who for other reasons have no address in London, the single men are accommodated at the Shelter itself, single women are handed over to the agent of the Jewish Ladies' Association and lodged in their home in Tenter Street North, and families are passed on to one or other of the private lodging-houses recognised for this purpose by the Shelter, where, if necessary, they are temporarily paid for. As a certain number of non-Jewish immigrants (e.g., Polish Catholics, Stundists, &c.) arrive from time to time among the immigrants, it is stated that special arrangements are made for their accommodation.

The distribution of immigrants having been carried out the following form is filled up and sent to the Port Sanitary

Authority, and also to the medical officers of the districts to which the immigrants have been taken :—

A.

THE POOR JEWS' TEMPORARY SHELTER, 84, Leman Street, Whitechapel, E.

London, _____ 189 .

To the Medical Officer of the_____District.

Dear Sir,

I beg to append the list of Names and Addresses to which immigrants arriving at the Port of London have this day been taken by our Immigrant Officer.

Yours faithfully,___ ___   _ ___Superintendent.

Taken off S.S._____ _ ____ _____Date of Arrival at the Shelter.

Original Number.	Name.	Address.	Remarks.

The following form is also sent to the Port Sanitary Authority at Greenwich giving the destinations where ascertained of the persons actually lodged in the institution and who afterwards have left it, a copy being sent to the Medical Officers of the Districts in which such places of destination (if in London) are situated.

B.

THE POOR JEWS' TEMPORARY SHELTER, 84, Leman Street, Whitechapel, E.

London,_____189 .

To the Sanitary Officer, Greenwich,

Dear Sir,

I beg to append the list of Names of Persons who have left the Institution and have appended their destinations, in such cases where this information was ascertainable.

Yours faithfully,   _____ ___   Superintendent.

On S.S.	Original Number.	Name.	Arrived at Shelter.	Left Shelter.	Gone to	Remarks.

By this arrangement the Port Sanitary Authority and the local medical officers are provided with information as to the location of those immigrants whose addresses were on arrival considered insufficient.

The Customs officer, as a rule, accompanies the ship from Gravesend to London and endeavours in the interval, with the aid of an interpreter, to obtain such additional information with regard to the immigrants as they are willing to afford in answer to questions.

It should be stated here that the medical inspection and the special inspection by a Customs official of all vessels bringing aliens is, at present, mainly confined to the Port of London. At other ports, e.g., Grimsby and Hull, the alien lists are checked by "special count" in the case of about one vessel in ten.*

There is a general agreement as to the care and accuracy with which as a rule the alien lists are kept.

With regard to the aliens distributed at once to their addresses by the shelter authorities no further statistical information is available. They are under the supervision of the local medical officer, but they often rapidly change their address and become lost to view, except in so far as they reappear as candidates for relief at the Jewish Board of Guardians or some other charitable body.

Further particulars, however, are obtained with regard to those (viz., single men, or married men unaccompanied by their families) without addresses in London, who actually stay in the Shelter.

History and Operations of the Jews' Shelter.—The Poor Jews' Temporary Shelter was opened in 1885 in temporary

---

* During the prevalence of cholera, of course medical inspection is in force, but at present this has been discontinued at these ports. At Grimsby, however, as a matter of fact the aliens on board nearly all vessels arriving are counted by a Customs officer.

premises, and was transferred in the spring of 1886 to its present building. The primary object was to break down the system under which the poor Jewish immigrants (who since 1881 were flocking in considerable numbers to London from Russia and Poland) were defrauded and robbed by "crimps," who met them on their arrival and detained them in their lodging-houses. For some time past a Jewish baker in East London had received a number of the immigrants free of charge out of compassion, but his premises were condemned as insanitary and closed in 1884. The Shelter has arrangements with four railway lines to be supplied with information as to the arrival of alien Jews in the Port of London or the departure for London of any of such aliens as have arrived at other ports. Since May 1893, as described above, a further arrangement has been in force with the Port Sanitary Authority.

The Shelter is not directly connected with the Jewish Board of Guardians, or any other charitable organisation, but is managed by a committee elected by subscribers.* It provides accommodation for 30 at a time, and when this number is exceeded the surplus inmates are lodged elsewhere at the cost of the Shelter where they take their meals. The manager is not authorised to make any charge to the inmates for board or lodging, the Shelter being entirely free. The maximum period during which any inmate may remain in the Shelter is 14 days. One of the principal aims of the Shelter is to facilitate the passing on to other countries of transmigrants. Many of these arrive with through tickets; others arriving with a certain amount of money but less than the necessary fare, are under certain circumstances assisted out of a special fund to complete the sum required for emigration.

The secretary states that employers are not, as a rule, allowed to apply at the Shelter for workmen, the exceptions not amounting to more than six in the year. Applications were more numerous at the beginning but the system had to be stopped for fear of encouraging "sweating."

The "Information and Location Bureau," conducted by the Russo-Jewish Committee, and described below, has no connexion with the Shelter, beyond the loan of a room, and the fact that the manager of the one institution happens to be the secretary of the other.

The following tables, giving particulars as to the inmates of the Shelter during the past six years, are based on the annual reports of the Shelter.†

---

* It has, however, been subsidised by the Russo-Jewish Committee on account of the assistance given by it to Russian refugees.

† The slight difference between the figures here given and those published in the reports is due to the fact that the tables here given represent *calendar years* instead of November—October as in the reports.

NUMBER of NEW INMATES admitted to the JEWISH SHELTER arriving from the following Places during the under-mentioned Years.

Years.	From Hamburg.	From United States.	Other Places.	Total.
1888 -	936	238	82	1,256
1889 -	563	196	100	859
1890 -	1,151	207	118	1,476
1891 -	1,913	95	20	2,028
1892 -	1,209*	154	27	1,390
1893 -	2,148*	58	—	2,206

NUMBER of INMATES who left SHELTER during the under-mentioned Years, with Place of Destination.

Years.	Went to United States.	Returned to Native Town.	Went to various Countries.	Remained in United Kingdom and unspecified.
1888 -	261	339	22	634
1889 -	96	268	18	477
1890 -	103	266	15	1,092
1891 -	532	269	439	788
1892 -	288	78	781	243
1893 -	370	105	1,410	324

It will be seen that during six years a total number of 9,215 persons have been inmates at the Shelter. This number, it may be repeated, includes only men arriving without women and children.

Out of the total, 948, or rather over 10 per cent., came from the United States, mostly, in the opinion of the secretary, *en route* for their homes in Eastern Europe. The remainder, about 90 per cent. of the whole number, came from Hamburg, Bremen, and other ports. As regards destinations, 1,650, or about 18 per cent., went on to the United States, 1,335, or 14 per cent., returned to their native town, 2,685, or 29 per cent., went to other countries, and 3,555, or 39 per cent., are returned as remaining in the United Kingdom or unspecified.

It is clear from the account of the operation of the Shelter given above that it deals at present more with transmigrants than with those intending to settle in this country. This has been very largely the case since the agreement with the Port Sanitary Authority. Thus families and all persons with a definite London address are usually simply taken to those addresses and do not figure in the returns, while those with

* From the Continent.

through tickets to other countries find a temporary resting place at the Shelter until their vessel sails. In the earlier days of the Shelter it appears to have dealt much more largely with intending settlers.

For example, in 1888 out of 1,256 persons admitted, 622 were passed forward or returned backward, leaving 634, or more than half, either remaining in the country or unspecified. In 1893, out of 2,206 persons, no fewer than 1,885 were sent forward or back, leaving only 321, or less than 15 per cent., not so accounted for.

For reasons given above caution is required in generalising as to the condition and destination of the general mass of alien immigrants from the statistics published by the Shelter, which apply solely to the class of migrants dealt with by them.

The following particulars as to the length of stay and alleged ages of inmates of the Shelter are based on the reports.

NUMBER of INMATES admitted to SHELTER from 1888 to 1893 who claimed to be of Ages within the following limits :—

Years.	Ages up to and including 20.	Ages from 21 to 40.	Ages from 41 to 60.	Ages from 61 and upwards.	Total.
1888 -	306	805	140	5	1,256
1889 -	191	555	101	12	859
1890 -	376	894	193	13	1,476
1891 -	569	1,261	192	6	2,028
1892 -	364	897	128	1	1,390
1893 -	610	1,396	193	7	2,206

LENGTH of STAY of INMATES each Year.

Years.	1 Day.	2–5 Days.	6–9 Days.	10–13 Days.	14 (Maximum).	Total.
1888 -	208	314	342	152	240	1,256
1889 -	47	168	235	130	279	859
1890 -	74	146	390	180	686	1,476
1891 -	2	202	706	729	389	2,028
1892 -	—	10	526	594	260	1,390
1893 -	—	109	486	994	617	2,206

The great bulk of the inmates appear to stay over a week, and the large proportion (no less than 27 per cent.) who stay the maximum time allowed is noticeable.

The reports of the Shelter tabulate the alleged previous occupations of the inmates, though it is doubtful how far the statements of the aliens on such points can be accepted as satisfactory. All that is certainly known is that those who stay in

London distribute themselves chiefly among a certain group of trades and handicrafts of which tailoring and bootmaking are the most important.

(iii.)—Position of the Immigrants in East London.

We may now leave the Shelter, which acts as a voluntary " immigration depôt " for receiving certain classes of immigrants and passing them on to their destinations in this country or elsewhere, and consider the position locally and industrially of those who remain in London, and the agencies and institutions by which they are assisted in various ways.

Foremost among these agencies stands the Jewish Board of Guardians, which combines the functions of a loan society and apprenticeship institution, a charity organisation society, and a voluntary outdoor relief agency, not to mention other forms of activity, such as the sanitary inspection of Jewish dwellings and workshops. As a general principle, however, the Jewish Board of Guardians does not grant relief to the immigrants until after a period of residence of six months, so that the newly arrived immigrant does not usually come at once directly into contact with this institution.

Should he, however, have come to this country owing to persecution in Russia (including under that term the enforcement of any regulations preventing him from living in the town or village which he had previously inhabited),* he can if distressed apply for assistance to the " Russo-Jewish Committee," which administers funds collected by public subscription after the passage of the Russian May Laws of 1881 and again after the increase in the stringency of their enforcement in 1891. The function of the Russo-Jewish Committee is to watch over the interests of the refugees who arrive, in or pass through this country. Its work includes: (1.) The relief of distress by grants and loans. (2.) Emigration or repatriation. (3.) The work of the " location and information bureau " for helping immigrants to find work and locating them outside the " congested districts " of East London. (4.) The " anglicising " of the immigrants by means of free adult classes for teaching them English. Relief and other assistance is sometimes made conditional on attendance at these classes. (5.) The subsidising of institutions which give assistance to refugees, e.g., provincial Jewish Boards of Guardians the Jews' Shelter, the Berlin Central Committee, &c.

Two main objects are kept in view by the Committee in dealing directly with the refugees :—to pass forward or backward to other countries as many of the immigrants as possible, and to accelerate in those who remain the process of " assimilation " with their English neighbours. Most of the immigrants arrive with no knowledge of the English language, and the extreme

* See pp. 36 and 52.

degree of concentration of the foreign Jewish colony in East London tends powerfully to retard assimilation.

This local concentration exercises so marked an influence on the conditions of life and progress among the foreign immigrants that it requires to be studied in some detail in connexion with its causes, and with the efforts made to counteract it by artificial means, before dealing in detail with the operations of the Jewish Relief Organisations.

(a.)—*Concentration in Special Districts.*—It has been indicated in another chapter in this volume that the great bulk of Russian and Polish immigrants in this country are to be found in certain quarters of a few large cities, especially London, Manchester, and Leeds. Between 1881 and 1891 this tendency, so far from being checked has increased, so that whereas in the former year about 76 per cent. of the total were living in the three large cities named above, the per-centage in 1891 had risen to nearly 81. Again, confining our attention to London we find that whereas in 1881 77½ per cent. of the total Russian and Polish population of London were living in Whitechapel, St. George's-in-the-East, and Mile End Old Town, the corresponding per-centage in 1891 was no less than 82. Thus the increase of numbers of immigrants has not been accompanied to any great extent by their wider dispersion over the country. As regards London, which is the main subject of this chapter, the three districts named above, covering an area of about two square miles, and containing in 1891 21,951 out of 26,742 Russians and Poles living in London, may be regarded for most purposes as sufficiently representative of the areas affected by the foreign influx. Within these districts whole streets and areas are nearly monopolised by the foreign Jewish colony, and the attraction of these "congested districts" on such Russian and Polish immigrants as arrive for settlement in London appears to have undergone no diminution. The causes of this attraction are indeed very powerful as will be seen below.

The Jewish colony in East London is nothing new, dating back as far as the time of the re-introduction of the Jews into England in the seventeenth century. When the influx from Eastern Europe began, it naturally directed itself towards the existing Jewish quarter, and since then the tendency towards concentration has grown, the attraction of community, of religion and customs being now reinforced by similarity of language and identity of nationality. A very large proportion of the immigrant Jews now go direct to relations in East London, but those who have no relations there often bring with them the address of someone in London who has previously arrived from the same town in Poland, or the "Pale,"* and from whom they are likely to receive a helping hand.

---

* The "Pale" includes fifteen Provinces of Western and South-Western Russia, to which as a rule Jews are now confined. See p. 52.

Another powerful influence tending towards concentration is the fact that the industries and handicrafts which offer the most likely means of livelihood to the untrained foreigner have become strongly rooted in Whitechapel and the adjacent districts, and hence tend to perpetuate and increase the attraction which these districts exercise on the Jewish poor. If we add to all these influences the proximity of Jewish institutions, both religious and secular, which are planted in or near Whitechapel —the synagogues and the charities connected therewith, the " chevras," the great Jews' Free School with its offer of free clothing and partially free board, the Jewish Board of Guardians, and the Jewish soup kitchen, not to speak of the proximity of the tradesmen who supply " Kosher meat " and other special forms of Jewish food —we shall arrive at some idea of the magnitude of the forces which make for local concentration, and which have to be reckoned with by those who desire to break up the Jewish colony and scatter its occupants more widely among the non-Jewish quarters of London, where they may come more rapidly and completely under "anglicising" influences.

For some time past the local concentration of the foreign Jews has afforded anxiety to the leaders of the Jewish community, and they have endeavoured so far as possible to reverse the tendency by planting institutions further east (e.g., the Stepney Jewish School) or outside the congested districts. They have recognised that the local congestion of newly arrived foreigners in streets and blocks of buildings, where nothing but " Yiddish " is spoken, tends to prevent the immigrants from learning the English language, which is the first and most essential step towards assimilation.

The adult classes for learning English established by the Russo-Jewish Committee were last winter held in the evening in seven centres (chiefly board schools), the average nightly attendance being 490, and the total cost about 578l.

With regard to these classes and the difficulties which they have to overcome, the last report of the Jewish Board of Guardians states : — " It is evident a long time must " elapse before the immigrants, stationed in the heart of the " foreign Jewish quarter, amid surroundings which give " them no opportunity to converse in English, but on the " contrary offer every temptation to speak their own native " jargon, will acquire the familiarity with English habits and " the English tongue which alone will overcome their reluctance " to seek for a livelihood away from their comrades and in " districts where they may encounter prejudice."*

A far more powerful instrument, however, for "anglicising" the foreign Jewish community is the great Jews' Free School in Bell Lane, Spitalfields, which, in the spring of 1893, was

* Report of Jewish Board of Guardians for 1893, p. 23.

attended by 3,582 Jewish children. Of these, 1,358 were actually born abroad, and of the remaining 2,224, no fewer than 1,628 were children of foreign-born fathers. Thus the proportion of children who may be described as of foreign extraction amounts to 83 per cent. of the whole number. This per-centage is somewhat in excess of the average for all the Jewish children attending schools in the East End. Information supplied to the Labour Department by 11 East London schools (excluding the Jews' Free School) largely attended by Jews, shows that of 8,403 Jewish children on the registers in the spring of 1893, 2,490 (or 30 per cent.) were born abroad, and 3,848 (or 46 per cent.) were English-born children with foreign-born fathers. In the Jews' Free School the corresponding per-centages are 38 and 45.

Every child in the Free School is clothed and shod free out of funds provided by a wealthy member of the Committee. All children who wish it can have free breakfast, and a certain number of the poorer children are provided also with a midday meal. It is therefore not surprising that the school, large as it is, is always quite full, with many names of applicants on the books waiting for admission; nor is it unnatural that the poorer members of the foreign Jewish community find it to their advantage to reside within its sphere of attraction. To the extent to which this great school tends to perpetuate the congestion of the Jewish population in its neighbourhood, it retards the progress of assimilation. So far, however, as its organisation and methods are concerned, it is the most efficient "anglicising" agency in the Jewish quarter of East London. As the children pass from the "A B C" class at the bottom, in which the energies of the teachers are mainly directed to teaching them the English language and something of English notions of cleanliness, upwards through the standards to the top of the school there is a most marked change in their appearance and habits. They enter the school Russians and Poles and emerge often almost undistinguishable from English children. A similar process is going on in the board schools in the neighbourhood which are attended by Jewish children.* All the teachers, however, regret the extent to which their efforts are hampered by the fact that the children are accustomed to hear nothing but a foreign language in their homes.

Thus the second generation of Jewish settlers are far more English in character than the first. Many of them become completely assimilated with the English-Jewish community, and gradually move out of the congested districts; others emigrate: while the Free School and other schools continue their work of anglicising a fresh contingent of immigrants from Eastern Europe.

---

* A few of these board schools seem even more foreign than the Free School itself. Thus in 1893 the Berner Street School had 925 Jews on the register, of whom 579 were born abroad, and 286 others had foreign fathers, and in the Hanbury Street School, out of 719 Jewish children, 406 were born abroad, and 291 others had foreign fathers.

The establishment by the Russo-Jewish Committee at the end of 1892 of an " Information and Location Bureau " was designed partly to overcome the initial difficulty which Russian refugees meet in finding work, owing to difficulties of language and want of training : partly to afford a " labour-test " by which to separate applicants for relief who are willing to work from those who are not willing: and partly " to disperse the refugees through " districts less overcrowded than the present nuclei of Jewish " population in the Metropolis."* With regard to the last-named object, however, the report states that " this part of their " expectation has not been realised to any great extent." In seven months ending September 13th, 1893, the Committee had taken in hand 162 cases, of whom it had only been able to plant 10 out of Whitechapel. The report ascribes the difficulty to:—

(1.) Indisposition on the part of the individual refugee to migrate to quarters where he would be mainly among strangers.
(2.) Local prejudices against foreigners, and especially refugee Jews, who are regarded as interlopers.
(3.) The persistent objection of some of the refugees to acquire a knowledge of English.
(4.) The objection to the schooling of the children outside Jewish influences.

The fact is that the forces tending to resist the dispersion of the immigrants on first arrival are so powerful as to be almost impossible to overcome. Another illustration of this is shown in the fact that the Stepney Jewish School planted outside the " congested districts " was attended in 1893 by 871 Jews, of whom, however, only 33 were born abroad, and only 100 others had foreign-born fathers. The tendency towards dispersion both east and west appears mainly to begin with the second generation, after the Free School and other schools of White-chapel and the neighbourhood have done their work.

The dispersal of the refugees is only a secondary object of the Information and Location Bureau of the Russo-Jewish Committee, the main aim of which is the placing of refugees in situations. This aspect of its work can best be dealt with after considering the general industrial position of the immigrants and their concentration in special trades.

(b.)—*Concentration in Special Trades.*—No less prominent a characteristic than the local congestion of the foreign Jewish community in East London is its industrial conges-tion. Not only do the immigrants confine themselves to special districts, but they flow (mainly) into a certain group of trades. It has been pointed out above that these two ten-dencies re-act on each other,—the necessity for pursuing certain highly localised trades tends to keep the immigrants in certain districts, and their presence in large numbers in those localities tends to force them into those special trades. The character-

---

* Report of Russo-Jewish Committee for 1892-3, p. 7.

istics of the trades chiefly affected—tailoring, boot, shoe, and slipper making, &c.—and the effects of immigrant labour thereon, are discussed in another section of this report. Like the local congestion, the concentration of the immigrants in a few crowded trades has been a matter which has caused anxiety to the leaders of the Jewish community, and it will be found below that their efforts, so far as they have had to do with the industrial condition of the immigrant poor, have been directed to scatter them more widely among other trades. Before noticing these efforts we may remark (as before when dealing with local congestion) that the forces which tend towards concentration in a few trades of peculiar organisation and character are many and powerful, and that up to 1891 at all events the tendency was rather increasing than diminishing. Thus in 1881 nearly 48 per cent. of all " occupied " Russians and Poles in England and Wales were returned as engaged in tailoring, boot and shoe making or cabinet making. In 1891 the corresponding percentage was 55.

The foreign Jew on arrival in East London is ignorant of the English language and often ignorant of any trade. Even where he has practised a skilled trade in Russia, he finds English methods of production so different that he has usually to begin again at the bottom of the scale. It is difficult for him as an adult to enter an organised trade as a learner, and he is not suited in physique and inclinations for a life of heavy outdoor labour. Moreover, if he could overcome all these obstacles and find a situation in an English factory or workshop or in some kind of outdoor work, he would find it very difficult to combine such labour with the due observance of the Jewish Sabbath and festivals. The Factory Acts make provision for Sunday work in the case of purely Jewish factories and workshops, but not in that of a few Jews working among a number of non-Jewish workmen, nor would it be profitable in the case of factories with steam power to keep the machinery working on Sunday for the sake of a small proportion of the workpeople.* The result is to prevent foreign Jews from mixing with English workmen, especially in factories, and to confine them on first arrival to trades in which the employers are Jewish, and in which the organisation is such as to admit of the entrance of untrained adult workers.

The practical outcome is that the immigrant Jew tends mainly to enter the small Jewish workshop producing certain cheap

---

* Even in the Jewish tailoring trade, in which " out-work " is most prevalent, the observance of the Sabbath is said to be greatly interfered with by the practice of the non-Jewish wholesale houses in requiring goods to be sent in at the end of the week. Until they are sent in they are not paid for, and the small master having little or no capital cannot pay his employees until he has received his money from the City house. Consequently even when the men do not work on Saturday they often have to go for their pay on that day, and on Friday evening are sometimes busy long after the Sabbath begins. The late Rabbi of the Federation of Minor Synagogues, from whom the above facts are derived, and many others have made great efforts to maintain Sabbath observance in the tailoring trade by the formation of leagues both of employers and employed, but he finds the task an uphill one.

qualities of clothing, boots, or furniture. His chief alternative is independent work as a hawker or petty dealer. Even from the boot trade he now finds himself to a considerable extent excluded by the "indoor" arrangement described in another chapter, whereby work formerly done at home is now performed on the employers' premises, and he finds it difficult to learn the trade except in the shop of the small Jewish "chamber-master" or of the "out-worker" working in defiance of the general agreement in the trade. The stream of immigrants has, therefore, been lately somewhat diverted from this trade, and those that still enter it do so under conditions which render them unpopular with the trade organisations by which the "indoor" system was inaugurated.

The above causes which induce the immigrants to work at home or in the small workshop rather than the factory are reinforced by one of their most characteristic tendencies, viz., the preference for a livelihood from petty profit to that derived from weekly wages. The foreign Jew is not by any means indisposed to handicraft, but he aspires from the first to become a small master, and he prefers a trade in which, owing to the smallness of its scale and of the capital required for carrying it on, the chances are greatest of achieving this aim. No trade offers such chances in this respect as the cheap clothing industry, especially that form of it known as "out-work," in which, the material being supplied by the warehouse or large manufactory, the capital required by the small master is reduced to its lowest point.

The foreign immigrants therefore tend naturally to gravitate towards the cheap clothing trades, and they are for several reasons especially fitted to pursue them with success. Thus, for example, the clothing trades are very intermittent and irregular in character, and the London trade is exposed to the very keen and probably growing competition of the large provincial factories. Under these circumstances the Jew is fitted to survive, as compared with the Englishman, by the extreme "elasticity" or indefiniteness of his standard of comfort.

This quality is the economic aspect of that persistence and pliancy under difficulties of environment which have always characterised the Jews.* The most noticeable point about the earnings of the Jewish workman is not their meagreness or their magnitude, but their extraordinary range. He passes from low wages to high and (if necessary) back to low without the disturbance and possible demoralisation which are so often the result of such changes on his neighbours. Under such circumstances the irregularity of the clothing trades has less terror for him than for them, and he cheerfully meets a depression by a lowering of piece-rates, when

* It must be understood that no opinion is expressed on the controversy as to how far such characteristics are really racial and how far they are the product of social circumstances. (See Jacob's "Racial Characteristics of the Jews," Anthropological Journal, Vol. XV., p. 23.)

the English trade unionist would starve in the effort to
maintain the "statement" intact. Moreover, the immigrant
Jew shows more resource than the English workman in the
organisation of the enforced leisure due to seasonal changes of
trade. Perhaps he turns to another branch of industry. The
slipper maker in spring takes to lasting or finishing, the tailor in
the autumn becomes a hawker, perhaps with the aid of a grant
for stock from the Jewish Board of Guardians (which he regards
like any other legitimate source of gain, and by which therefore
he is not easily "pauperised").* Or if such material resources
fail him, he will often occupy the spare time left him by the slackness of his trade in the study or discussion of the Talmud or other
Jewish literature. In the immediate neighbourhood of Booth
Street buildings in Whitechapel (the block of dwellings which
more perhaps than any others is occupied by foreign "greeners"
on their first arrival) is a "chevra" or Jews' club and "minor
synagogue," which is the resort of Russian and Polish Jews, and,
unlike most of the "chevras," is open every day. The dwellings are in the heart of the tailoring trade, and the neighbour-
ing buildings are honeycombed with small Jewish workshops.
In the slack times of the clothing trades this "chevra" may be
found crowded with the poorest foreign Jews, eagerly intent on
the discussion of the Talmud, which is read and expounded
from a raised desk in the middle of the room by one of themselves. This double life of the Jew, the concentration of half
his thoughts on material gain and the other half on his race, its
history, and its literature, must be understood in order to grasp
the position he takes in the industrial world. He is thus
enabled to survive and find an interest in life under conditions
which, to an English workman, would be intolerable, while the
continual study through many generations of the casuistry of
the rabbinical law, in the opinion of those who are entitled to
speak with the greatest authority on such a subject, has been
no mean instrument in sharpening those faculties which make him
so formidable a competitor in industry. The English skilled
workman often finds in his trade union, with its ideals of the
amelioration of the conditions of labour, the satisfaction for a
great part of his social and even religious instincts. With the
foreign Jew, the two sides of life are kept more apart—in
industry he is a purely "economic" competitor, while his "com-
munistic" feelings run into the channel of race patriotism rather
than of trade organisation.

The foreign Jew is, therefore, not popular as a workman
among English workmen. He is thought (not without some
reason) to have no feeling of the dignity of his trade, to care little
for the general standard of its organisation, and to evade any
agreements generally arrived at for its improvement.

The fact is that to this class of immigrant the very conception
of a "standard" wage is wanting. It corresponds to no clearly

---

* *See* pp. 50 and 53.

formed idea of a definite standard of comfort or subsistence. "As much as can be got" is the only formula which would express the notion of the Russian Jew as to the "certain amount " of the necessaries, comforts, and luxuries of life" which are embodied in the so-called "standard of comfort" of various classes of labourers. The newly arrived "greeners" will work cheerfully for the first few months for the barest subsistence; in some cases close observers are of opinion that they work at first considerably below subsistence point, with the result of permanently reducing their mental and physical powers. They will do this, not only because they cannot protect themselves or even because of the extreme pressure of competition, but because while learning a trade they must be content with the wages of learners. As soon as a chance of improvement is seen it is eagerly grasped, and the same individual, within the space of a few years, may excite the hostility of his English neighbours for his "pauperism" and their indignation for his wealth. "A " foreign Jew is always either a sweatee or a sweater" was the form in which this quality was described by an official of a Union connected with one of the trades into which the immigrants flow, and who was consulted during the course of this inquiry, and though the statement is too sweeping, there is some foundation for the idea which he sought to convey.

It is now easy to understand how it comes about that foreign Jews tend to be concentrated in certain special trades, and how their presence in these trades (however little they may interfere directly with English labour) is sometimes resented by English workmen. It is also not difficult to account for the apparently contradictory accounts which are given by different observers of their industrial condition. To the observer who meets the vessels in which they arrive, travel stained, with no money and no knowledge of a trade, they appear as "paupers" likely to become a public burden; to those who see the "greeners," working early and late for the barest subsistence while learning the rudiments of a trade, they are the helpless victims of the "sweater"; to those who watch the growth of the Jewish trades, they are a persistent and tenacious race which can thrive while others cannot live—not "paupers," but the cause of pauperism in others. None of these views represent the complete truth; but it is easy to understand how each of them has arisen and has found its adherents.

We may now turn from the description of the industrial congestion of the foreign Jews to the efforts made to counteract the tendency. The first place must be given to the Apprenticing Department of the Jewish Board of Guardians, which apprentices about 100 boys and a few girls every year to various trades.* In choosing the trades, the desirability of dispersion

---

* There is also a workroom where 10 or 50 girls or women are taught needle-work, &c.

over a large number of industries is especially kept in view.
The result is seen in the list of 92 trades in which the apprentices were employed at the end of 1893, which is printed in full
on pp. 142 and 143.

During 1893, 126 boys and 5 girls were apprenticed to 53
different trades. The Board also may exercise some degree of
control over the trades entered by applicants for business loans
or grants for stock.   Except in these respects, and in the promo-
tion of attendance at technical classes by the apprentices, the
Jewish Board of Guardians does not directly touch the industrial
life of the Jewish community.

The technical classes such as those connected with the Jews'
Free School and the Stepney Jewish School are also to be noted
as an attempt to divert the stream of children from exclusively
flowing into particular trades.

The Russo-Jewish Committee, as noted above, has established
a "bureau" with the object of finding situations for a certain
proportion of the Russian refugees who apply for assistance.
The aim is to overcome in this way the initial difficulty of
obtaining work offered by ignorance of the English language,
and sometimes of a trade.   The placing of applicants is not done
through establishing a labour registry to which employers
apply, but by personal canvass of employers by the secretary,
aided, where necessary, by the payment of a small premium to
compensate the employer for teaching the immigrant his trade.

This experiment, of the results of which "it is too early to
speak confidently,"* has been looked upon with considerable
misgiving among some of the leaders of the Jewish community.†
At present its operations are on a limited scale and cannot
appreciably affect either the labour market or the condition of
the mass of immigrants.   During the first seven months in
1893, 69 situations were found by the bureau for 58 persons.
In 24 cases the situations were refused either at once or after a
short trial.   In 26 cases the results are stated to have been
apparently successful, the persons remaining in the same
situations and earning a fair living.   A list of the 26 cases
stated to have been successfully dealt with by the bureau is
printed in the last report of the Russo-Jewish Committee.*   Out
of 34 individuals placed in work, 9 have been placed in some
department of the boot and slipper trade, 7 in the skin and hide
industry, 4 in tailoring, 6 in other branches of the clothing
trades, 2 set up as hawkers and dealers, and the remaining 6
placed in various miscellaneous industries.

The questions discussed above—of language, of locality, and
of trades—are perhaps the three most important points to be
considered in connection with the problem of the "assimilation"
of the foreign immigrants to their surroundings.

---

* Report of Russo-Jewish Committee for 1892-93.
† See Reports of Jewish Board of Guardians for 1892 and 1893.

As regards assimilation of customs and ideas there is a process continually going on—too fast for some of the stricter of the community—by which the newcomers absorb the ideas and learn to imitate the practices of Western Europe. The sudden change from despotic rule and police surveillance to the complete liberty of this country produces in some cases a complete and violent break up of social and religious ideas. Apart from such cases, which are comparatively few, the process of assimilation goes on gradually—slowly with the adults, much faster with the children—until it reaches or may even pass the limits prescribed by the customs and observances of the Jewish community as such. The children of the rawest "greener" are often as English as the oldest established native Jew.

(iv.)—"Pauperism" and the Jewish Relief Organisations.

In the above sketch of some of the influences at work in the East London Jewish community incidental reference has been made to certain departments of the work of the Jewish Board of Guardians and the Russo-Jewish Committee. It is now desirable to describe more fully the work of these organisations, in relation to the relief of distress among the Jewish poor. This is the more necessary in view of the common practice of loosely applying the term "paupers" to the immigrant Jews, and of treating the great Jewish relief organisation as though it were in fact as in name merely a Board of Guardians.

As a matter of fact, very few foreign Jews come upon the rates for relief. In Whitechapel, in the last week of March 1894, 9 Russian and Polish Jews were in the workhouse, 9 in the infirmary, and 6 in receipt of medical relief only. In St. George's-in-the-East, in the same week, 4 Russian and Polish Jews were in the workhouse, and 19 in receipt of medical relief only. In Mile End Old Town in the same week there were 2 Russian Jews in the workhouse and about nine Russian and Polish Jews in receipt of medical relief.

The above numbers are trifling if we take into account the total number of foreign Jews and the volume of pauperism in these districts. During the whole of 1893, 5,240 persons* were admitted to the Whitechapel workhouse, of whom 40 were of Russian or Polish nationality; 5,864 were admitted to the infirmary, of whom 59 were Russians and Poles. Thus while forming 18 per cent. of the population of Whitechapel, the Russians and Poles contribute less than 1 per cent. of the pauperism.

In the strict legal sense of the term, therefore, hardly any of the alien Jews are "paupers." The reason is not the absence of distress, nor yet (entirely) the reluctance of the immigrants

---

* The number given refers to *admissions*, not to separate individuals.

to avail themselves of rate aid, but the fact that Jewish poverty is effectually relieved in a more eligible way by voluntary Jewish organisations. The Jew is reluctant to enter the work-house, partly owing to the importance attached (especially by foreign Jews) to ceremonial observances, special food or methods of preparing it, and other matters of the kind.* This objection is one which appeals strongly to the charitable rich in the Jewish community, with whom the assistance of the poor is a religious duty, and the result in the past was the multiplication of overlapping agencies for the distribution of relief which led to much demoralisation. It was as an attempt to organise the distribution of relief to the Jews on better principles that the Jewish Board of Guardians was formed in 1859 by the three city " Ashkenazite "† congregations.

In addition to the industrial functions of the Board already alluded to, and its sanitary work mentioned below, the Board as a relief agency is compelled from the nature of the case to combine two functions which it is usually the aim of administrators of the poor law and of charitable funds to keep as far as possible distinct, viz., the permanent assistance of " helpable " cases and the relief of destitution as such. The latter function is that of the poor law, the former is that undertaken by the Charity Organisation Society and kindred voluntary institutions, which can sift their applicants and refer those whom they see no chance of permanently benefiting to the relief provided by the rates.

The Jewish Board of Guardians has to provide by the same machinery for both classes of cases. It does not make mere destitution its test, but it cannot reject, as a rule, the destitute or the improvident, since (granting the validity of the objection to the workhouse) there is no poor law to fall back upon. Moreover, the Jewish Board of Guardians in its dealings with " paupers " acts entirely as an outdoor relief agency, and employs no labour tests.‡

The more elaborate of the application forms used by the Board are almost exactly reproduced from the case papers of the Charity Organisation Society. The degree, however, to which verification is carried in ordinary cases is naturally much less than is possible in the case of a society dealing with a much

---

* The Whitechapel Guardians have taken steps to meet the difficulty by providing special food, &c. for Jewish inmates. This has not, however, led to any great number of foreign Jews applying for admission.

† i.e. The Jews coming from Central and North-Eastern Europe, who form nine-tenths or more of the whole Jewish body in England. The Spanish or Portuguese Jews have a small Board of Guardians of their own, but its work has no relation to the influx.

‡ A special sub-committee appointed during 1892 to consider the advisability of opening a wood-cutting yard for the purpose of a labour test, reported against the proposal on certain grounds, some of which illustrate the extent to which the policy of the Board is influenced by the possibility of attracting immigrants (p. 13, Report 1892).

smaller number of cases, while the rota system makes continuity of treatment more difficult.

Inquiries are made by paid investigators and voluntary visitors, and on their reports the cases are decided by the members of the committee sitting in rotation.

The following statistics as to the cases dealt with in recent years are based on the annual reports of the Jewish Board of Guardians. During 1893, 4,881 individual cases were relieved,* of whom 2,543 were foreigners who had been in England less than seven years, 1,886 foreigners who had been here over seven years, and 452 were natives of the United Kingdom. The 4,881 cases comprised 18,852 individuals (including 10,833 dependent children); 1,826, or 37 per cent., of the cases were new, the remaining 3,055, or 63 per cent., having been relieved in the previous or prior years. In addition to the above, 297 cases were investigated and refused relief in 1893.

The following table gives a classification of the cases relieved during the last five years, according to nationality :—

	1889.	1890.	1891.	1892.	1893.
(i.) Natives of United Kingdom - -	455	419	451	448	452
(ii.) Foreigners resident more than seven years in the United Kingdom :					
Russians and Poles - -	822	821	914	1,008	1,444
Germans - - - -	83	118	121	124	163
Dutch - - - -	275	244	267	351	271
Others - - - -	17	9	16	15	8
Total - - -	1,197	1,192	1,318	1,498	1,886
(iii.) Foreigners resident less than seven years in the United Kingdom:					
Russians and Poles - -	1,096	1,483	2,462	2,137	2,242
Germans - - - -	146	183	150	146	205
Dutch - - - -	16	36	53	61	63
Others - - - -	70	38	40	23	33
Total - - -	1,328	1,740	2,705	2,367	2,543
Grand total - -	2,980	3,351	4,474	4,313	4,881

This table makes it clear that the overwhelming majority of foreign Jews who are relieved by the Board of Guardians (viz., 3,686 out of 4,429 in 1893) are natives of Russia and Poland. Of the 1,826 new cases which were relieved in 1893, 1,404 were Russians and Poles.

The table also shows that, roughly, one half of those relieved in the year had been resident in the country less than seven years. The only figures available showing the proportion of

---

* Excluding the work of the Loan, Industrial, and Sanitary Departments. Also excluding the Russian Conjoint Committee work, for which *see* p. 51.

persons relieved during the same year in which they arrived in the country apply solely to the *new* cases, which may be classified as follows :—

	1890.	1891.	1892.	1893.
Foreigners arrived during the year -	270	323	141	245
Foreigners arrived before the year but resident less than seven years.	850	1,435	1,071	1,121
Foreigners resident over seven years -	113	231	234	343
Natives - - - - -	86	103	81	117
Total *new* cases - -	1,319	2,092	1,527	1,826

The rule of the Jewish Board of Guardians not to relieve persons who have been less ·than six months in the country, accounts for the small numbers who appear from the above table to have been relieved during the year of arrival.
The stated occupations of the persons in receipt of "ordinary relief" set out in the following table, are based on more detailed figures published by the Jewish Board of Guardians.

TABLE showing the OCCUPATIONS of the ORDINARY RECIPIENTS of RELIEF from the JEWISH BOARD OF GUARDIANS in the Six Years 1888–93.

Occupations.	No. of Recipients of Relief in					
	1888.	1889.	1890.	1891.	1892.	1893.
Building trades - - -	137	121	115	131	134	112
Engineering and metal trades -	14	10	17	19	23	15
Clothing trades :—						
Boot finishers and rivetters -	217	169	190	205	205	271
Boot lasters - -	2	21	22	41	33	41
Other boot and shoe trades -	53	61	64	85	85	85
Slipper makers and sellers -	62	59	85	132	143	171
Tailors and tailoresses* -	676	580	666	904	921	1,070
Cap makers - - -	31	37	31	47	51	54
Furriers - - -	49	48	52	68	62	50
Dress, millinery and mantle makers	14	11	11	17	23	13
Other clothing trades -	35	29	34	40	60	55
Cabinet makers, &c. - -	43	25	44	95	85	95
Bakers, confectioners, &c. -	21	18	23	40	48	58
Butchers - - -	16	13	8	17	17	17
Retail tradesmen - -	238	237	160	207	194	239
Hawkers, rag sorters, &c. -	228	189	245	316	327	366
Cigar makers - -	132	115	129	140	146	162
Stick and umbrella makers -	31	24	30	27	41	39
Domestic servants, waiters, &c. -	65	58	79	90	92	106
Miscellaneous skilled occupations	30	27	29	41	49	48
Others - - - -	74	69	74	92	95	62
Unspecified - - -	513	764	433	511	777	814
Total ordinary recipients of relief	2,681	2,681	2,541	3,265	3,611	3,943

* Including " machinists," some of whom may be machinists in the boot or other trades.

The greater part of the " unspecified " are stated to be widows or old men.

It will be seen from this table that the trades which contribute most largely to the number of applicants are tailors and tailoresses* (1,070); boot, shoe, and slipper makers (568), and hawkers, rag-sorters, &c. (366); which among them contributed over 64 per cent. of the total number whose occupations were ascertained. In the previous year the same trades contributed slightly over 60 per cent. of the cases.

Turning from the nationality and occupations of the applicants to the causes which induce them to apply for relief, we have the following classification :—

Classification of Cases.	1892.		1893.	
	Cases Relieved.	Dependent Wives and Children.	Cases Relieved.	Dependent Wives and Children.
(i.) Permanently helpless cases -	46	66	36	59
(ii.) Widows - - -	543	973	577	808
(iii.) Wives in distress through crime or misfortune of husband :—				
(a.) Husband in gaol -	8	28	11	15
(b.) Husband in lunatic asylum - -	7	11	10	26
(c.) Deserted by husband	353	903	346	851
(iv.) Unmarried women - -	85	—	70	—
(v.) Orphans and deserted children, and cases of illegitimacy -	20	41	19	43
Total of classes I.–V. -	1,062	2,025	1,069	1,805
(vi.) Assisted to emigrate only -	376	151	548	409
(vii.) Women assisted only to join husbands or to return to native country - -	75	141	171	284
Total of classes VI. and VII.	451	292	719	693
(viii.) General body of cases not included in the above, and having an adult male as head of family - -	2,800	10,171	3,093	11,473
Grand total of cases -	4,313	12,488	4,881	13,971
	16,801		18,852	

* Including 105 "machinists," some of whom may be machinists in the boot or other trades.

The character of the relief given to various classes of cases may be thus classified for the year 1893 :—

	Number of Cases.	Amount of Relief per Case.
		£ s. d.
(1.) Cases of emigration which have not received any other relief - - - - -	719	1 13 11
(2.) Persons who have received special relief only, i.e., assistance in confinement or mourning, medical stimulants, surgical instruments, &c., but who have not applied for any other relief -	436	0 16 5
(3.) Persons assisted with tools or money to start business - - - - -	694	3 2 4½
(4.) Ordinary recurrent cases (including such as also received special relief or relief for business purposes) - - - - -	2,813	2 5 8¼
(5.) Fixed allowances - - - -	219	12 13 11
Grand total of cases - - -	4,881	—

The recurrent cases were relieved partly in money and partly by tickets for necessaries of life, the total amount so expended in 1893 being 6,416l.

During 1893 219 cases were relieved by "fixed allowances" (i.e., weekly allowances of a fixed amount, but subject to periodical revision) amounting on an average to about 12l. 14s. a year each. All of these recipients had resided over seven years in the country, and 88 of them were natives by birth. 244 cases were assisted by "periodical allowances" (i.e., weekly allowances of a certain amount for a certain definite period). Taking the cases assisted by "fixed" and "periodical" allowances together we find that in 53 out of the total 463 cases, the allowance was of the nature of an old-age pension, in 125 it was given on account of illness; 181 recipients were widows, 65 deserted children or orphans, 7 deserted wives, 9 wives whose husbands were in lunatic asylums, and 23 single women.

A most important part of the Board's operations, and one of the most interesting from the point of view of this inquiry, consists in emigrating persons, either by helping them to proceed to America, the Cape or Australia, or by sending them back to the Continent.

The following table shows the number of cases dealt with in this way in the last few years :—

(1.) *Emigrated.*

	To United States.	To Cape.	To Australia.	Returned to Continent.	Total Cases.
1887 - - -	215	2	14	305	536
1888 - - -	317	1	18	340	676
1889 - - -	143	8	36	234	421
1890 - - -	144	12	19	418	593
1891 - - -	344	2	11	662	1,019
1892 - - -	138	10	8	330	486
1893 - - -	267	14	21	419	721
Total for 7 years -	1,568	49	127	2,708	4,452
Yearly average -	224	7	18	387	636

(2.) *Migrated to other parts of Great Britain.*

1887	-	-	-	-	-	32
1888	-	-	-	-	-	25
1889	-	-	-	-	-	20
1890	-	-	-	-	-	28
1891	-	-	-	-	-	24
1892	-	-	-	-	-	34
1893	-	-	-	-	-	38

The total number of cases thus removed from London by emigration or migration during the last seven years was 4,653, giving a yearly average of 665.

The cases included 8,430 individuals, or a yearly average of 1,204.

Large as this number is it would be greatly increased if we added the individuals annually assisted to emigrate by the " Conjoint Committee of the Jewish Board of Guardians and the Russo-Jewish Committee." The average for the years 1887–1893 of the number of persons helped onwards or to return to the Continent by this committee was 628. During the year 1893 this number was 1,182, or, including 24 persons migrated to the provinces, 1,206. Thus during 1893 the total number of *individuals* forwarded, returned, or migrated by the two agencies was 2,738, almost the whole of whom were foreigners.*

Besides assisting emigration, the Board takes such steps as it can from time to time to stem the tide of immigration by causing paragraphs describing the overcrowded state of the British labour market to be inserted in Russian and other foreign papers which circulate among foreign Jews.

It should be added that the emigration operations of the Board are stated to have lately been rendered more costly by the rise of fares which has taken place to the United States, owing to the restrictions there imposed.

* There is also a Jewish Emigration Society which annually sends away from 200 to 300 persons.

Russo-Jewish Committee.—It is unnecessary to describe in detail the relief operations of the Russo-Jewish Committee. Though the money is drawn from specially collected funds the administration of the relief is entrusted to a conjoint committee of the Russian Committee and the Jewish Board of Guardians. The staff of visitors employed is now the same, the cases are dealt with in the offices of the Board of Guardians, and the principles of administration do not materially differ from those of the Board itself, except for the fact that the benefit of the fund is confined to cases of "persecuted" Russian Jews, that the six months' residential qualification is not required, and that the committee employ from time to time the machinery of the "Information and Location Bureau" as a labour test or as a means of placing applicants in situations.

Among "persecuted refugees" are usually included persons compelled to leave their homes in Russia by the Administration, either because they had been living in a part of Russia outside the "Pale," to which all Jews except those possessing certain qualifications are confined, or because within the Pale they had been living in villages, from which since the May laws Jews have been excluded. These laws were not at once stringently enforced in all districts, so that many Jews continued to live for some time without interference in districts or villages, in which they were not legally entitled to reside. In 1891 the stringency with which the laws were enforced was considerably increased, with the result of expelling large numbers of Jews from places where they had long resided. In some cases Jews migrating from Russia to avoid conscription or even as deserters from the army are treated as "persecuted cases" by the Russo-Jewish Committee, it being stated that the conscription is made to press with undue severity on the Jews in Russia.

The total number of cases dealt with in 1893 was 1,409 (3,984 individuals) compared with 1,697 in 1892 (4,450 individuals). The total outlay of the Committee in 1893 was 5,781*l*.

Of the 1,409 cases, 1,155, representing 2,649 individuals, were new, and 254, representing 1,335 individuals, were old cases which re-presented themselves. 294 cases (740 individuals) were emigrated, 297 cases (442 individuals) were returned to their homes on the continent, 7 cases (24 individuals), were migrated to other places in the United Kingdom; 604 cases (2,262 individuals) remained in London, and were relieved, and the remaining 207 cases (516 individuals) were remanded or refused.

Causes of Distress and Destitution.—The causes of distress among the ordinary "recurrent" cases are not analysed in detail in the annual reports of the Jewish Board of Guardians, but the examination of the records of a certain proportion of cases visited by one of the Board's visitors leads to the conclusion that the most prevalent causes of application for relief are sickness, or inability to make a livelihood either on account

of low wages or of slackness of employment. The difficulty which the petty dealer or hawker finds in making a
living by selling to people nearly as poor as himself, supplies an
important cause of poverty, as is not unnatural when it is
remembered that large numbers of Jewish tailors, bootmakers,
and others look to hawking as a resource in the slack seasons of
their own trades. This tendency may perhaps to some extent
be encouraged by the grants made for stock to enable applicants
whether belonging to other trades or not to try their fortune as
hawkers. If this mode of relief does not fail with the poor Jew
as it has usually failed with the English poor,* this fact is itself
evidence of the differences in the nature of the problem of Jewish
as compared with ordinary poverty, to which further attention is
called below.

Another cause of distress which appears very frequently, owing
to the special circumstances of an immigrant and transmigrant
population, is wife desertion. The husband goes on to America
or elsewhere promising to send for his family, and in some cases
is not heard of again, the wife and family being thus left destitute.

Gambling appears to be a well marked cause of Jewish
destitution, but the two most prominent and incurable defects
which lead to English pauperism, viz., drink and laziness, appear
almost absent in the case of the Jews. The most difficult
of all the cases with which the Russian Committee has to
deal are said to be those of professional or business men, who
have been forced to leave Russia, who can find no opening for
their talents in this country, and who are too old to learn another
occupation.

Cost of Jewish Relief.—The total net expenditure of the
Jewish Board of Guardians and the Russian Conjoint Committee
during 1893 on the relief and assistance of the Jewish poor was
roughly 26,000*l.* This includes current office and administrative
expenses, and such items of the expenditure of the Loan, Industrial, Sanitary and other Committees (not directly engaged in
relief operations), as are not repayable, but excludes loans, &c.,
which are recoverable. It includes expenditure on emigration,
and an amount of nearly 3,500*l.* disbursed by the Board of
Guardians in relief to special cases on account of private individuals. Taking the number of the Jewish population of
London as 80,000† (a rough estimate which is probably as close
as can be made on the very imperfect data available), this would
give a payment of about 6s. 6d. per head per annum. If the
expenditure on administration, emigration, and other items not
of the nature of relief be deducted the amount expended on relief
by the two organisations appears to have been about 18,000*l.*, or
about 4s. 6d. per head of the Jewish population of London.
This estimate is of course only approximate.

See "Report on Agencies and Methods for dealing with the Unemployed," p. 261.
† See Booth's "Life and Labour of the People" vol. III., p. 166; Jacob's
"Statistics of Jewish Population in London" (1894), p. 3; "Jewish Chronicle,"
May 25, 1894. p. 9.

In London, the total amount expended in 1891–2 on poor relief, including maintenance of in-door paupers, out-door relief, maintenance of lunatics, cost of administration, medical relief, and all other expenses, except repayment of loans, was 2,349,372*l.*, or over 11*s.* per head of the population. If we deduct from this the cost of administration, interest on loans, maintenance of lunatics, and all other expenses, except in-door, out-door, and medical relief, we find that the total so expended in 1891–2 was 1,011,399*l.*, or 4*s.* 10*d.* per head of the population—very nearly the same figure as that representing the expenditure of the Jewish Board of Guardians and the Russian Committee on the relief of the Jewish poor. Considering the poverty of the greater part of the Jews living in London, the above figures certainly do not support the idea of any exceptional degree of dependence on public funds on the part of the Jewish community, even if all the amount expended in relief by the Jewish organisations be considered as equivalent to poor relief, while on the other hand no account is taken of the large expenditure on the relief of the non-Jewish poor by non-official charitable agencies.

"*Pauperism*" *among the Immigrants.* — The question remains How far ought the recipients of relief from the Jewish agencies described above to be described as "paupers"? In the strict legal sense not at all, since they are not a charge on the rates. But the question may be pushed further. How far do they show the characteristics which in the British poor are usually regarded as the marks of "pauperism," considered as denoting a defect of character rather than a particular legal status?

The answer (so far as any answer can be given to so speculative a question) appears to be that they show some of these marks, but not all. So far as to be "pauperised" means to acquire the habit of coming for assistance as often as possible, a considerable section of the East London Jewish poor are pauperised. They have hardly their full share of the feeling which makes the independent poor dread and avoid the receipt of public charity and relief. Partly it may be that they regard themselves as having the right to assistance from their richer co-religionists whom they are helping to discharge their duty by receiving their alms. Partly it may be that the relief given carries with it no civil disabilities, and is given in an acceptable form. But the fact remains that a large section of the East End Jews are willing to have recourse to the relief given by the Jewish relief organisations, that many of them apply again and again as often as they are allowed by the Board to do so,* and that they some-

* As regards the proportion of "chronic" cases the following figures, published by the Jewish Board of Guardians are of interest :—In 1893 out of 4,881 cases relieved 1,826 were new applications, leaving 3,055 cases which had been dealt with in the previous or prior years. Of the latter number 2,558 had been relieved in the previous year. During 1893 the average number of times on which the same case received relief was 6·5 or eliminating the recipients of fixed allowances and those assisted to emigrate only, 5·3, compared with 4·6 in 1892, 4·5 in 1891, and 4·2 in 1890. The Jewish Board of Guardians and the Conjoint Committee regard it as a great object to be kept in mind in giving relief to diminish the frequency of application.

times continue their applications after they are well removed
from all fear of want. As an example of this may be quoted the
case of a man who came to England with a wife, married son
(with wife and baby), and two unmarried children. They were
Russian refugees and applied for aid to the Russian Committee.
Places were found through the " Bureau " for the two sons who
were taught a trade, and the family was helped in other ways.
A short time ago the man applied for relief. He acknowledged
on being questioned an income amounting for the whole family
to 2l. 2s. 0d. a week. On being asked what he wanted he
replied merely " Help." Needless to say he was unsuccessful.
Again one of the most prominent classes of frequently recurrent
cases is that of hawkers who replenish their stock out of grants
or loans, and then after exhausting it apply again.

The idea, however, implied by the use of the term "pauperised" usually includes not only the disposition to apply
persistently for relief, but the relaxation of individual energy
and the gradual deterioration of character which is produced
by the habit of relying upon assistance from others. From this
last-mentioned characteristic of the " pauper," the foreign Jew
appears, on the whole, to be freer than the English poor. He
will take what help he can get, but he does not therefore necessarily slacken in his pursuit of gain. Perhaps this fact, as well
as that mentioned before, are both to be explained by the
" elasticity " of the Jew's standard of comfort which is alluded
to above. As the possession of sufficient wages does not always
deter him from seeking further assistance, so the acceptance
of assistance does not deter him from seeking his advantage by
other means. In fact, the help given by the Jewish Board of
Guardians is often looked on simply as one out of many
means by which the applicant can improve his position. There
are, of course, many hopeless and helpless cases among the
Jewish poor, but the impression left by the evidence is that the
proportion of cases in which they lose their power of self-help
when they accept the Board's assistance is smaller among the
Jewish than among the non-Jewish poor of East London. If
this be true, the proportion of "pauper cases " among the Jews
is, in this sense, below the average.

It is of course to be remembered that the definition of
" paupers " here adopted would, if similarly applied to the
native poor, include not only those legally so called but a large
number of the recipients of charitable assistance.

It is doubtless the fact of the presence in the foreign Jewish
population of the characteristics alluded to above, of tenacity
of purpose and elasticity of standard, which makes possible
without the risk of wholesale "pauperisation" the system of
relief administered by the Jewish Board of Guardians, which,
dealing with a congested and poverty-stricken population largely
composed of immigrants acts as a purely " out-relief " agency
without being able to fall back upon the workhouse test

It is not proper, in a report like this, to discuss the questions of policy and administration of relief which have lately aroused much interest and divergence of opinion among the leaders of the Jewish community. How far it is possible to replace "doles" by a more adequate system of treatment; whether cases should be visited and advised, or left to shift for themselves and to apply for help when forced to do so; whether the Board should be regarded as a purely eleemosynary institution or whether its functions should have a wider scope—all these are questions on which there is difference of opinion. The proper treatment of ordinary "out-of-work" cases, is a question on which such differences are felt. There is no doubt that the policy of helping such cases, either by grants of money or food or by loans or grants to enable them to set up as hawkers may to some extent make more tolerable, and hence encourage, the irregularity of some of the "sweated" trades besides possibly acting as a rate in aid of wages. Another mode of treatment —by means of a "bureau"—has aroused divergence of opinion on different grounds. It is to be remarked that in the discussion of questions of relief within the community, it is regarded as an axiom by all parties that nothing should be done which would encourage immigration. The recent influx has strained severely the resources of the Jewish Board of Guardians, the last report of which speaks of its financial position as being extremely precarious. Under these circumstances the reduction of immigration is strongly desired by many of the Jewish community, and some would regard with equanimity or active approval any measure of legislative restriction (if such a measure could be devised) which would exclude the class of undesirable immigrants who, at present, are so heavy a tax on the resources of the Jewish organisations, and at the same time offer no obstacle to the free entrance of refugees from political or religious persecution. Difficulty, however, is presented by the vagueness of the term "persecution" and by the fact that among the class of refugees who would still be admitted are to be found some of the most difficult of the "pauper" cases dealt with.

(v.)—Sanitary Condition of the Immigrants.

A question which may well be considered here, as closely connected with the habits, the local concentration, and the trade congestion of the foreign Jewish population in this country, is that of the sanitary conditions under which they live. There is no question that these conditions leave much to be desired. So much, however, has already been written on this subject in the reports of the Lords' Committee on Sweating and elsewhere, that it is unnecessary to go over the ground again. It will therefore suffice to indicate briefly the results of the present inquiry with regard to the recent changes which have taken place in this respect.

Inquiries have been made of the Medical Officers of Health in Whitechapel, Mile End Old Town, and St. George's-in-the-East, with regard to the present sanitary condition of the dwellings and workshops occupied by foreign Jews in those districts compared both with their condition a few years ago, and with the state of the dwellings and workshops of the surrounding non-Jewish population. Mr. Lakeman, H.M. Superintending Inspector of Workshops, and his staff of assistants, and the Medical Officers of Health of the London County Council, who have recently made inspections of selected workshops, have also given valuable information with regard to the sanitary condition of East London workshops.

Besides the evidence obtained from the above authorities, a large amount of valuable information with regard to the sanitary condition of Jewish dwellings is to be found in the recent reports of the Sanitary Committee of the Jewish Board of Guardians.

The Russian and Polish immigrants come to Great Britain for the most part accustomed to a far lower standard of cleanliness than prevails among the majority of the inhabitants of this country. On arrival, after a long and tedious journey overland, they are probably seen at their worst, but in the opinion of the medical inspectors who were consulted at Gravesend, as well as of the Custom House officials who meet the vessels which bring alien Jews to London, there has been a marked improvement of late in the appearance of the immigrants on arrival. This improvement is thought to date from the enforcement of medical inspection at the time of the prevalence of cholera in 1892-93, which (as described above) is still carried out in the port of London.

There is a general consensus of opinion that the overcrowding of workshops has been checked during the past year or two, though it still occurs to a considerable extent. The medical officer in Whitechapel states that they do not there find overcrowding of workshops a very serious difficulty, the Jews and foreigners being more amenable to pressure than the English when they have learnt the requirements of the law. The report for 1893 of the medical officer in Mile End Old Town gives particulars of all workshops known to the local authority in the district. All these workshops were visited by sanitary inspectors, most of them at least twice during the year. On the whole, 362 visits * were paid to 200 workshops, of which the majority were Jewish. On 22 occasions the workshop is stated to have been found overcrowded. The whole of these cases of overcrowding were in the western part of Mile End, which is affected by the influx. There is some difficulty in drawing inferences even from the results of

_____

* Besides 42 cases in which the workshop visited was found to be unoccupied

two visits, since some of the trades (e.g., slipper-making) in which overcrowding is complained of are of a seasonal character. That some improvement, however, has taken place is evident from the results of the recent inspection of selected workshops in East London by an officer appointed by the London County Council (under Sections 100 and 101 (1) of the Public Health (London) Act, 1891). The list of workshops to be visited was prepared by the Sanitary Committee of the Jewish Board of Guardians, and included only certain Jewish workshops which had recently come under observation, many of which were believed to be faulty in one or more respects. Of 110 East London workshops inspected during 1892, 55 were found to be overcrowded. Of these 55, 35 which showed the most glaring defects were re-inspected in April and May, 1893. In seven cases the rooms were found to be no longer used as work-rooms; in 17 the overcrowding had been remedied, and in seven some attempt to remedy the evil had been made, but some degree of overcrowding was still present. In the remaining four cases (i.e., two in Whitechapel and two in St. George's-in-the-East) the rooms were still overcrowded, but "there were no instances discovered " of such gross overcrowding as was seen last December; in " fact, the masters of the workshops seem now to be alive to the " fact that there is a limit to the extent to which they may " crowd workers into the rooms."*

Classifying the workshops originally inspected by trades we find that 99 tailoring workshops visited in East London and the Strand, 37 were found to allow less than 250 cubic feet for each person found employed at the time of inspection. Of these three provided less than 150 cubic feet. The average number of cubic feet per head in all the tailoring workshops was 324, and in the "overcrowded" shops (i.e., those with less than 250 cubic feet) 202. Of 12 boot and shoe workshops, no fewer than eight contained less than the "minimum" of 250 cubic feet, the average for the whole number of boot workshops being 235 feet, and for the "overcrowded" workshops 175 feet. This evidence is very limited, but so far as it goes the state of over-crowding in the boot and shoe shops appears to be the worst.

The Medical Officer of the London County Council is of opinion that overcrowding is far the most serious sanitary defect in the Jewish workshops.

As regards the general cleanliness of workshops, the most complete statistical record for any single district is afforded by the tabular statement referred to above, of the results of the inspection in 1893 of the whole of the workshops known to the local authority of Mile End. The 362 visits to workshops may

---

* London County Council (Public Health Department) Report on Workshops, May 4th, 1893.

be classified as follows according to the description given in the report :—

Class of Workshops.	Described as " Good."	Described as " Dirty."	Described as " over-crowded."*	Total.
Tailoring - - - - -	212	38	21	271
Boot, shoe and slipper making -	34	5	1	40
Cap making - - - -	7	—	—	7
Dressmakers and milliners - -	26	1	—	27
Others - - - - -	14	3	—	17
Total - - -	293	47	22	362

In Whitechapel and St. George's-in-the-East there are too few English workshops to make any kind of comparison between them and Jewish workshops possible. In both districts, however, the medical officers state that the sanitary condition of Jewish workshops has improved since 1888 (when the inquiries of the Lords' Committee on Sweating were held), under the pressure of sanitary inspection. The bootmaking shops are stated to be the worst. Mr. Lakeman attributes this largely to the fact that in the boot trade so large a proportion of workshops do not contain any "protected persons" (i.e., women or young persons) and consequently escape the control of the factory and workshop inspectors. Some particulars as to the sanitary condition of boot and shoe workshops visited in the course of this inquiry are given on pp. 171 to 181. On the whole the majority of those workshops visited seemed in fair sanitary condition, and some were very good. A certain proportion, however, were very bad, in some cases totally unfit for occupation.

Turning from workshops to dwellings, a consensus of opinion is found that the rooms inhabited by the immigrants on their first arrival in London (e.g., in Booth Street Buildings) are very defective from a sanitary point of view. After some period of settlement, however, the immigrants tend to improve in these respects, and they then often pass on from Whitechapel or St. George's to Mile End or other parts of London, or elsewhere. Thus the congested districts of Whitechapel are to some extent only a temporary halting ground for the newly-arrived aliens, and the sanitary condition of their homes in these districts is to this extent typical of the condition of the foreign Jews at the time of their arrival in this country rather than after they have become "anglicised." The process of assimilation, however, frequently takes a long time. Little complaint is made of the sanitary condition of the homes of the old settled Jews.

On this point the best detailed information is that published by the Sanitary Committee of the Jewish Board of Guardians, by

* Including cases of overcrowded and dirty workshops.

which a large number of the more defective dwellings are inspected. In 1893, 5,209 visits were paid by the officer of this committee to 1,746 dwellings chiefly in Whitechapel, St. George's-in the-East, Mile End and Bethnal Green. Of these, 986 dwellings or considerably more than half were found to be below the standard of the local authority. In the great majority of cases the defects discovered were remedied during the year, but the report makes strong complaint of the condition of certain blocks of tenement houses particularly Booth Street Buildings, which house over 1,300 persons, and (as stated above) are chiefly inhabited by newly-arrived immigrants. The report states that the owners of the greater part of this property cannot be induced " to take steps " adequate to secure that the premises shall be kept in something " like a decent and sanitary state."

In spite of the unsatisfactory condition of certain spots like that alluded to above, there appears to be a consensus of opinion that on the whole the sanitary condition of the Jewish districts of East London has shown an improvement during the past five or six years.

(vi.)—Condition as regards Crime.

A census carried out for the purpose of this inquiry by the Home Office throughout all the local and convict prisons in England and Wales shows that on January 11th, 1894, there were 56 persons of Russian or Polish nationality in those prisons, viz., 13 in convict prisons, and 43 in local prisons. Of the latter, 4 were under remand or awaiting trial, leaving 39 under sentence, viz., 21 in London and 18 in the provinces. The degree of gravity of the offences may be gathered from the following analysis of the length of sentences in all cases in which sentences had been pronounced :—

	Provinces.	London.	Total.
Penal servitude.—10 years - - -	1	—	1
7 years - - -	3	—	3
5 years - - -	6	—	6
3 years - - -	3	1	4
Imprisonment.—1 year or more - -	1	5	6
6 months and under 1 year -	5	3	8
3 months and under 6 months	5	3	8
1 month and under 3 months -	3*	9	12
under 1 month - -	4†	—	4
Total under sentence - -	31	21	52

Of the 56 persons in prison, 11 were charged with offences of violence and assault of various kinds, 8 with burglary, house-

* In one case with alternative of sureties.
† In three cases with alternative of fine.

breaking &c., 3 with forgery, 1 with arson, 1 with abduction, 21 with theft, fraud, or receiving stolen goods, 2 with offences connected with the coinage, and the remaining 9 with various minor offences.

In order to make some kind of rough comparison between the extent of criminality of this class of immigrants, and that of the corresponding native population, it is necessary to compare the total number in prison in a given locality with the number of the population from which they are drawn. For this purpose it is best to take London (or rather the area that commits prisoners to London prisons) as the area of comparison, since it is here that the majority of Russians and Poles are concentrated and we are enabled to compare them with a large surrounding city population exposed to somewhat similar conditions as regards crime. Moreover, the statistics published by the Commissioners of Prisons show that only 39 occupants of London prisons (or less than one per cent.) were under the age of 16 on March 31st, 1893.* The population therefore with which the number should be compared is not the total population of all ages, but the number of persons over the age of (say) 15. This correction is of importance in estimating the criminality of foreigners since these do not include their full proportion of children. Thus only slightly over 15 per cent. of the Russians and Poles in England and Wales are shown by the Census to be under the age of 15. Applying this percentage to London, we find that there were in 1891, 22,711 Russians and Russian Poles in London over the age of 15.† 21 were in prison at the beginning of 1894, giving a proportion of 1 in 1,081.

Now, roughly speaking, the population over the age of 15 of the entire district from which prisoners are committed to London prisons is about 4,000,000. On an average 4,027 were in prison on any one day during 1893, giving a proportion of 1 in 993, a slightly greater proportion than in the case of the Russians and Poles. In this comparison no account has been taken of the fact that since 1891 the foreign Russian and Polish population of London has probably grown at a faster rate than the total population.

Without laying too much stress on the actual figures (which in dealing with so small a number of Russian and Polish prisoners may possibly be somewhat misleading), it may be stated generally that the evidence shows that the amount of crime traceable to this class of immigrants is small in actual volume, and that its proportion to the numbers of the immigrants is probably less rather than greater than the normal

* Sixteenth Report, part 1, p. 23.
† There are also a small number of Russians and Poles in the extra-metropolitan districts which commit to London prisons. Their number, however, cannot be exactly ascertained, and may be neglected without serious error.

proportion among the whole population of London and the neighbourhood.

This result confirms the view which has often been expressed by persons conversant with the habits of the foreign Jews, that they are on the whole a peaceful and law-abiding community.

PART II.—THE INDUSTRIAL POSITION OF THE IMMIGRANTS IN CERTAIN TRADES.

§ (*a*) GENERAL INTRODUCTION.

Distribution of Immigrants among Trades.—On pp. 148 to 156 a statistical table is given showing the distribution of the class of immigrants under consideration among different trades and industries.

For reasons given in the last section it has been thought sufficient to confine this analysis to persons born in Russia and Poland and living in each sub-district of East London,* Manchester, and Leeds. The materials on which the table is based are extracted, by permission of the Registrar General, from the unpublished occupation sheets of the Census of 1891.

Whatever doubts may be entertained as to the absolute accuracy of the total figures, there is no reason to doubt their substantial correctness, so far as relates to the relative distribution of the aliens among the chief groups of trades and occupations, on the day to which the Census relates. A difficulty, however, is afforded by the seasonal character of many of the trades affected, which seriously stands in the way of a very accurate detailed enumeration of persons engaged in some of the trades pursued. Thus the London slipper-making is an almost purely seasonal trade, being very largely confined to the last six months of the year. The result is that the Census (taken in April), shows a total of only 172 Russians and Poles in East London engaged in this trade, which in the season must afford occupation to a much greater number, a certain proportion of whom work at some other branch of the boot trade in the slack season. Again, the number returned as hawkers, travellers, &c., in the same districts is only 198, compared with 309 who were actually relieved by the Jewish Board of Guardians during the same year. One reason for the discrepancy is undoubtedly the fact that a certain number of tailors and others, whose busy season is in the spring when the Census was taken, become petty dealers in the slack season, and appear as applicants for relief in this capacity.

There is, however, no possibility of mistaking the general deductions to be drawn from the table on page 154. The two main groups of manual trades in which the Russian and Polish Jews in East London are engaged are tailoring (5,727), and boot, shoe, and slipper making (1,763). These are followed at a considerable distance by cabinet-makers (690), furriers (409), cap-makers (406), cigar-makers (364), dress and mantle-makers (302), stick-makers (200), and bakers (143). Retail tradesmen and shop assistants number 510, and hawkers 198, though for reasons given above this last number is probably largely understated.

---

* *i.e.*, the Tower Hamlets and Hackney.

Rough, heavy, or out-door labour hardly attracts any of this class of immigrants. Thus only eight are returned as general labourers, three as carmen, and one as railway worker.

The vast majority are engaged in petty handicrafts, i.e., handicrafts conducted in small workshops or at home, and requiring no great exercise of physical power, and no high degree of skill.

As regards local distribution, Russian and Polish tailors and tailoresses are chiefly found in Whitechapel, the northern part of St. George's-in-the-East, the western part of Mile End Old Town, and the southern corner of Bethnal Green. These districts, covering an area of 938 acres, account for 5,601 out of the 5,727 Russians and Poles engaged in these trades in the whole of East London and Hackney. Of this number, 4,336 are males and 1,265 females. Foreign Jewish boot, shoe and slipper makers are chiefly confined to the same area as tailors, 1,660 Russians and Poles, (viz., 1,629 males and 31 females), being resident therein out of a total of 1,763 Russians and Poles pursuing these trades throughout East London and Hackney.

Russians and Poles engaged in cabinet making are most largely found in the northern part of Whitechapel and the southern part of Bethnal Green, the four registration sub-districts covering this area accounting for 530 out of a total of 690 (nearly all males) for the whole of East London and Hackney.

The distribution in East London of foreign Jewish cap-makers, dress and mantle makers, and persons engaged in the other main Jewish trades does not materially differ from the above.

Turning to the Russians and Poles in Manchester, we find that tailoring, as in London, easily heads the list of industries so far as regards the numbers engaged, no fewer than 1,123 of this class of foreigners being employed in that trade. The next trade in order of magnitude is cap-making, which employs 281. Slipper-making accounts for 171, cabinet-making for 139, and boot and shoe making for only 67. Hawkers number 242.

In Leeds the proportion of tailors is yet more marked than in London or Manchester, this trade accounting for no fewer than 1,882 out of 4,540 Russians and Poles resident in the district. Slipper-making follows at a great distance with 185, boot and shoe-making with 145, and hawkers with 89. Cabinet-making, cap-making, and other handicrafts practised by foreign Jews in London and Manchester, do not appear to be carried on by them to any appreciable extent in Leeds, where the wholesale clothing trade nearly monopolises the labour of this class of aliens.

Character and Limits of the Present Inquiry.—It is clear from the above that for the purpose of considering the economic effects, if any, of the competition with British labour of this class of aliens, it will be sufficient to deal with the clothing trades, including tailoring, boot-making, cap-making, &c., and the furniture trades. There is one other industry—that of hawking and petty dealing—into which they enter to a considerable extent, often as a supplementary resource. In an unorganised and casual employment, however, such as this it is very difficult to arrive at any definite conclusions as to the effect on British labour of foreign immigrants.

The industrial position of foreigners in the clothing trades in 1888–1890 was dealt with by the Lords' Committee on Sweating, and also less elaborately by the House of Commons Committee on Immigration and Emigration in 1888. It was also the subject of a Memorandum by the Labour Correspondent of the Board of Trade in 1887. Moreover, it was carefully investigated about the same time in the course of the unofficial inquiry into the Labour and Life of the People in London, instituted by Mr. Charles Booth and his co-workers. So far, therefore, as the situation five years ago is concerned, we are in possession of much information. Since that time, so far as the inquiries of the Labour Department have shown, the methods of organisation of the tailoring and furniture trades, the extent and character of the foreign competition in these trades, and the departments of labour which it chiefly affects, have not undergone any sufficient transformation to make it necessary to cover the whole ground again by a fresh detailed inquiry. With regard, however, to the tailoring, cap-making, and kindred trades, which employ large numbers of women, the present inquiry has been directed to an examination of the industrial position of the women workers, both foreign and English, and of the character of their competition with one another and with foreign and English men. In the course of this inquiry, which was conducted by Miss Collet (the lady Labour Correspondent of the Labour Department), a considerable amount of information has been incidentally obtained as to the position of foreigners generally in the tailoring trade. Miss Collet's report will be found on pp. 95 to 133.

The boot and shoe trade stands in a somewhat different position, inasmuch as since the publication of the reports above alluded to* a considerable change has taken place in the organisation of the trade in the direction of the substitution of " indoor labour " in factories and workshops for outdoor labour in small workshops and the homes of the operatives. This change, which applies chiefly to the lasting and finishing departments, has had effects on the industrial position of foreign labour which require to be somewhat fully discussed. The boot and shoe trades have therefore been selected for special inquiry in connexion with the present report, both because of the changes which they have recently undergone, and because it is in this group of industries that English and foreign immigrant labour seem to come into the most direct relations, and in which consequently the chief complaints are

* An elaborate inquiry into the state of the East London boot and shoe trade was made in 1888-9 by Mr. D. F. Schloss, the results being published both in Mr. Booth's volume and in a separate form.

heard of the injurious effects of foreign immigration. The
Lords' Committee on Sweating reported that " the cheap boot-
" making trade in London is that which attracts the largest
" number of 'greeners,' and in no trade, not even that of
" tailoring, does the sweating system find a more unlimited field
" for its action."*

It is in the boot and shoe trade that competition between
native and alien labour is said to reach its acutest phase, and
consequently this industry is even more suited for detailed
inquiry than the tailoring trade, which on the whole employs a
larger number of alien workers. Thus in most branches of
tailoring (so far at least as male labour is concerned) the field
is divided more or less completely into departments, some almost
monopolised by English labour, and others almost monopolised
by foreigners. In boot-making the dividing line appears to be
not in all cases so sharply drawn.

It has been stated that foreign labour has had a detrimental
effect on some branches of the boot trade, especially in London, both
in crippling the power of the men's unions by supplying a reservoir
of cheap labour on which employers who have a dispute with the
unions can draw, and in monopolising the cheaper branches of
work on which British workmen formerly learnt the trade. No
allegation is made of actual diminution in the rates of wages of
British bootmakers, but it has been suggested that the competition of the foreigners has tended to break down the recent
agreement for the provision of indoor workshops, and to induce
a reversion to the old outdoor system. It is also stated that the
rates at which newly-arrived foreigners work are often far
below the piece rates recognised by the associations of employers
and of employed for the cheapest class of work to which the
piece " statement " applies.

In order to deal adequately with the points here enumerated,
it will be necessary to describe somewhat fully the general
conditions under which the boot and shoe trade is carried on,
especially in London, and the recent changes that have taken
place in its organisation. In making this inquiry, the results
of which are given in the following section, the Department has
to acknowledge the valuable co-operation of H.M. Inspectors of
Factories and Workshops, especially of H.M. Superintending
Inspector of Workshops and his assistants, and also of the Secretary of the London Boot and Shoe Manufacturers' Association,
of the officials of the Metropolitan Branches of the Trade Unions
concerned, and of others possessing special knowledge on the
subjects dealt with.

---

* Final Report, p. lxviii.

§ (b.) ALIEN IMMIGRATION IN RELATION TO THE BOOT AND SHOE TRADE.

Present Position and Local Distribution of the Boot and Shoe Trade.

—The Census of 1891 showed that 248,789 persons were then engaged in various branches of the boot, shoe, and slipper trade in England and Wales,* viz., 202,648 males and 46,141 females. Of these 38,989 were in London, 24,159 in Leicester, 13,138 in Northampton, 7,662 in Leeds, 6,384 in Norwich, 4,874 in Bristol, and the remainder in various other districts. Out of the total, 3,778 (viz., 3,608 males and 170 females) were born in foreign European countries, and of this foreign contingent 2,609 (viz., 2,515 males and 94 females) were natives of Russia or Russian Poland; 1,763, or 68 per cent., of the total natives of Russia and Poland engaged in these trades in England and Wales were living in East London and Hackney.

It is to the London trade, therefore, that in the main this inquiry may be confined.

It would be a mistake to suppose that all the above centres of the boot trade are competing directly with one another for the production of the same class of goods. In common with Leicester, Bristol, Norwich, and certain other provincial centres, London is a centre for the manufacture of very varied classes and qualities of boots and shoes, largely, but not entirely, for women's wear. On the other hand, there are districts, like Leeds and Kingswood (near Bristol), which are mainly centres of the "heavy" trade, i.e., the making of men's heavy hobnailed boots.

The chief centres for the production of the very commonest classes of goods are East London, where they are made largely by Jews, and the outlying villages of Leicestershire, where they are produced largely on the domestic system by families working at home.

Tables are given on pp. 186 to 193 showing the magnitude of the exports and imports of boots and shoes from and to the United Kingdom for the last 20 years, from which it is evident that the manufacture for export is a large and growing branch of the trade. In 1893, 693,049 dozens of pairs of boots, valued at 1,697,232l., were exported from the United Kingdom, mainly to British possessions. The tables are further discussed on pp. 90 and 91.

The largest boot factories are in the provinces, chiefly in Leicester and Northampton. The London trade is mainly in the hands of small and medium employers, who number between 300 and 400, in addition to some 200 "chamber-masters," mainly foreign Jews.†

* 21,749 persons are shown by the Census to have been engaged in the boot and shoe trade in Scotland and 21,506 in Ireland in 1891. Of this number only 56 were foreigners, viz., 34 in Scotland and 22 in Ireland. These parts of the United Kingdom may therefore be left out of account in the present inquiry.
† See p. 86.

Among the 70 London employers who have kindly supplied full particulars of the numbers of various classes of workpeople whom they employ, 6 employ less than 10 persons on their premises; 44 employ from 10 to 49 persons, 18 employ from 50 to 99, and only 2 employ over 100 on the premises, the average number employed indoors by each of the employers making returns being about 45. As will be seen below, a certain number of outworkers must be added to this number.

The chief organisations in the London trade are the London Boot and Shoe Manufacturers' Association, including 139 employers; the Metropolitan Branches of the National Union of Boot and Shoe Operatives, including about 5,250 members, chiefly lasters and finishers, and clickers and rough stuff cutters engaged in the machine-sewn trade; and the London Branches of the Amalgamated Society of Boot and Shoe Makers, with about 1,700 members, chiefly engaged in the hand-sewn trade. Hardly any women belong to the Unions. A certain number of foreign Jews belong to the National Union.

Recent Tendencies in the Boot and Shoe Trade.—

In common with tailoring and furniture making, the other two industries in which foreign Jewish labour chiefly abounds, the boot-making industry is in a state of gradual economic transformation. From the condition of a pure handicraft, in which each article was made throughout by the hand labour of one worker or group of workers, all these trades have been gradually changed in character by the introduction of machinery, which has converted them from crafts into wholesale industries, carried on under the conditions of subdivision of labour. In all the branches which have undergone or are undergoing this process of transformation the subdivision of labour has had the effect of graduating the skill required, so that in place of a set of workers of more or less uniform degrees of skill, the operatives engaged in the trades have become classified in different groups, ranging from a low to a high degree of skill, the door being thus opened to a less skilled class of labourers than formerly worked at the trades. Meanwhile the old handicraft method of production has gone on side by side with the newer machine industry, though gradually shrinking in bulk.

The newer or wholesale branches of the trade tend to become concentrated in factories, owing largely to the use of power, but the process of transformation being as yet incomplete there are important processes or subdivisions of the industry which are still largely carried on by hand without the aid of machinery, and which virtually constitute a new species of handicraft (e.g., boot-lasting or finishing*), which can equally well be done out of the factory. While, therefore, in most centres where factories can flourish the great factory is swallowing up the

---

* For explanation of these terms see p. 74.

small workshop, there has been a counter tendency to the multiplication of small workshops often in the homes of the workers for the carrying out of certain subdivisions of the trade, the work being given out for this purpose from the main factory or workshop, and returned after the completion of the process. Thus by the side of or in place of the small maker has grown up the "outworker" dependent on the factory. The changes here described have been independent of any pressure of competition from foreign labourers, being the natural result of the economic changes affecting the trade in all parts of the country alike. The above description applies, to some extent, to tailoring as well as to bootmaking. In the bootmaking trade, however, the tendency towards the outdoor system of work has been lately checked, and in most districts reversed by the operation of two distinct influences. In the first place, the abuses to which it gave rise, both of a sanitary and economic character, led to a protest against it by the Operatives' Unions, which claimed the provision by all employers of sanitary workshops. This "indoor" movement in the trade began in London, about four years ago, and since then agreements for the establishment of the "indoor" system for most branches of the trade previously carried on out of doors have been made between the Unions and the Employers' Associations in London, Leicester, Bristol, Northampton, and elsewhere. The second, and in the long run the more powerful, influence which has encouraged the concentration in factories and workshops of the branches of work formerly carried on outdoors has been the gradual introduction, into the finishing and lasting processes, of machinery with its accompanying subdivision of labour. This transition from hand-lasting and finishing to machine work is yet far from complete, but it is a change which may be said already to have determined, so far as the future is concerned, the question of factory *versus* domestic labour in the lasting and finishing branches, at least for all districts in which factories can flourish. Whether this new subdivision will in its turn develop a fresh form of outwork—in the shape of those particular sub-departments of finishing which "follow" the machines, and are entirely worked by hand—is a question which could only be answered by those possessing expert knowledge of the trade. For the immediate future there is little doubt that the introduction of finishing machinery driven by power will tend more and more to concentrate this department of work in factories. Of lasting the same may be said with some reservations. Lasting machinery is still in its infancy, and a recent tendency has shown itself towards subdivision of the handwork without recourse to machinery, the lasters working in teams of three or more following each other. This is the "team" system, which is still in dispute between the representatives of the operatives and the employers. It appears, however, to be essentially a transitional rather than a permanent mode of labour organisation in the trade, being almost certainly destined to disappear as machinery becomes more perfected.

While, on the one hand, the advent of machinery gives an impetus to the adoption of the indoor system of working, the latter in its turn facilitates the introduction of machinery.

The above general sketch indicates broadly some of the economic forces which are at present at play in determining the evolution of the boot and shoe trade. Briefly speaking, the opposing forces are the influence of machinery tending towards concentration, and, on the other hand, the possibility of a longer working day, of family help, and of freedom with regard to the particular hours of working which tend to make outwork popular with certain classes of workpeople, while it reduces some items of expense to the employer and lessens his responsibility. It has been indicated above that in this contest of rival tendencies the forces which tend towards concentration are on the whole the most powerful. It is evident, however, that the relative force of the two tendencies will vary very greatly according to the circumstances of each district and the character of the population. Thus (to take a single example) in the Bristol district, which is an important centre of the boot and shoe trade, the indoor system has lately been established with the general concurrence of both parties, while a few miles off, at Kingswood, the industry is almost entirely carried on on the "outdoor" principle, in small workshops built at the back of the operatives' houses, and at present there is no very strong movement in the direction of indoor work ; the habits of many of the operatives in this somewhat isolated district being opposed to the regularity and constraint of factory hours.

Thus it happens that while there is, on the whole, a general tendency to indoor work, showing itself most strongly in districts where (as, for example, in Leicester) there is a factory population, there are also other districts which form "backwaters" with regard to the general current, and in which, for various reasons, depending on the industrial circumstances and character of the population, the forces are very evenly balanced or in which the tendency towards the multiplication of small workshops is on the whole stronger. London is the most important of these "backwaters," and the reasons for this fact and the influence of foreign labour in the matter demand the most careful attention.

Before, however, going in detail into the position of the London boot trade it should be remembered that the mutual competition of different districts, e.g., Leeds with Kingswood, London with Leicester, Norwich, Bristol, and other centres, is very keen, and that this competition acts as a constant pressure on the backward districts to conform to the more advanced methods under penalty of losing part of their trade.

It must be repeated that the general character of the evolution of the boot and shoe trade has been entirely independent of foreign immigration, though some of its symptoms have often been mistaken for results of the competition of alien labour. Certain methods of labour division, which will be described below (e.g., the subdivision of hand-finishing between the "knifer" and the finisher proper), are apparently due to the foreign Jew, but they are probably "transitional" features of the trade, which disappear with the minute and more scientific subdivision which accompanies machinery. The modern tendency towards machinery in the trade comes from America and not from Russia and Poland. If it be desired to summarise in a word the influence of the Russian and Polish Jew on the character (as apart from the remuneration) of the boot and shoe trade in this country it may be said to consist in this—that it has somewhat prolonged the intermediate stage of transition from hand labour in small workshops to machine labour in factories, by the provision of a supply of labourers specially adapted to petty handicraft on the small scale, and with sufficient powers of endurance and a sufficiently low standard of living to enable them to make head (for a time at least) against the enormously superior odds of the great machine industry.

The direct competition of the "sweating" workshop in London is not with the handsewn trade; but, in the first instance, with the large factory (mainly in the provinces), and, in the second instance, and to a far smaller extent, with bootmakers abroad. It competes with the provincial or London factory, in so far as the higher qualities of the work carried out in the sweater's shop overlap the lower qualities made indoors in factories and workshops regulated by the "uniform statement." For a still lower class of goods its competitors are said to be abroad. It is asserted by the employers that the lowest class of shoes cannot be profitably made in this country under the existing scale of prices, and that it forms a floating margin of the trade, being carried on here or abroad according to the increase or decrease of the facilities in England for the engagement of "cheap" labour unrestricted by the "uniform statement."[*]

Besides the direct competition referred to above (i.e., the competition between different classes of workmen, or workmen in different places offering to execute the same class of work), there is an "indirect" competition to be taken into account between the wholesale and the old "handsewn" trade.

The "handsewn" and the "machine" operatives do not, for the most part, meet directly as competitors. In many cases neither class could, as a fact, do the work of the other. But the market for handsewn boots has gradually contracted, owing to the competition of the cheaper machine-made article. This form of competition, acting through demand rather than through supply, is very powerful in its ultimate effects on the industry

---

[*] It should, however, be stated that this view is not entirely admitted by the Union. The point is discussed on p. 83.

affected, but in this present case it has tended rather to diminish the numbers engaged in the handsewn branch than to reduce their rates of wages, which, as a matter of fact, have risen appreciably in recent years, especially in East London.

Meaning of "Changes of Wages" and "Displacement of Labour."—From the above sketch of the forces which keep the boot and shoe trade in a state of unstable equilibrium we can realise the difficulty and complexity of the question of determining the precise influence on wages and displacement of British labour caused by the competition of a particular class of workpeople, e.g., alien immigrants.

With what scale of wages is the comparison to be made in a trade which is in a condition of rapid internal evolution, in which there is a continual re-adjustment going on of the functions of each set of operatives? And how is it possible to make accurate comparisons with regard to a class of work which is oscillating between England and foreign countries?

A perfectly accurate comparison of wages at two different periods must compare like with like: either the class of operatives or the class of work must have remained the same. Confusion and misunderstandings are frequently caused by the application of the same term "change of wages" to an alteration in the scale of pay for particular classes of work, and an alteration in the proportion which the more and less highly paid branches of the industry bear one to another. Thus it would be said that wages in the boot trade have risen or fallen if the scale of piece rates recognised in the "statements" have been raised or lowered, and for certain purposes this is the most accurate mode of comparison. But those who assert that there has been a rise or fall of wages often mean something quite different, viz., that the tendency has been for the proportion of the higher class of work to increase (or decrease) compared with the lower branches of the trade. This mode of approaching the question has much to be said for it if the classes of operatives engaged in the different branches of the trade are similar as regards skill and grade. Where, however (as in the boot trade), this is not the case, this way of looking at changes of wages may be seriously misleading. Can wages be said in any real sense to have fallen if (say) the foreign Jews have introduced a very cheap and low paid class of work, provided the wages of those engaged in other classes of work remain untouched?

A good illustration of the confusion above alluded to is afforded by a disputed question which was recently before the London Boot and Shoe Trade Arbitration Board, but which has not been brought to an issue, viz., as to the recognition of a special rate of pay below the present "minimum" for the making of what are known in the trade as "lasting" shoes. The employers claim that this class of shoe was not provided for in the "statement" of wages agreed to in 1890, and regard the fixing of a lower price for them as merely an extension of the range of the statement. The men contend that the statement included all classes of boots and shoes, and look on the employers' demand as a proposal for reduction.

In view of the different standpoints from which such questions may be regarded, it is not difficult to understand how the most widely differing statements may be made apparently with equal authority as to changes in wages, which are equally difficult to prove or disprove.

The difficulty appears still more clearly if we try to attach a definite meaning to the term "displacement." The most frequent charge against the alien Jew is that he "displaces" British labour. Now a labourer unquestionably "displaces" another if he settles down by his side and offers to take the work which he is doing at a lower price, provided that the condition of the industry at the time is a stable one and the demand for its products constant approximately. In this case the new comer getting the work will deprive the first man of it, while (*ex hypothesi*) the cheaper price at which he does it will not extend the demand sufficiently to provide work for both.

But the case is altogether different if the demand instead of being constant is a peculiarly elastic one, especially if, as is the case in the boot trade, the new comer concentrates his attention largely on that part of the trade in which the demand is most elastic, viz., the export trade. The question becomes a nice one, whether ho has " displaced " native labourers (*i.e.*, is doing work which but for his presence they would have done), or whether he has introduced a new trade (*i.e.*, is making for a demand which he has created, and which, had it not been for his arrival, would either have remained unsatisfied or have been supplied by producers abroad).

Still more difficult is it to establish the fact of the displacement of labour in any particular district. The London boot and shoe operative who complains that he is being displaced by aliens means that he would otherwise have been doing the work which they are doing. But in the state of constant and un-remitting competition among different districts, the alternative to the Jewish sweater's shop in Whitechapel may conceivably be, not the London factory employing native labour but the provincial factories in Norwich or Bristol, or the home-workers in Leicestershire villages.

This is a fact which is often not realised. The London work-man who sees the Jewish "sweater" taking out a low class of work at prices below the recognised scale entertains no doubt that, but for this "unfair" competition, this work would have fallen to him to do at the higher rate of pay, whereas the real stress of competition may not be between himself and the "sweater" at all, but between the "sweater" and provincial or foreign workers. The Leicester factory, with its 98 distinct processes and 59 distinct machines through which a boot has to pass, is in the long run a far more potent instrument of competition than the sweater's workshop, however low may be his piece-rates and however long his hours of work.

Keeping in mind the above considerations, we may now turn to a more detailed account of the recent history and present position of the London boot trade as affected by alien immigration.

It is desirable in the first place to define in general terms the main divisions of the trade, the system under which each is carried on, and the classes of operatives concerned, specifying the branches in which foreign workers are chiefly engaged. In what follows no attempt is made at a complete and accurate technical description of the industry, the object being merely to give a sufficient indication of the character and sub-division of processes to throw light on the position of foreign workers in the trade.

Character and Division of Processes.—Generally speaking the chief operations connected with the making of boots and shoes may be divided into four main classes : (1) "clicking," or the cutting out of the leather for the "uppers," and "rough-stuff cutting," or the cutting-out of the "stuff" for the heel and sole ; (2) the sewing or "closing" of the uppers ; (3) the "lasting" of the boot or shoe, i.e., the bringing together of upper and sole on the last ; (4) the "finishing" of the boot or shoe, including the paring of the sole and heel with a knife, and various subsidiary finishing operations, e.g., blacking the heel, polishing or burnishing the edges of the sole and heel, &c.

In the "machine," as distinct from the "handsewn" trade, these operations are usually confided to different sets of operatives, and some of them are often further subdivided. The limits of subdivision are determined partly by the class of work, partly by the size and equipment of the factory or workshop. It is naturally carried furthest in the case of the great factories employing the newest machinery.

"Clicking" is a hand operation, almost invariably carried on on the premises of the employer. "Rough-stuff cutting," or the cutting out of the material for sole and heel, is usually done by machinery, also on the employer's premises. Machining, or sewing the uppers, is done chiefly by English women, but partly by foreign men, usually, though not invariably, off the premises of the employer. In the lasting and finishing departments there has been a recent contest between the "outdoor" and "indoor" systems of working, which will be described more in detail below.

The only subdivision of labour usual in the clicking depart-ment is in the separation of pattern cutting from the actual cutting out of the leather, and the employment of boys in cutting linings.

"Closing" is subdivided into "fitting," "machining," and the work of "table hands," including buttonholing, the addition of bows, buckles, &c. The process of "machining" itself is often subdivided, each machine being confined to the sewing of particular parts of the upper, or the lining.

"Lasting," as distinct from sole sewing and the attaching of the heel, is not usually subdivided in the ordinary London workshop, but two forms of subdivision are to be noted : (1) the "team" system, whereby hand lasters have been employed in certain provincial factories on the premises in groups of three, at time rates of wages, instead of each man "lasting" throughout at a piece-rate : (2) the system of subdivision in force in the Jewish "outdoor" system, by which a small master takes out lasting at a piece price, and employs subordinate workers, (usually youths) sometimes on time wages, sometimes at a certain graduated share of the piece-rate.

"Finishing" is now almost invariably, among Jewish workers, divided into at least two subdivisions—"knifing" and "finishing" proper, the former being the more skilled operation. On the other hand English finishers as a rule, knife and finish throughout without subdivision.

The above organisation is considerably modified in those establishments which have introduced "lasting" and "finishing" machinery. Thus, for example, finishing machinery in the largest factories in the provinces may split up the processes of finishing not into two, but into more than twenty consecutive processes with corresponding subdivision of labour. On pp. 162 to 164 is given a list of the 98 operations through which a boot passes from the beginning to the end of its construction in a large boot and shoe factory working with the newest machinery.

As regards the relative numerical importance of the four groups of workers indicated above, returns have been received from 70 establishments in London, employing 3,160 operatives indoors as well as 644 outworkers. Of the indoor hands 541 (or 17 per cent.) are clickers and roughstuff cutters, 351 (or 11 per cent.) machinists, 1,054 (or 33 per cent.) lasters, 868 (or 28 per cent.) finishers, the remaining 11 per cent. being employed in various miscellaneous operations not included in the above groups. The precise number of individuals engaged on outwork for these firms cannot be ascertained, since some of the 644 outworkers doubtless employ subordinate labour. 35 of the outworkers are finishers and 9 lasters (all working out of doors by special arrangement, and employing no labour), 188* are machinists, 398 "sew-round" and "handsewn" hands, 9 sole sewers, and 5 miscellaneous or unspecified.

Though the firms represented in the returns just summarised only employ a fraction of the total labour engaged in the London boot trade, the proportions of workers engaged in the various operations may be regarded as fairly typical of that part of the trade (including the great majority of firms) which is subject to

---

* Besides machinists working in the country for one firm. (Number unspecified.)

the recognised agreement. The detailed particulars with regard to these firms are given on pp. 158 to 161.

The departments of the trade chiefly affected by foreign labour are the lasting and finishing branches, which, as will be seen above, absorb 61 per cent. of the total indoor workers employed by the firms making returns. Comparatively few foreigners are employed as clickers, but a few foreign Jewish men are engaged in machining.

The above outline must only be regarded as affording a very rough and general description of the trade as usually carried on in London. A more detailed account of recent changes in the last few years is given below.

Recent Changes in the Organisation of the London Trade.—In September 1889, the London Metropolitan Branch of the National Union of Boot and Shoe Rivetters and Finishers,* which at that time chiefly consisted of lasters and finishers, resolved to make three demands from the employers : (1) to alter the " second-class " statement of piece prices, and to extend its application to all firms who either compete with or supply the firms paying " statement " wages, (2) to prohibit lasters and finishers from working with assistants other than their sons, and (3) to provide workshops on or off the premises of the employers, who should pay all expenses of rent, light, &c. It was further resolved to enter on a strike if the last-named concession were not granted before March 24th, 1890. Somewhat similar resolutions were adopted by the City (" women's ") Branch of the Amalgamated Boot and Shoemakers', the Jewish Masters', and the Jewish Journeymen Finishers' and Lasters' Societies. At a conference held early in 1890 between the trade union executives and the employers' section of the Conciliation Board, it was resolved to recommend the concurrent adoption of the workshop system and of the principle of arbitration, June 25th being named as the date by which the workshops should be provided. Owing, however, to various causes, this conference did not avert a widespread and prolonged strike, which affected the whole of the London boot and shoe trade from the end of March to June, 1890. In this strike the men were supported by the Union of Jewish Masters or so-called " sweaters," and eventually terms of settlement were agreed to, which should be quoted in full, owing to their widespread influence on the recent course of development of the trade :—

(1.) That the manufacturers will open workshops for the men at the earliest possible date.
(2.) That matters relating to classification and all other questions, excluding direct reduction of wages, be referred to arbitration.
(3.) That a uniform statement of wages be forthwith prepared for all shops except the present first and second-class statement houses.

---

* Now the " National Union of Boot and Shoe Operatives."

(1.) That a joint board of conciliation and arbitration be forthwith appointed, to consist of seven employers and seven workmen, and that one arbitrator (who shall be a practical man) be elected by the employers, and one arbitrator (who shall be a practical man) shall be elected by the workmen, who, when appointed, shall elect a third arbitrator, who will act when called upon.

The above settlement applied solely to the lasters and finishers in the boot and shoe trade. Clickers and rough stuff cutters were already working on the premises of the employers, and machinists (who are largely women) have continued to work as outworkers. The agreement, moreover, has not affected the so-called " sew-round " trade, i.e., the manufacture of fancy shoes and slippers, of which East London is an important centre. The limits of the indoor agreement must be carefully remembered in what follows.

The settlement with regard to the provision of workshops for lasters and finishers was agreed to by 385 employers, representing practically the whole of the trade.

Under the agreement no lasters or finishers were allowed to work at home except for special reasons (e.g., age) with a permit from the Joint Board.*

The effect of the change was to sweep into the employers' factories and workshops the great mass of those who had hitherto worked as "outworkers," including many of the Jewish "sweating" masters, who now took their place as ordinary journeymen lasters or knifers. There were, however, some of these small masters who were unable to find places as journeymen, and who were practically ruined by the change. The Jewish Masters' Union became a branch of the National Union of Boot and Shoe Operatives. Its former secretary (now the secretary of the branch), now works as a journeyman knifer and finisher in a workshop. Before the change came about he described to the Lords' Committee on Sweating the state of the boot-finishing industry at that time. Under the old "sweating" system the small master who took out boots to finish did the " knifing " or paring the soles and heels himself, and employed a team varying from two to four less skilled assistants to complete the operation of finishing. Usually there was only one subdivision of labour, i.e., between the knifer and finisher, but a skilled knifer could work fast enough to " feed " several finishers. In some cases, however, where learners or " greeners " were employed, there was further sub-division among the finishers proper who worked in a " team," the new-comer doing the least important part of the work. The mode of division of the joint earnings was simple. The knifer provided the workroom, light, firing, " grinding," tools and materials, did the knifing, and took half the price, the remainder being divided among the subordinate

* Altogether 209 such permits have been granted. For the form and conditions, see p. 170. No subordinate labour may be employed by outworkers with permits.

labourers. Under this system it is stated that a highly skilled
knifer, working long hours and aided by his wife in "shopping"
the goods, could make 5l. a week as his share of the gross
earnings. The same man, working under the "statement" as a
journeyman knifer, can now earn 2l. or more a week nett. Under
the statement the division of the piece price between knifer and
finishers, is in the proportion of 7 : 17 (i.e., 3½d. to 8½d. out of
every shilling) intead of 1 : 1, but the price thus divided is a
nett and not a gross price, the rent of workroom, &c., being no
longer a charge on the knifer. Whether the knifer's position
has improved or deteriorated by the change is a matter of individual opinion. In the opinion of some the shorter and fixed
hours of the workshop, the absence of responsibility, and the fact
that a man's house is now his own, and is not turned into a
workshop, are considerations which more than compensate for
the lowered earnings. Others doubtless regret the change. But
whatever be the position of the knifer, there can be little doubt
of the improved position of the "finisher" proper, who can now,
if possessed of fair skill, earn higher wages while working moderate
hours in a sanitary workshop.* How far the change affects the
pocket of the employer it is not easy to judge. Some think that
it has unquestionably increased the cost of production, while
others are of opinion that better work can be obtained under
the indoor system. It is, however, generally agreed that under
the indoor system firms governed by the recognised "statement"
no longer find it profitable to employ low class or untrained
adult labour. The opportunity which the "greener" used to
find of taking his place at the bottom of the scale in the team of
subordinate labourers in the finishers' back parlour, and of
gradually working his way up to the top, and of becoming a
small master in his turn, is now much diminished, so far as the
workshops conforming to the agreement are concerned. He is
shut out by the barrier of the standard wage. The only capacity
in which "greeners" could enter the workshops would be as
learners—like boys, and this door has now been almost closed
by the action of the union soon after the new agreement. Since
then its members decline to teach the trade to any immigrants
who have not already practised some branch of it in their native
country. The result is that "greeners" can no longer learn the
trade or find a place in the workshops over which the union has
any control.

It should be stated that the sub-division of labour between
knifer and finisher to which (except in the case of sons employed
by their fathers) the union objected under the old "outwork"
system is now recognised in the workshops, knifing and finishing
being frequently carried out in different parts of the building,
and regarded as separate departments of labour. The subdivi-

---

* He loses, however, the doubtful advantage of being able to employ members of
his family.

sion, however, is mainly confined to the Jews, who had formerly practised it under the "outwork" system.

The case is different with "lasting," the commoner branches of which were, during the continuance of the outdoor system, carried on to a considerable extent by "teams." As in the case of finishing, the unions discountenanced sub-division except between father and son, and English lasters rarely employed adult subordinate labour, the "team" system being almost exclusively adopted by foreign Jewish masters. Now that lasting is performed indoors there is, as a general rule, no sub-division, each man lasting throughout.

Such being a brief description of the changes in the position of lasters and finishers caused by the introduction of the indoor system, it remains to give a short account of the history of the system since its introduction, and the difficulties with which it has met, and finally to attempt a picture of the existing state of the trade and the present outlook.

For the first year, after the agreement of 1890, few complaints were heard of breaches of the agreement. From July 1891 onwards, however, disputes have taken place with regard to outwork, chiefly with small employers, and in some cases with employers who did not belong to the Employers' Association, or who had begun business since the agreement. The number of shops "blocked" by the union owing to disputes about outwork or other matters since the agreement came into force has only been 25. In a few cases an understanding has subsequently been arrived at, leaving 16 employers stated in the official report of the union to be "blocked" at the present time (April 1894).

That there has been a certain revival of outwork pure and simple is clear, but it does not appear to be of great dimensions at present, though naturally giving rise to anxiety. The question is dealt with statistically on pp. 86, 87. A characteristic example of the way in which the revival has come about in some cases is afforded by a Polish Jew, whose workshop I visited in East London in January 1894. He takes out finishing and himself does the knifing, at which he is expert. Four finishers (all foreign Jews) are employed to follow him. According to his assertion he has himself been in the country seven years; of the others two have been here for two years, and the others one year and six months respectively. Formerly he was a finisher (not a knifer) in a team which worked out of doors for an important manufacturer. When the indoor agreement came into force he worked indoors as a finisher for the same manufacturer and thus learned to knife. He has now come out again as a small master employing a subordinate team, alleging that owing to the introduction of finishing machinery he was no longer able to make a living indoors.

A comparatively small proportion, however, of the boot and shoe trade (as distinct from sew-rounds), as carried on at present in small workshops, is outwork pure and simple. Of 51 small workshops recently visited in East London, mostly Jewish, 17 turned out to be those of manufacturers of boots and shoes, 3 slipper manufacturers, 8 to be "sew-round" hands, 9 machinists, 3 finishers, 2 lasters and finishers, and 9 lasters. Thus, excluding the machinists and sew-rounds (in which branches outwork is recognised), we have 14 out of the whole number who are outworkers proper.

The large proportion of small makers, however, suggests a form which the small "sweating" shop may assume under the pressure of the agreement prohibiting outwork.

The growth of a business from small beginnings to a comparatively large scale, has in former times been very common in the London boot trade, and there has probably never been a time when there have not been scattered about London a number of small boot workshops making on a comparatively small scale, either for the retail shops or for "factors," or even for the purpose of hawking.

Recent changes may, however, in some ways tend to stimulate this form of workshop. In the first place firms which pay the "statement" price may no longer be able to produce profitably the cheapest class of boots and shoes, and as it is important for them to be able to supply these boots, along with the higher qualities which they manufacture, to their retail customers or to sell them in the retail shops which are often connected with their establishments, they act as factors as well as producers, buying up in the open market the produce of the small workshop which is unfettered by the "statement." This is no new feature of the trade, but it has probably grown in importance in recent years.

The system may lead easily to evasion of the outwork agreement. I have interviewed a foreign Jewish laster and finisher who alleges that he *buys* the "uppers" ready made from a certain firm (which itself conforms nominally to the agreement), lasts and finishes them, and then *re-sells* them to the same firm "or to others." It was impossible to say with certainty how far there was an agreement to re-sell, but some understanding of the kind is exceedingly probable.*

Apart from all question of the evasion of the agreement, the development of the "factor" system gives an impulse to the multiplication of small masters, whose workshops are not in all cases any more sanitary than those of outworkers proper. We have here an illustration of the fact, on which the Lords' Committee on Sweating laid stress, that "the middleman is found to " be absent in many cases in which the evils complained of " abound."

---

* I am informed that the Conciliation and Arbitration Board has stopped some cases of evasion of this kind.

Another impulse to the multiplication of small makers as distinct from outworkers has been given by the practical closing of the workshops which conform to the "statement," against the newly arrived and untrained foreign Jew. The causes of this closing have been discussed above. One effect is that the greener has difficulty in learning his trade, except either in the employment of the outworker (and the opportunities for this have, of course, been enormously restricted) or in the small shop of a fellow countryman who is unaffected by the statement. These small shops are themselves the parents of a new system of outwork on a very petty scale, several small masters giving out part or all of the lasting and finishing to the same "outworker."

After the above sketch of recent changes we are in a position to consider more precisely the relation of foreign immigration to wages, displacement of labour, and general condition of the trade at the present time.

Wages and Methods of Remuneration.—As a general rule it may be said that piece-work prevails in the boot and shoe trade, except in the case of operatives working machinery, who are usually paid at time rates.

The piece rates payable for each operation in various classes of goods and by various classes of manufacturers are fixed by "statements" agreed upon between the employers and workmen.

The earlier statements referred naturally to the hand-sewn trade, the manufacturers being roughly classified into four grades, according to the character of the goods principally made by them. The grade to which an employer is held to belong determines the "ground work" price which he has to pay, i.e., the price for the making of the simplest possible form of boot. To this "ground-work" price may be added various allowances according to the nature of the materials used, or the additional work put into it, or on the other hand it may be subject to certain deductions.

The first "statement" drawn up in London in 1872 for the wholesale trade was based on the grading not of employers but of classes of boots, the classification depending on the nature of the material. This statement embraced some fifteen firms producing the highest class goods in the wholesale trade.

In 1875 a new "second-class" statement was introduced, applicable to about 25 employers turning out goods on the whole inferior to but competing with those manufactured by employers working on the former statement. As in the "first-class" statement the graduation of the boots is based on material.

Until 1890 the firms outside the limits of the various statements specified above (i.e., the great bulk of the makers of the medium and lower class goods) escaped all general regulation as to piece prices, though a few were induced to adopt special agreements (or "shop statements") with wages scales lower than the second-class statement. In 1884 an abortive attempt was made to bring the lower-class firms under regulation, but it was not until the re-organisation of the trade in 1890, with the accompaniment of indoor workshops and the formation of an arbitration board, that a uniform statement was introduced.

Thus at present the manufacturers in the wholesale (like the handsewn) trade are classified for purposes of determining piece-rates into three groups, according to the character of the goods chiefly produced. Within each group the classes of boots produced are further classified, the graduation depending chiefly on the materials used.

A specimen of the " statements" is printed in full on pp. 164 to 169.

It will readily be understood that the adjustment of rates, according to material, is a fertile source of disputes, especially since in the course of time materials formerly used in high-class boots are used in commoner qualities, or are imitated, or go out of fashion altogether, while new materials are introduced.

But besides the constant friction due to differences as to classification, the introduction of machinery for lasting and finishing threatens in the near future to make the piece state-ments to some extent inapplicable. Already there are large factories in the provinces in which almost all the workers are on time-wages.

As regards the London trade, it may be said generally, that, at present, all members of the Manufacturers' Association pay and all members at least of the unions receive the rates de-termined by the various statements so far as they are applicable. There are also a large number of non-union men receiving full " statement " wages. The only employers not paying the state-ment rates are some of those who are outside the association, including a few fairly sized houses, but chiefly small " chamber-masters " in East London engaged on an inferior class of work.

Members of the association, however, are not prohibited from acting as " factors " and buying up the produce of the " non-statement" workshops, and this is done to a considerable extent. There is also a class of " factors," pure and simple, who buy up the goods made by the " chamber-masters," without themselves engaging in manufacture at all.

On pp. 171 to 182 are given some notes on the outworkers and small makers in East London lately visited for the purposes of this inquiry. In most cases no information could be obtained as to piece prices, and in the remainder the figures given rest on the statements of the occupier. As, however, some of the rates are derived from " outworkers " receiving them, and some from small makers paying them, and the results agree fairly well, there is less reason to doubt their substantial accuracy. So far as these facts are trustworthy it would appear that there is a very con-siderable gulf between the lowest piece prices current for the cheaper forms of " outwork " and the *minimum* rates in the statement scale. Thus we find the rates for lasting performed in or given out by the small non-statement shops as low as 2s. 6d. a dozen pairs, a common rate being 3s. 6d., compared with 4s. 6d. a dozen which is the minimum "statement" rate for the very commonest class of goods provided for in the scale.* Finishers again have been found receiving as little as 2s. a dozen, compared with the minimum of 3s. in the "statement."* Of course it must not be assumed that there is necessarily an equal discrepancy between the weekly earnings of lasters and finishers in "sweating" and "statement" shops, since it is possible that the lower class goods may be produced more rapidly than the higher qualities.

It is, however, sufficiently clear that many of the "chamber-masters" and other non-associated employers are getting work done at lower piece rates than are possible in "statement" firms, and that the bulk of the workmen employed by such masters are foreign Jews. The question remains, how far the goods made under the different sets of conditions are really comparable. It has been indicated above that it is a disputed question how far the commonest class of shoes was provided for under the uniform statement. The so-called "lasting" shoes, to which the controversy mainly refers, are a cheap class of women's house shoes, the uppers of which, made of a fabric known as "lasting," are imported ready closed from Germany. A few of these shoes are made at present in London in statement shops; but the greater part are made up by small chamber-masters employing Jewish labour, to whom they are given out by factors. Moreover, the whole volume of production of this class of goods in London has greatly decreased of late years. The Employers' Association asserts that the trade has been driven into the hands of the non-statement masters or abroad, by the fact that the lowest prices provided in the statement prohibit the profitable production of this class of shoe.† It appears that the question of embodying a special lower scale for "lasting" shoes in the uniform statement came up before the Board of Conciliation and Arbitration when the statement was being drawn up. It was then agreed to omit it "subject to special " consideration of this material in a lower quality if required."‡ The employers subsequently pressed for the provision of a special class below the existing minimum so as to embrace this kind of shoe. The union has never, however, admitted its necessity, its contention being that the minimum in the statement already admits of the making of "lasting" shoes (which

---

* i.e., for "lasting" shoes classed as "H," for which the ground-work price is 5s. for lasting and 4s. 6d. for finishing, subject to deductions reducing the prices to 4s. 6d. and 3s. respectively. See p. 165.

† Letter from Secretary of Boot and Shoe Manufacturers' Association to arbitrators, quoted in evidence before Royal Commission on Labour, Section C., Q. 15,857.

‡ See Minutes of Board, 16th December 1890.

as a fact, are so made in certain quantities), and moreover that
what has driven away the trade has been partly a change in
fashion, "lasting" being partly replaced by sheep skin and other
cheap materials.

Between these rival views it is not proposed to attempt to
decide. The question at issue, however, is of interest as
illustrating the two views which may be held as to the relation
of many of the low paid Jewish workers to the union operatives
—the one view being that they are "under-cutting" British
labour, the other that they are working at specially low rates on
a different class of goods. Possibly neither view can be
exclusively accepted as furnishing a complete account of the
matter.

To turn from a comparison of wages in the "statement" and
"sweating" shops respectively to the question of general
changes of wages during the past few years, it will be evident
that such changes are not easy to estimate. The first and
second class "statements" have undergone no material alteration
during the past ten years, so far as the actual piece-rates
embodied in them are concerned. The change, therefore, from
outdoor to indoor labour in 1890, was equivalent to a clear
rise in wages, seeing that the cost of rent, light, &c., has since
fallen on the employer instead of the operative, and hence is no
longer a deduction from the latter's earnings.

It is evident, therefore, that no prejudicial effect has been
produced by the foreign influx on the rates of wages current in
the higher branches of the trade, in which, indeed, little or no
Jewish labour is to be found.

As regards the remainder of the trade, the uniform statement
only came into force in 1890, since when it has not been
altered. Before that date there were no generally recognised
rates, and there are therefore no satisfactory data for any
trustworthy calculation as to the relative weekly or yearly
earnings of those engaged in the commoner branches of the
trade at the present time compared with ten or fifteen years ago.
Earnings are affected as much by irregularity of work as by
changes in piece rates, and (with the exception of the figures
showing the recent growth of the export trade) no materials
exist for measuring the fluctuations in the demand for labour,
much less for separating those fluctuations due to the general
conditions of trade from those to be ascribed to other special
causes.

As is stated below, in dealing with the branch of the trade
known as "sew-rounds," the "sew-round" hands employed by 54
firms obtained a rise of about 12½ per cent. in wages in
1890. This rise only affected those engaged on the better class of
"sew-round" work, and left untouched the low class sew-round
trade in which foreign Jews largely abound. It is, however, a
proof that the presence of foreign Jews in the lower grades of

the trade has not had the effect of lowering the rates current for English operatives in the higher and medium branches.

Relation of Foreign Immigrants to Trade Disputes.

—Allusion has been made above to the possibility of the Union being weakened in trade disputes with employers by the presence of a reservoir of "cheap" foreign labourers, by which the strikers' places can readily be taken. As a matter of fact, however, apart from the cases already alluded to of a few employers who seceded from the agreement as soon as practicable, and have since been "blocked" by the Union, foreign labour has been a very small factor in actual recent disputes in the boot and shoe trade. This will be seen from the table on pp. 183 and 184, giving a list of the disputes reported to the Board of Trade as having taken place in the London boot and shoe trade since the introduction of the "indoor" system of work in 1890. Since that time it will be remembered there has been in operation a board of conciliation and arbitration to which all questions other than direct reduction of wages have been referred. Only 13 actual disputes have been recorded in London during the period referred to, the most important being the lock-out of operatives by 150 firms in October, 1891, resulting from a strike of the employees of one firm on the question of the alleged delay of the board in dealing with their grievances. The strike was in defiance of the union, which compelled the men to return to work, and the lock-out was then withdrawn. The only other dispute of large dimensions was the strike of "sew-round" hands employed by 54 firms in September, 1890, which was followed by an advance of about $12\frac{1}{2}$ per cent. in wages for the better class of sew-round makers. Of the remaining disputes, two were strikes of bootmakers for advance of wages, of which one was successful, and the other partially successful the men in those shops which did not concede the advance returning to work on the old terms, and not being replaced by others. Two other successful wages disputes were a strike in March, 1891, of the rivetters and finishers employed by three firms against the refusal of employers to agree to the advanced price list which had been generally accepted, and a strike of boot and shoe operatives in September, 1893, against the alleged refusal of one employer to pay according to the London statement. Two other disputes, viz., a strike of finishers in April, 1891, while the question of a revised statement was under consideration, and a strike of lasters and finishers in August, 1891, against the dismissal of certain colleagues, were disapproved by the Union. Another small strike of East London operatives took place in June 1893, for a reduction of hours.

The remaining four disputes are to be classed as unsuccessful, the strikers being replaced by others. Of these, two were small strikes of clickers, one involving 11 persons, in February, 1891, against the alleged excessive employment of boys, the other involving 17 persons in August, 1892, against the discharge of

four clickers for refusal to accept reduced prices. It is to be
remembered that clicking is not a branch of the trade in which
the encroachment of foreign labour is felt as a serious grievance.
There remain but two disputes of boot and shoe operatives (in
May, 1892, and September, 1893) each affecting a single firm.
The cause was the alleged refusal of the employers to pay
" list " prices or classify their work on the accepted scale. Sixty
persons were affected by one of these disputes, and forty or
fifty by the other. They ended in the defeat of the Union and
the replacement of " Union " men by others.

It appears from the above that the part played by foreign
labourers in taking the places of boot and shoe operatives
engaged in recent trade disputes has been comparatively small,
a conclusion which confirms the impression left by other evidence
that the extent to which the two classes of workers overlap is
on the whole less than is often supposed.

Magnitude of the Recent Revival of " Out-work."
—In the sketch given above of the recent history of the London
boot and shoe trade it has been indicated that since the agreement of 1890 for the provision of workshops by employers there
has been a certain, though limited, revival of " out-work " in the
branches of the trade included in the agreement, and that the
majority of the " out-workers " in the lasting and finishing
branches appear to be foreign Jews. It is therefore of interest
to inquire how far the revival has gone, and how far it threatens
the permanence of the general agreement by which the trade
has been so conspicuously benefited.

The materials for a calculation of the present number of
persons working as " out-workers " in the prohibited branches
are not completely satisfactory, and any estimate that is founded
on them must be regarded as a rough approximation only.

The employers who are possibly giving out lasting and
finishing may be divided into three classes : (1) the firms which
have seceded from the agreement, who have left or been
expelled from the Manufacturers' Association, and who are now
" blocked " by the Union ; (2) a few firms which have come into
existence since 1890 and have never come within the agreement ;
(3) small " chamber-masters " (chiefly Russian and Polish Jews).

The firms included under the first head number 16, and the
Secretary of the Manufacturers' Association estimates that,
including those who come under the second head, the number of
firms other than small " chamber-masters " giving out-work is
not more than 30. The number of " chamber-masters " cannot
be exactly stated, but from evidence collected from leather
merchants and others it appears likely that they number at
least 200, some of whom are doubtless giving outwork, though
on a small scale.

Through the courtesy of the Factory Department of the
Home Office complete lists have been drawn up of outworkers
to whom work is given out by 18 of the above firms (other

than chamber-masters) taken at random. These lists show that work is given out by the 18 firms to 202 outworkers, viz., 134 men (of whom 67 appear to be Jews) and 68 women, all English. The women are doubtless all machinists, and need not be further considered. The men may be divided into " sew-round " hands, machinists and sole-sewers, lasters, and finishers. The returns do not in all cases distinguish these different classes, but if those returns in which the distinction is made are typical of the whole number, we should conclude that about 60 of the Jewish outworkers returned are lasters and finishers.

A considerable proportion of the English outworkers are also lasters and finishers, but in most cases apparently working alone. If, further, we assume that the employers to whom the lists apply are typical of the whole number of firms (other than chamber-masters) giving out lasting and finishing, we should conclude that these 30 employers among them give out lasting and finishing to about 100 Jewish outworkers. These outworkers in most cases employ subordinate labour. The 14 workplaces occupied by lasters and finishers visited for the purpose of this inquiry were found to contain 55 workers at the time of the visit,* or an average of about four each. Applying this proportion to the whole number of outworkers we should arrive at a total of about 400 lasters and finishers employed on the "outwork" principle through the 30 employers referred to above.

As regards the out-work performed for the chamber-masters, we have the evidence of the visits paid to the workshops enumerated on pp. 171 to 176. In 12 small shops coming within this designation, 107 persons were found employed, including 23 clickers and rough-stuff cutters, 51 lasters, 22 finishers, and 11 others. Bearing in mind the proportions (given on p. 75) which the various classes of operatives usually bear to each other, this would indicate that, so far as the shoes are concerned for which the clicking is done on the premises, little or no lasting is given out, but that about 20 finishers are employed off the premises in the 12 shops. Probably, therefore, on the whole, between 300 and 400 individual finishers and lasters may be employed as "outworkers" by the total number of chamber-masters, on work for which the "clicking" is done on the premises. To this number we must add a conjectural number of "outworkers" employed by chamber-masters in lasting and finishing boots of which the uppers are imported and given out by "factors." Technically, the chamber-masters who receive these uppers are not "outworkers," but some of them may sub-let a certain proportion of the lasting and finishing to outworkers.

After making an allowance for this class of outworkers, it is probable that the total number of foreign Jews working at lasting and finishing on the "outdoor" system in London lies

---

* See pp. 177 to 179.

between 800 and 900, a number considerable in itself, but bearing a small proportion to the total number of lasters and finishers employed in the London trade.

Thus the "indoor" agreement may be said to be intact so far as the great bulk of the trade is concerned.

Alien Immigration in relation to Other Branches of the Trade.

—There are certain branches of the boot and shoe trade to which the "indoor" agreement does not apply, and which are carried on entirely or partly by outworkers. It is therefore necessary to note the effects, if any, of alien competition in these departments of the industry.

(1.) *Boot Machining.*—The "closing" of the uppers of boots and shoes by the sewing machine is, to a large extent, given out to be done by English women in their own homes or in small workshops, though a good many manufacturers employ women machinists on their premises. A certain amount of "outdoor" machining is, however, done by foreign Jewish men who thus come into direct competition with English women as in the tailoring trade. Examples of the two classes of workers are given on pp. 179 and 180, showing particulars of workshops visited in East London.

The number of men employed in machining is, however, small, and they appear to be losing rather than gaining ground compared with the English women. The manager of a company which supplies a large number of bootshops in East London with sewing machines on loan, and so has an intimate knowledge of the course of the trade, gives it as his opinion that the work of closing uppers so far from tending to fall into the hands of the Jews of East London has a tendency to leave London for the provinces.

(2.) *The Sew-round Trade.*—A branch of the boot and shoe trade which has recently attained considerable proportions in London is the so-called "sew-round" branch, which is concerned with the making of light shoes and slippers. This department of the trade has been hardly affected by the recent changes in the organisation of the industry and is still almost entirely an "outdoor" trade, the uppers already cut out and "closed" by the machines being given out to makers who work in small workshops or in their own homes. In the West End the system of associated workshops prevails to some extent among the workmen engaged on the better classes of "sew-rounds." The whole of the industry is a season trade, the busy period being from July to January or February. The sew-round trade in East London may be divided somewhat sharply into two sections which scarcely overlap at all, viz., the better and medium qualities made by English operatives, and the lower classes of goods, the production of which is monopolised by foreign Jews.

A reference to the particulars of Jewish workshops on pp. 180 to 182 will give some idea of the character of the lower branch of the trade, which has largely grown up during the years in which the influx of foreign Jews has taken place. It is in the cheap sew-round and slipper trade that some of the worst abuses of "sweating" are found, in the way of long hours, low earnings, and irregularity of work. The shoes and slippers are made partly for home consumption, partly for export. They appear to have created a new demand, chiefly for fancy wear, and not to have taken the place of any other form of shoe. A few English workers are engaged in the cheap slipper trade, but the number is not appreciable.

On the other hand, the Jews do not to any appreciable extent enter the higher branches of the East London sew-round trade, which are governed by a special "statement" of piece-prices agreed to by employers and employed. In the opinion of one of the Branch Secretaries of the Amalgamated Society of Boot and Shoemakers, about 800 men are engaged in these branches in the East London district of whom very few are Jews, though there are two or three Jewish employers (employing English workmen) engaged in the trade and paying the "statement" rates of wages. He can only recollect one case of attempted "under-cutting" of prices by two Jewish workmen, and this was successfully resisted.

There is therefore little direct competition between Jewish and English workmen in the sew-round and slipper trade. Nor does there appear to have been any great indirect competition through the encroachment of the cheaper qualities of goods produced by the Jews on the market supplied by goods of English make. On the contrary, the English sew-round trade is itself a recent creation, having mainly grown up during the last 10 years (i.e., during the period of the influx). Before that time this class of shoes and slippers were largely imported from France : but London has now become an important centre for their production, which appears to be still extending, both for home use and export.

Most of the goods produced in London are hand-sewn, but in some provincial centres (e.g., Norwich and Leicester) machine-sewn work is now being turned out. There is a cheap slipper trade in Manchester and Leeds, but the chief provincial competition appears to come from Norwich and this applies only to certain grades of work.

The trade in London was unaffected by the "indoor move-ment," partly owing to its want of organisation, partly owing to the absence of machinery.

In 1890 a considerable rise in wages took place in the higher class sew-round trade in London which has since been main-tained, and many of the most skilled men receive very high wages. The chief evil in the trade is that of long hours, due to the system of family work at home.

Neither the Union nor the "statement" embraces any part of the "sweated" trade.

In the London "sew-round" and slipper trade we have therefore a good example of an industry divided into two almost
"non-competing" sections. In the one is found the skilled
English workman making for one market, in the other the
low-skilled foreign Jew supplying another. Neither the workers
nor the markets appear to any great extent to overlap or to
affect each other. Both branches of the trade have grown
rapidly during the same period, and the English workers have
recently materially raised their wages.

In this trade, therefore, while the evils of "sweating" from
which the Jewish branch suffers acutely are greatly to be
deplored in the interest of the foreign Jews themselves, the
English workers have no complaint against them for interfering
either directly or indirectly with their labour.

Relation of Immigrants to Growth of Foreign
Trade.—In view of the question how far the Jewish alien
immigrants have economically displaced British labourers and
overrun their industries, and how far, on the other hand
the real effect of the influx has been to create or at least
largely to augment an important trade in cheap clothing,
especially for export, it is of interest to analyse the statistics
of exports of boots and shoes during the period covered by
the influx and the few years preceding it. If statistics were
available for the home trade the comparison would of course be
more complete, but as the rapid growth of the cheap clothing
industries of late years has been largely a growth in the export
branches, the statistics of foreign trade are of considerable value
for the purpose of comparison.

A detailed table is printed on pp. 186 to 189 showing for each
of the 21 years, 1873-1893, the total quantities and values of
boots and shoes exported from the United Kingdom to each
country or British Possession. The influx began in 1881, and
it is therefore convenient to group the years into periods of six,
viz., 1875-1880, 1881-1886, and 1887-1892.

The yearly average of the total quantities exported during
these periods is as follows:—

	Period.	Yearly Average Exports of Boots and Shoes (in Dozens of Pairs).
Six years immediately preceding the influx -	1875–1880	437,689
First six years of influx - - - -	1881–1886	553,167
Second six years - - - - -	1887–1892	665,460
Increase of average of last period over that of first - -		227,771
Ditto. ditto per cent. - - - -		52

It is evident, then, that the influx has been accompanied by a rapid expansion of the export branch of the wholesale boot trade. It does not, of course, follow from the above figures that it has been *due* to the influx, nor is it likely that so limited a cause could account entirely for so large an increase of trade. It must be remembered that, as pointed out above, the boot trade has been undergoing a transformation by machinery which has been quite independent of the influx of foreigners, and to this transformation the remarkable development indicated by the figures must be largely due.

The figures, however, do not certainly lend any support to the suggestion that has often been made, that the export trade has suffered from the influx owing to the inferior quality of goods produced.

A table is added on pp. 190 to 193 showing for the same period the quantities and values of boots and shoes imported into the United Kingdom. The average yearly quantities for the various periods are as follows:—

Period.	Yearly Average Imports of Boots and Shoes (in Dozens of Pairs).
1875–1880	103,284
1881–1886	106,166
1887–1892	115,200

The great growth in the import trade in boots and shoes within recent years was between 1873 and 1876, when it increased from 40,304 dozen pairs to 109,896 dozen. Since 1876 on the whole the imports have remained nearly stationary, the imports in 1892 being 118,386, and in 1893 122,219 dozen pairs. It appears likely, therefore, that the influx of foreigners has done something to check the growth of importation of boots and shoes.

General Summary.

The general conclusions to be drawn from the above investigation with regard to the influence of foreign Jews on the boot and shoe trade may be thus summarised:—

(1.) The boot trade being (in common with the slop clothing and other industries to which foreign Jews chiefly resort) in a state of steady but uncompleted economic transformation, owing to the introduction of machinery and other causes, it is a matter of extreme difficulty to disentangle the effects on wages and conditions of labour of any special cause (such as foreign immigration) from the general effects produced by the process of revolution which the trades are undergoing. It is clear, however, that the presence of foreign Jewish labour in certain departments of the boot and shoe industry, while it may be a symptom of one stage of the evolution of the trade, is in no sense the cause of the transformation itself.

(2.) The main bulk of the foreign Jews employed in boot and shoe making in the United Kingdom reside in East London, where they are chiefly engaged in the production of the commonest qualities of boots, shoes, and slippers.

(3.) Some of them work on the "indoor system" on the premises of manufacturers, but more often they are either small "chamber masters" selling to retail shops or to "factors," or "outworkers" engaged in lasting, finishing, or (to a more limited extent) machining, or in the "sew-round" trade.

(4.) Some of these foreign Jews work according to the recognised "statement" prices, but in many cases, especially among the "outworkers" and "chamber masters," the piece-rates current are considerably below those generally observed in the trade for the lowest quality of goods to which those rates apply.

(5.) Up to 1890 most of the "lasting" and "finishing" (which between them employ the majority of boot and shoe operatives) was given out to be done off the manufacturers' premises. In that year, however, a great change took place in the organisation of these branches of the trade. A general agreement was arrived at between the employers and employed for the provision by the employers of workshops for these branches of work: a uniform statement of prices was also compiled applicable to the whole of the trade not covered by former lists, and an arbitration and conciliation board was set up for the settlement of differences.

(6.) Since that date a certain number of manufacturers have broken away from the agreement and again given out "lasting" and "finishing." The total number of employers, however, other than small "chambermasters" not observing the indoor agreement is probably less than 10 per cent. of the total, and the numbers employed by many of them are comparatively small. There has thus been a partial revival of "outwork," chiefly among the foreign Jews, but as regards the bulk of the trade the agreement is observed. The total number of foreign Jews working at lasting or finishing on the "outdoor" system is probably between 800 and 900.

(7.) The number of foreign Jews engaged in the trade in East London has largely increased during the 10 years between 1881 and 1891, but since 1890 the flow of newly-arrived Jews into the trade has been checked by the operation of the "indoor" agreement and the "minimum statement" of piece-rates, combined with the refusal of the Union to allow immigrants who have not been engaged in bootmaking before arriving in the country to enter the workshops as learners. It has thus become impracticable for "greeners" to learn bootmaking in many of the workshops governed by the agreement.

(8.) This check has apparently diverted somewhat the flow of "raw" foreign labour from bootmaking to other trades. The agreement of 1890, however, does not touch the "sew-round" hands, the lower grades of whom are almost entirely foreign Jews, and the outdoor system here prevails almost exclusively. The inability of foreign untrained Jews to enter "statement" workshops may also have tended to stimulate to some extent the multiplication of small Jewish masters and outworkers ungoverned by the agreement.

(9.) Many of the small Jewish workshops are insanitary and overcrowded: the earnings, at least of newly-arrived foreigners, are low and the hours long. The sanitary condition, however, has improved during the last few years, and the local authorities are taking action with regard to overcrowding.

(10.) The competition of the alien Jews has not affected the piece-rates recognised generally in the trade, which have not been substantially altered since their establishment. The English sew-round hands (engaged in the better class of work) actually gained a considerable rise in wages during 1890, while the introduction of the indoor system has been equivalent to a rise of wages for lasters and finishers in workshops governed by the first and second class statements.

(11.) The foreign Jews are to a large extent engaged on a common class of boots and shoes, some of which probably could not profitably be made by English labour under the existing statement, and might hence cease to be produced, or at least leave London (either for the provinces or abroad), were it not for the presence of Jewish labour.

(12.) In the machining department, where foreign men compete with English women, the latter are gaining ground on the former.

(13.) The above conclusions are confirmed by the great increase
(amounting to 52 per cent.) which has taken place in
the total annual exports of boots and shoes from the
United Kingdom, if we compare the average of the
last six years (1887–92) with that of the six years
(1875–80) immediately preceding the influx.

(14.) Since the agreement of 1890 there have been comparatively few important strikes in the London boot and
shoe trade, and in very few of these, affecting a small
number of persons, has the presence of foreign labour
been a considerable factor in the dispute.

(15.) The gradual introduction of finishing and lasting
machinery acts as a powerful influence, tending to
maintain the "indoor" factory system. This machinery has been more extensively introduced in the
provinces than in London, and the main stress of
competition on the part of the foreign Jew is probably rather with the provincial factory than with
the London operative.

PART III.—FOREIGN IMMIGRATION IN RELATION TO WOMEN'S LABOUR.

(Report by Miss Collet.)

§ (a) INTRODUCTION.

I.—OBJECT AND SCOPE OF INQUIRY.

The object of the inquiry was to ascertain the extent to which foreigners compete with English women in different industries of importance, with special reference to the effects, which might be expected to follow in cases where foreigners destitute of the means of support endeavoured to obtain employment.

Two aspects of the question were to be kept in view :—

(a.) The competition of foreign women with English women ; and

(b.) The competition of foreign men with English women.

On the one hand, therefore, it was necessary to investigate the conditions under which immigrant foreign women arrive in England in order to measure the extent to which they might be expected to enter the labour market as wage earners.

On the other, it was necessary to make some survey of the trades in which foreign women were chiefly to be found, to compare the work done and the wages earned by English and foreign women in these trades, to contrast these earnings with those of English women and girls in trades in which no foreign women were to be found and finally to note any branches of trade in which foreign men were employed on work generally performed by women in establishments managed by English employers.

The ground to be covered by my inquiry was therefore but a limited portion of that already covered previously to 1890 by Governmental and private investigation. The Reports from the Select Committee on the Emigration and Immigration of Foreigners for 1888 and 1889 in addition to the general evidence on the subject contain a summary of statistics of wages in 1886–87 in the tailoring and trouser-making trade at the East End of London, compiled from schedules distributed and collected and in part filled up after personal communication with employers by the Labour Correspondent of the Board of Trade. Mr. Burnett supplemented his inquiries for the Board of Trade by further personal investigation in East London and Leeds, the results of which are to be found in Appendix G. to the Second Report, and in Appendix O. to the Fourth Report, of the Select Committee of the House of Lords on the Sweating System, and in Mr. Burnett's evidence before the Select Committee. The Reports of the House of Lords Committee on the Sweating System contain the evidence given in 1888 and 1889 of large numbers of persons in London, Leeds, Manchester, Birmingham, Hull, Sheffield, Newcastle, Glasgow, and other towns as to the effect of the employment of foreigners on the system of sweating. Contemporaneously with the investigation carried on by the Government, Mr. Charles Booth was superintending a special inquiry into East London industries and published the result in " Life and Labour of the People," Vol. IV., devoting separate chapters to the study of the Boot and Shoe Trade, the Tailoring Trade, the Cigar Trade, and the Cabinet-making Trades, the four industries in which Jewish labour was most largely found. Only one of these trades, the tailoring trade, at that time involved the employment of any considerable number of foreign women, although the cigar trade employed a certain number. The chapter on the tailoring trade, contributed by Miss Beatrice Potter, together with the reports of Mr. Burnett to the Board of Trade and the evidence on the tailoring trade given before the Select Committee on the Sweating System, contain nearly all the trustworthy evidence as to the employment of foreign women available previous to 1890.

In none of the inquiries referred to was any definite attempt made to consider the industrial position of foreign women as distinct from that of foreign men nor to estimate exactly the extent to which foreign men entered into competition with English women as distinct from English men. But the evidence on the tailoring trade referred to above gave indications that such distinctions would need to be drawn in order to arrive at a clear understanding of the persons affected by foreign immigration or liable to be affected by restrictions on immigration.

My instructions were, therefore, to concentrate attention on these two aspects of the effects of foreign immigration, and, after personal investigation, to re-state the position for 1893 and to give supplementary evidence on points merely touched upon in previous inquiries.

II.—METHODS PURSUED AND MATERIALS FOR INQUIRY.

(a.) Tracing of Individual Immigrants.

The Select Committee on Emigration and Immigration (Foreigners), 1889, recommended "that measures should be " adopted to provide for a record of the names, sexes, ages, " occupations, nationalities, and destination of all alien steerage " and deck passengers arriving at ports of the United Kingdom " and not in possession of through tickets to other countries." In accordance with this recommendation the Act 6 Will. IV. c. 11, requiring every master of a ship arriving in this country with aliens on board to hand in a list of the names and descriptions of those aliens to the Customs authorities has been enforced at all the principal and many of the minor ports since 1890. Since the early part of 1891, officers of Customs at the several ports concerned have been specially charged with the duty of making personally an actual count of all the aliens on board a certain proportion of the vessels arriving with such passengers in order to test the substantial accuracy of the lists handed in. Furthermore, since June 1891, it has been the special duty of an officer of Customs to visit vessels arriving in the port of London from Hamburg likely to have destitute aliens on board.

The lists supplied by this officer of Customs contain the nationality, sex, civil condition of aliens on board without through tickets for places not in the United Kingdom, and also the addresses and names of relatives or friends to whom the immigrants profess to be going together with the sums of money which they allege that they have in their possession. To these lists I was allowed access, and from them I extracted the names and alleged destinations of a number of foreign women who landed in London in 1892. All the women, 80 in number, who landed from Hamburg during the first fortnight in May 1892, and the women, 37 in number, who came over in one vessel on July 4th, 1892, were selected, the former group as representative of immigrants arriving during a period of normal immigration, the latter as representative of immigrants arriving in large numbers close upon each other.

Of these selected immigrant women 25 were passed over as giving for their destination parts of London or elsewhere too far distant from each other to make inquiry profitable. Of the remaining 92 I endeavoured to discover the history subsequent to landing in London. The addresses given in each case were visited by me, accompanied by an interpreter acquainted with Yiddish. Every assistance was rendered to me by the Jewish Board of Guardians, who searched carefully through their registers and those of the Russo-Jewish and Board of Guardians Conjoint Committee to discover whether any of these 92 women had come before them for assistance, and the Secretary of the Poor Jews' Temporary Shelter performed the same service. The register of the Home for Jewish Girls was also searched, and information most readily given by one of the lady managers of the home. The results of this inquiry are given in full in the Report.

(b.) Occupations of Poor Jewesses.

The London Jewish Board of Guardians placed at my disposal at their offices in Devonshire Square the application sheets of all persons applying to them for relief for the first time from July 1st, 1892, to January 31st, 1893, thus enabling me to obtain exact information as to the means by which destitute Jewesses endeavoured to obtain a living. Similar information was supplied me by the Secretary of the Leeds Jewish Board of Guardians.

(*c.*) *Reports of the London, Manchester and Leeds Jewish
Boards of Guardians.*

The London Jewish Board of Guardians publishes annually
details of applicants for assistance and of persons emigrated,
showing their nationality, length of residence in England, civil
condition and occupations. The Manchester Board publishes
very similar information. The Leeds Jewish Board has hitherto
been unable to make these returns. Until 1892 the various
congregations in Leeds expended a certain amount in charity
without the intervention of the Board ; during the last year the
amounts thus subscribed have been paid direct to the Board, the
machinery for relief being thus assimilated to that of London
and Manchester.

(*d.*) *Trade Inquiry.*

In this part of my inquiry I have to acknowledge most
valuable assistance rendered by H.M. Chief Inspector of
Factories, and by H.M. Inspectors of Factories Mr. Lakeman, Mr.
Gould, Mr. Hine, and Mr. C. W. Shaw, who furnished me with
information as to the trades in which foreign women were to be
found, and supplied me with lists of workshops under inspection
in the East and the West End of London, in Leeds, and in
Manchester. The industries of main importance proved to
be the tailoring, waterproof-making, cap-making, cigar-making,
and fur-sewing trades. I am especially indebted to the Singer
Manufacturing Company, by whose managers and agents in
East London, Leeds, and Manchester, no pains were spared
and no labour grudged in giving the results of their wide
experience as suppliers of sewing machines on hire ; I have also
to thank Dr. Murphy, Chief Medical Officer to the London
County Council ; Dr. W. H. Hamer, Assistant Medical Officer to
the County Council ; Dr. Tatham, Medical Officer of Health at
Manchester ; and Dr. Cameron, Medical Officer of Health at
Leeds, for assistance given me in visiting workshops.

From evidence from various sources and from the census
returns for 1891 it appeared that London, Manchester, and
Leeds were the largest centres to which the poorest foreigners,
the Russian and Polish Jews resorted, the trades pursued by
them in smaller towns being exactly the same as in the three
above mentioned. In London, accompanied by Dr. W. H.
Hamer, I visited 166 small tailors' workshops in the West End,
and in the East End the workshops of 54 coat-makers, 7 vest-
makers, 4 trouser-makers, 4 mantle-makers, 3 dressmakers
(men), 19 cap-makers, and 12 furriers, making 269 workshops
in all. In Leeds, accompanied by a sanitary inspector, I visited
75 tailors' workshops, and in Manchester, also accompanied by a
sanitary inspector, 61 tailors' workshops, 18 cap-makers, 4
waterproof-makers, and 2 slipper-makers. In the 166 West
End workshops particulars of sex and nationality were noted.

In the remaining 263 workshops visited particulars were obtained whenever possible as to numbers employed in each branch, wages paid, civil condition of women employed, race, and length of residence in England. Information was also asked for and obtained from a few wholesale clothiers and manufacturers in London, Leeds, and Manchester.

§ (b.) RESULTS OF STATISTICAL INQUIRY.

1. POSITION OF FOREIGN IMMIGRANT WOMEN ON ARRIVAL IN LONDON.

The Board of Trade reports on emigration and immigration from and into the United Kingdom in the years 1891 and 1892 show that the Russians and Poles and the Germans supply the largest number of foreign immigrants into London.

From these returns it appears that during the last two years the number of women immigrants from Russia and Poland is about half that of the men, and that the Russian and Polish immigrants more than equal in numbers the immigrants of all other nationalities.

According to the census returns of 1891 the number of Russians and Poles in London included 14,773 males and 11,969 females, while that of the Germans in London included 16,440 males and 10,480 females. The numbers of female immigrants are in both cases smaller than those of male immigrants, and were the children classified apart from the adults the disproportion would appear still greater. The majority of the adult women would therefore probably be married, and it remained to be seen whether as married women they entered the labour market.

No facts presented themselves which might have rendered an inquiry into the occupations of non-Jewish German immigrant women necessary. Partly owing to their distribution over a wider area of London than occurs with the Russians and Poles, and partly to the demand for German domestic servants, partly to the fact that large numbers of Germans are clerks whose wives do not enter the labour market, no complaints have been made so far as I am aware of their competition with English working women.

In order to ascertain whether the Russian and Polish female immigrants came to London without any home prepared for them by relatives or friends, and were therefore liable to accept work at very low rates through destitution, a list of female immigrants was drawn up, and efforts made to trace them. For reasons already stated this list included the names of the 80 women who landed from 12 vessels arriving in London in the first fortnight of May 1892, and 37 who came in one vessel on the 4th July 1892. It was compiled from the alien lists furnished to the Customs, and contained the address to which the immigrant professed to be going, the relative or friend who was to receive her and the sum of money she stated to be in her possession. The 117 names were submitted to the Jewish Board of Guardians, who after the most careful search through their registers could only identify eight as persons who had come under their notice as being in need of relief for themselves or members of their families : of these three had been sent to the United States. A similar search was made through the registers of the Poor Jews' Shelter with the result that one name was recognised as that of a woman sent to America by the society. Twenty-five women on the list had given addresses in different parts of London at some distance from the Jewish quarter in Whitechapel and St. George's, and no attempt was made to trace them.

The results of the inquiry into the remaining 92 cases are given in detail in the tabular Appendix XII. (pp. 196 to 201).

They may be summarised as follows :—

(a.) Numbers traced.

Of remaining 92 women—

56 were married women or widows.
36 were unmarried women.

Of the 56 married women or widows—

5 gave either no address or an insufficient or incorrect one, and were not heard of elsewhere.
28 could not be traced.
3 were known to have been met by relatives on landing.
20 were traced.

Of the 36 single women—

4 gave either no address or an insufficient or incorrect one, and were not heard of elsewhere.
5 could not be traced.
1 was known to have been met on landing by a relative.
26 were traced.

(b.) Position of Women traced.

Of the 20 married women or widows traced—

11 were known to be supported by their husbands or relatives and to have no wage-earning occupation.
1 was known to be with her husband.

3 were known to be living apart from their husbands and
to be earning wages by washing, cleaning, or nursing.

2 had been sent to the United States.

2 had received assistance from the Jewish Board of Guardians.

1 was living entirely on the charity of neighbours.

Of the 26 single women traced —

6 had been given into the charge of relatives in London and
had not since been heard of.

2 were married shortly after arrival.

5 obtained situations as domestic servants.

3 obtained work as tailoresses.

1 obtained work as capmaker.

1 obtained work as cigarette maker.

1 obtained work as fur sewer.

3 were known to be wage earners, but the kind of work
was not known.

2 had been sent to the United States.

1 had been sent home.

1 was in a lunatic asylum.

(c.) Married or Widowed Women not traced.

Of the 28 married or widowed women not traced—

5 landed in England with their husbands.

3 landed in England with some adult male relative.

20 were unaccompanied by any male relative ; of these 13
professed to be going to their husbands, 5 to their children,
1 to a sister, and may have been met on landing : 1 appeared to have no friend in London.

None of these could be found on the registers of the Jewish
Board of Guardians or the Poor Jews' Temporary Shelter
as having applied for relief, and if assisted must have applied
under some other name.

Further information with regard to unmarried immigrant
women is afforded by the records of the " Home for Jewish Girls."

The agent of the Jewish Ladies' Association meets every
immigrant ship and ascertains the number of single women
on board. Those who are not met by friends are taken to the
Jewish Home for Girls. Their friends, if they have any, are
found for them, and if they have none they stay in the home
until employment has been obtained for them. Particulars of all
girls thus received between July 1st, 1892, and January 1st, 1893,
were furnished and are given in detail in the table on pp. 201
and 202.

The following is a summary of these particulars :—

24 were received into the Home. Of these

7 obtained situations as domestic servants.

3 obtained work as dressmakers.

2 obtained work as glovemakers.

2 obtained work as tailoresses.

1 obtained work as umbrella maker

3 were sent to the United States.

5 were given into the charge of relatives or friends and had not since been heard of.

1, who was not Jewish, was transferred to the Travellers' Aid Society.

2. OCCUPATIONS OF MARRIED JEWESSES.

(a.) Occupations of Jewesses who received Assistance from Jewish Boards of Guardians.

In the foregoing inquiries there was no indication of any tendency amongst poor married Jewesses to enter the labour market, but the scope was too limited to draw any conclusions from this. A very much better test was furnished by the Jewish Board of Guardians, who placed at my disposal the application sheets of all persons applying to them for relief for the first time between July 1st 1892 and February 1st 1893, who were assisted. The number of cases of persons assisted for the first time during these seven months who had only been in London one year or less than one year was 98 out of a total of several hundred cases assisted during that period. Of these, 17 were cases of men who were either unmarried or had left their wives in Russia or Poland. In the 81 remaining cases there were altogether only 10 women or girls who were attempting to earn a living. These cases were as follows :—

Occupation.	Civil Condition.	Occupation of Husband.	No. of Children.
(1) Charwoman	Married	Hawker	3
(2) Cook	Widow	—	Pregnant.
(3) Washing	Married	Ill	2
(4) Needlewoman	(?)	—	1
(5) Learning mantle making.	Single	} Assisted to join brother in United States.	
(6) Learning mantle making.	,,		
(7) Learning mantle making.	,,		
(8) Charwoman	Widow	—	1
(9) Servant	Single (17)	—	—
(10) Needlewoman	Widow	—	—

Here there is only one case of a woman with an able-bodied husband to support her. In all the other cases where the husband applied for relief the wife was not a wage-earner.

During these seven months there were several hundred cases of persons assisted for the first time who had been more than one year in England. Of the applicants or wives of applicants there were only 30 wage-earning women and girls. These 30 cases were as follows:—

Occupation.	Civil Condition.	Occupation of Husband.	No. of Children.
(1) Tailoress	Deserted wife	—	2
(2) Washing	(?)	—	—
(3) Bonnet maker (age 45, wanted spectacles).	Single	—	—
(4) Needlewoman (a cripple).	Single	—	—
(5) Needlewoman	Deserted wife	—	1
(6) Charwoman	,, ,,	—	3
(7) Dressmaker	Widow	—	(?)
(8) Tailoress	Deserted wife	—	3
(9) Needlewoman	Married	In U. S. A.	—
(10) Washing	,,	,, ,,	2
(11) Washing	,,	Cabinet maker, out of work.	4
(12) "A little felling"	,,	Cabinet maker, out of work.	1
(13) Buttonholer	Deserted wife	—	5
(14) "A little dressmaking"	Married	"Not in London"	2
(15) Needlewoman	Deserted wife	—	—
(16) Hawker (aged 68)	(?)	—	—
(17) Umbrella maker (bad sight).	Single	—	—
(18) Shopkeeper	Widow	—	7
(19) Charwoman	Married	"Not in London"	2
(20) Needlewoman	Deserted wife	—	2
(21) Slipper-sock making	Married	Tailor, out of work	2
(22) "A little washing"	,,	,,	3
(23) Needlewoman (paralysed).	Single	—	—
(24) Charwoman	Widow	—	1
(25) Tailoress	Deserted wife	—	1
(26) Nurse	Single	—	1
(27) Mantle maker	Widow	—	1
(28) "A little charing"	,,	—	2
(29) Nurse	Divorced	—	1
(30) Trouser maker (hand injured).	Single	—	A sister (age 6) to support.

It will be noticed that of these 30 women only four had husbands living with them, and that these four were only doing work of a casual kind while their husbands were out of work. The rarity of industrial employment among Jewish married women may be inferred from the fact that in the form of application there is no place for stating the wife's occupation, such information being supplied in the few cases in which it is necessary in the notes of the agent who makes inquiries. On the other hand, it is possible that the absence of such a heading may result, to some extent, in a neglect to ask the question. The same inference may be drawn from the experience of the Jewish Boards of Guardians in Leeds and Manchester.

At the time of my visit to Leeds, about the end of March 1893, 70 persons were on the register as receiving relief at the time, and the occupations of the persons relieved were given me. Of these, 35 had been pensioners for a long time. Of the 70 relieved 27 were widows, of whom nine were too old to work and 10 partially supported themselves and their children by hawking (2 cases), shopkeeping (3 cases), cleaning (2 cases), slipper binding, tailoring, and taking in lodgers (1 case each). Fourteen were deserted wives, of whom seven were from some cause unable to work and seven partially supported themselves and their children by washing and cleaning (4 cases), tailoring (2 cases), and taking lodgers. In the remaining 29 cases the husband was either ill or out of work, and in only two of these cases did the wife attempt to earn money.

In Leeds, therefore, as in London, it appeared that among the recipients of charity, at least, a Jewish wife living with her husband makes no attempt to become a wage earner.

The Jewish Board of Guardians in Manchester stated that, as in London and in Leeds, married Jewesses living with their husbands, even when extremely poor, rarely attempted to earn money except by casual employment in domestic services.

(b.) Married Women in Jewish Workshops.

The absence of married Jewesses in the workshops which I visited in the course of the trade inquiry detailed below was very noticeable. The results may advantageously be summarised here.

In London out of 205 Jewesses engaged in 39 coat and vest shops 5 were married and 2 were widows. Out of 25 non-Jewish women in these workshops 7 were married and 2 were widows.

Of the 83 Jewesses employed in 19 capmaking workshops only one was married ; of the 103 non-Jewish women and girls in the same workshops 6 were married.

In Leeds out of 307 Jewesses employed in 37 tailoring workshops, 17 were married or widowed. Out of 224 non-Jewish women and girls in these workshops, 48 were married or widowed.

In Manchester out of 161 Jewesses employed in 60 tailoring workshops only 1 was married. Of the 19 non-Jewish women and girls 9 were married.

In the capmaking trade but few adult women were employed. Out of 624 non-Jewish women and girls and 243 Jewesses, there were according to the statements of the employers only 4 married women and these were non-Jewish.

Out of 37 Jewesses engaged in waterproof establishments, 1 was married : out of about 400 non-Jewish women and girls, 50 were married.

The evidence, therefore, derived from actual visits to workshops supports the conclusions drawn from the experience of Jewish organisations to the effect that the competition of married Jewesses in the labour market as regular workers is so slight as to be negligeable for the purposes of this inquiry.

So far, therefore, as industrial competition of immigrant women is concerned we need only pay attention to the unmarried women and girls together with a few deserted wives.

§ (c.) RESULTS OF TRADE INQUIRY.

In approaching the subject from the trade side the points of inquiry were—

(1.) The numbers of male and female persons employed in each branch.

(2.) The nationality and race of persons employed.

(3.) The number of married women.

(4.) The number of women and girls in England but a short time.

(5.) Wages in each branch.

Of the trades in which Jewesses are to be found in considerable numbers the tailoring trade is the most important, and is therefore dealt with first.

I.—TAILORING TRADE.

(a.) East London.

Statistics of Workshops visited.—Particulars were obtained by visits from 54 Jewish coat-makers, seven Jewish vest-makers, four trouser-makers, and four Jewish mantle-makers in East London. The particulars with regard to number, race, sex, and occupation of persons employed therein are given below :—

(i.) NUMBER, RACE, SEX, and OCCUPATION of PERSONS employed by 54 JEWISH COAT-MAKERS in EAST LONDON.

Total Number.		Race.		Branch of Work.						
Men and Boys.	Women and Girls.	Jewish.	Non-Jewish.	Press-ers.	Tailors.	Ma-chinists (Male).	Ma-chinists (Fe-male).	Button-holers.	Fellers and Finish-ers.	Errand Boys and Girls.
374	247	585 (doubt-ful).	33	50	130	118	8	78	145	23

Of the 33 non-Jewish females, eight were errand girls, three were machinists. The three whose race was not ascertained were errand girls, and were most probably non-Jewish. The other non-Jewish women and girls were all fellers, finishers, or general hands, none being employed on button-holes only.

(ii.) NUMBER, RACE, SEX, and OCCUPATION of PERSONS employed by seven JEWISH VEST-MAKERS in EAST LONDON.

Total Number.		Race.		Branch of Work.						
Men and Boys.	Women and Girls.	Jewish.	Non-Jewish.	Press-ers.	Tailors.	Ma-chinists (Male).	Ma-chinists (Fe-male).	Button-holers.	Fellers and Finish-ers.	Errand Boys and Girls.
35	48	76	7	9	5	21	1	16	28	3

Of the seven non-Jewish persons, two were errand girls, and five were fellers and finishers.

(iii.) NUMBER, RACE, SEX, and OCCUPATION of PERSONS employed by four TROUSER-MAKERS in EAST LONDON.

Total Number.		Race.		Branch of Work.		
Men and Boys.	Women and Girls.	Jewish.	Non-Jewish.	Pressers.	Hands workers (Female).	Machinists (Female).
7	61	—	68	7	53	8

One of the employers was Jewish, the others were German. Two of the women were German, the rest were English or Irish.

(iv.) NUMBER, RACE, SEX, and OCCUPATION of PERSONS employed by four JEWISH MANTLE-MAKERS in EAST LONDON.

Total Number.		Race.		Branch of Work.				
Men and Boys.	Women and Girls.	Jewish.	Non-Jewish.	Pressers.	Tailors.	Machi-nists (Male).	Button-holers.	Fellers and Finishers.
26	8	31	—	3	10	13	(nearly all given out.)	7

In three Jewish dressmakers' workshops, seven Jews, nine Jewesses, and two non-Jewish women were employed.

Proportion of Married Women in Tailoring Workshops.— Particulars' were, asked as to the status of women as regards marriage in 39 coat and vest workshops. In these, out of a total of 25 non-Jewish women and girls employed, seven were married, and two were widowed. Out of a total of 205 Jewesses five were married and two were widowed. In two trouser workshops, the employers professed not to know whether the women (all non-Jewish) were married or single : in a third, out of 11 women, one was married, and two were widowed : in the fourth, managed by a Jewish employer, in which, however, no Jewesses were employed, out of 20 women, eight were married.

Very rarely was a middle-aged Jewess to be seen in any of these workshops : the few non-Jewish workers in them, with the exception of the errand girls, seemed in nearly every case older than the majority of the Jewesses, very few of whom looked over 23 years of age. The small number of young Jewish girls who seemed under 16 years of age, was also remarkable. In the coat, vest, and dressmaking workshops, not one woman had been in England less than one year. One mantle-maker employed four women, of whom three were married women ; two of the three had been in England less than one year.

Classification of Workshops by Size.—By classifying the coat workshops according to numbers employed some idea of the difference in organisation may be obtained.

OCCUPATIONS of PERSONS employed in 53 COAT WORKSHOPS of DIFFERENT SIZES in EAST LONDON ; and of the CLASS of WORK done in such WORKSHOPS.

Class of Workshop.	Machinists.	Pressers.	Tailors.	Buttonholers.	Fellers and Finishers.	Errand Boys and Girls.	Men and Boys.	Women and Girls.	Workshops.	Class of Work Done.			
										Order.	Stock.	Order & Stock.	Doubtful.
Workshops employing—													
10 persons and upwards.	98	54	87	49	98	18	240	164	26	7	10	6	3
6 to 10 persons	32	14	25	14	31	4	71	49	15	5	7	3	—
Under 6 persons	13	7	19	8	4	—	39	12	12	5	4	1	2
	143	75	131	71	133	22	350	225	53	17	21	10	5

In the smallest workshops, the persons employed were generally members of the employer's family, the employer himself often being both tailor and presser. In most of the workshops the employer was actually at work himself when I called, sometimes being a presser, more often the fixer in the establishment, and occasionally a machinist. The only exceptions were in cases where the employer had just come back from the warehouse. Even in the small family workshops there was only one instance of the employer's wife working at the trade, and her assistance was only given at intervals during the day.

Wages in Jewish Coat Workshops.—The information on wages given below was in nearly every case given by the employer; whenever the wage stated seemed exceptionally high for a woman, I asked the woman herself what she earned. In the smaller workshops, several of the workpeople heard the statements made by their employer. In a few cases the information was refused, and in many cases the manner in which the other information was given, or the suspicion with which I was regarded, convinced me that it was useless to ask questions as to wages. Such facts about wages as were given exactly, relate to nearly two-fifths of the whole number, and were given, as it appeared to me, straightforwardly and truthfully. The wages of the buttonholers on piecework were obtained from the girls themselves. The recognised daily hours of work for men in East London were in most cases 12 hours exclusive of meal times, overtime, however, being frequently worked. In some workshops a day's work for men was longer still, but here the machinists and pressers were paid by the piece and are not included in the table of wages given below.

TABLE showing the NUMBERS of PERSONS of various OCCUPATIONS earning the under-mentioned RATES of WAGES per DAY in COAT WORKSHOPS (Men 12 Hours, and Women 10½ Hours per Day).

Occupation.	Number earning										
	Under 2s.	2s. to 3s.	3s. to 4s.	4s. to 5s.	5s to 6s.	6s. to 7s.	7s. to 8s.	8s. to 9s.	9s. to 10s.	10s. Total	Average Wage per Day.
MEN and BOYS.											
Machinists	—	1	4	10	12	10	7	9	4	1	58	*s. d.* 6 0
Pressers	—	—	—	1	8	—	11	10	1	—	31	6 11
Tailors	—	—	2	4	7	12	7	5	1	—	38	6 3
WOMEN and GIRLS.											
Fellers and Finishers	6	27	12	5	—	—	—	—	—	—	80	*s. d.* 2 10
Buttonholers (piece)	—	—	4	6	1	—	—	—	—	—	11	4 2
Machinists	—	—	1	2	1	1	—	—	—	—	5	4 8

In one workshop the wages were entirely given me by the workpeople themselves: here one head machinist averaged on a full day's work 11s. to 12s. net, working from 8 a.m. to 9 p.m., with one hour for dinner, the other from 9s. to 10s. The assistant machinists were two youths, 20 and 19 years of age, and two women who were paid by their own account 6s. 6d., 5s. 6d., 5s. 4d., and 3s. 4d., a day respectively, the women's day being only ten and a half hours. Although the work done here was only stock work, it will be seen that the principal piece-worker earned more for a day's work than anyone in all the workshops where the machinists were paid by the day.

If it be assumed that these average rates hold good for the workshops in which information as to wages was not given (omitting the largest workshop from consideration, owing to special circumstances which make it unlikely that the wages therein paid would be representative of others) the average rate of wages for men in these Jewish coat shops, comes to 6s. 3d. for a day of 12 hours, and for women to 3s. 4d. for a day of ten and a half hours: from this must frequently be deducted charges for twist, thread, &c. The rate of payment for buttonholes, made by hand averaged ½d. and ¾d. a hole according to the class of work, and the cost of twist came to about 1d. in the 1s.; 2d. for five holes was the lowest rate paid. Buttonholes were in some cases given out to be done at home, or in one or two work-shops used exclusively for machining buttonholes: the rate for these machined holes ranged from 2s. to 2s. 6d. per 100 holes, the only work thus given out being stock work.

In five out of eight workshops in which ordered work was being done, and in which information as to wages was given, the machinists and pressers were paid by the piece. This piece-work system was only adopted in two out of sixteen such workshops, in which stock work was being done. The average wages of the few pressers and machinists paid day wages on order work in three workshops are therefore by no means representative, but are given in the table below for what they are worth, together with those paid to other workers on stock or order work.

TABLE showing the NUMBER and AVERAGE WAGES per DAY in the following EMPLOYMENTS in COAT WORKSHOPS.

Class of Work.	Machinists.		Pressers.		Tailors.		Fellers and Finishers.	
	No.	Average.	No.	Average.	No.	Average.	No.	Average.
		s. d.		s. d.		s. d.		s. d.
Order	5	6 7	5	6 11	11	5 8	13	3 2
Order and Stock	13	6 3	8	6 9	5	6 8	11	3 4
Stock	32	5 10	13	7 2	16	6 5	48	2 9

The average wages of tailors on stock work seem fairly high: this is in some measure due to the employment of women included amongst fellers and finishers on work which usually would be done by youths. The only fact which comes out clearly from the above table is the difference in the rate earned by female hand workers on order work and on stock work.

It is one of the special features of the Jewish system of sub-division to give no part of a garment to a woman to do which a

man or boy could do better, and no part to a man which a
woman could do better, always provided enough workers of
either sex can be obtained.   Male labour happens to be abun-
dant: skilled female labour is comparatively scarce.   Men
making button holes are slower than women, and would earn
less if paid at the same rate, therefore women in Jewish shops
make the buttonholes.   In working the machine without steam-
power men are physically better adapted to the work than
women, and Jewesses very rarely compete for this work.   But
whenever women can do the same work as youths or men, they
seem to be paid in the Jewish workshops exactly the same as a
man would be paid for the work.   Although day wages prevail
in London they are fixed according to quantity of work done,
and in the few instances in which female machinists were employed they earned high wages, reaching in one case 6s. 6d. a
day.   In London, in Leeds, and in Manchester, the impression
left on me was that the Jewish employers in choosing their
workpeople give the preference to capacity rather than to
cheapness; that they engage the man or woman who can do the
most work in the time, not the one who asks the lowest pay
for it.

That the Jewish employers take out coats at a much lower
rate than would be permitted by the Amalgamated Society of
Tailors is indisputable; but the assertion that the Jew is
content with much lower earnings for his day's work is more
questionable.   The order work made in the workshops which I
visited was of a class worn by well-to-do artisans and others
who, in the majority of cases, if the prices of the coats were
much higher, would fall back on ready-made coats.   A comparison of the daily earnings of the Jewish men making these
coats on the sub-division of labour system, with those of the
English tailor making them without any assistance, except from
a woman or two, does not fall within the scope of my inquiry.
But the average daily earnings of the women and girls in the
Jewish workshops may be compared with those mentioned in
the following paragraph of the report of the London Tailoresses'
Trade Union for the year ending June 1892:—"About this
" time the London County Council had requested that a com-
" mittee of clothing trades should draw up a wage log, suitable
" for contract work.   The Amalgamated Society of Tailors
" called together such a committee, to which our society sent
" two representatives.   That log is now complete; and as the
" County Council have recently passed a resolution to pay trade
" union wages, we may hope soon to see it in force.   The wages
" for tailoresses in that log are stated as 24s. for machinists
" and first-class tailoresses, 18s. second class, and 14s. learners
" for a week of 54½ hours."   The London Tailoresses' Trade
Union consists almost entirely of West End tailoresses engaged
on a better class of work than was being made in the Jewish
workshops visited.   It would be difficult to say whether they or

the Jewish tailoresses suffered most from slack time. On the other hand the hours stated in the log just given are only 54½, whereas the Jewish tailoresses' week is 59½ hours. Nearly all the tailoresses in the West End, however, actually work as long as this.

Wages in Vest Workshops.—The number of Jewish vest and trouser makers is very small. The Jewish coat-makers account for this on the ground that it is "impossible to make a living on vests and trousers." Of the seven vest-makers visited one employed 32 persons and three employed less than six persons. In the largest of these workshops the head machinist was paid 6s. 8d. a day, six others being employed whose wages were not mentioned : in another, where there were four machinists, the two best were paid 7s. and 5s. a day : in a third workshop the employer himself was head machinist, one was paid 6s. 6d. a day and the other 12s. a week whether he worked or not ; in a fourth the employer was head machinist and his assistant was paid 4s. 6d. a day : in a fifth the employer did all the machining : in a sixth, he did machining, pressing, and tailoring by himself. In the seventh the daily wages paid to the five machinists were 6s. 5d., 5s. 0d., 4s. 6d., 3s. 6d., 3s. 6d. Eight of the nine pressers employed were paid by the piece : one only was paid by the day and received 4s. a day. The employers did the tailoring except in two shops, where the five tailors received from 6s. to 4s. a day. Buttonholers were paid at 2d. for six holes on an average in two workshops, 3d. a dozen in two other workshops ; in two cases the holes were given out to be machined, and in one the employer's sister was making them and the rate was not stated. In the largest workshop nine fellers and finishers were employed, who earned about 2s. to 2s. 6d. per day : in three others the average earned by 12 women and girls was 2s. 4d., 3s. being the highest and 1s. the lowest paid. Of the seven non-Jewish women in these vest shops, two were errand girls and three were married women : of the 41 Jewesses one only was married.

Wages in Trouser Workshops.— As already stated, the 61 women employed in the four trouser workshops visited were all non-Jewish. Men were only employed as pressers. The women handworkers, made the trousers throughout with the exception of the machining. In one workshop the 19 handworkers were paid 1s., 1s. 1d., and 1s. 3d. a pair, and the two machinists, if at work the full week with overtime on three nights, would earn about 22s. each, or about 3s. for an ordinary day. In another trouser shop the 16 handworkers were generally paid 1s. a pair and extras : three machinists were paid 3s. 4d., 3s., and 2s. a day respectively, and a fourth was there as a learner. In a third trouser shop the 10 handworkers were paid 1s. a pair and extras up to 1s. 6d. a pair. One of these workshops managed by a German (not Jewish) was more overcrowded than any other one visited, there being eight persons too many in the rooms.

Statements of Managers of Wholesale Clothing Firms.—The following information mainly based on statements by the managers of four wholesale clothing firms is interesting as throwing further light on the East London tailoring trade. As a rule vests are taken out from the city warehouses by English women, the pay varying with the class of work and sinking to a very low rate. Trousers are taken out by English and Germans, both men and women, the women then employed by them being almost invariably English or Irish. The evidence of the managers of four city firms all employing Jewish labour in East London shows that in this respect the state of things shown to be prevalent in 1888 still obtains and that Jewesses do not compete for the less profitable branches of the tailoring trade.

Employer A. said that his firm employed 50 to 60 men in their city tailoring workshop; these were nearly all English or Irish. He could not give exact figures of the amount given out in 1888 as compared with 1893. But ever since the Sweating Committee they had endeavoured to get the work done on the premises. Roughly speaking about 75 per cent. of the work that was given out then was now done on the premises, while the whole of the trouser making was done inside, from 80 to 100 persons (principally females) being employed in a new workshop of theirs. They still gave out coats to about 8 or 10 Jewish masters. They also gave out vests to women, all English, none Jewish. In their workshop they had once employed two Jewesses and would be quite ready to take them if they applied and would allow them to stay away on Saturday; but so far as he knew they never did apply. He found it most difficult to get as much female labour as he wanted.

Employer B. stated that within the last four years, the firm had established a workshop on their premises in which they made trousers; in it there were 15 men and 110 women, of whom one was a Jewess. Since then other workrooms had been opened: in one about 70 women and girls and 12 men were making coats, no Jewish labour being employed; in another about 80 women and girls were making vests. Altogether in their tailoring department 260 women and girls were doing inside what in 1888 was being done outside; but trousers had nearly always been made outside by non-Jewish men and women, and vests were always made by women. This left, therefore, about 70 women and 12 men doing, on the premises, work which would in 1888 have been done by Jews outside. They still gave out coats to about 14 Jews, and vests to three Jews and 13 non-Jewish women.

Employer C. said that the customers of his firm were principally working-men; their trade consisted largely in supplying clothing made to measure according to country orders. They began to make coats and trousers on their own premises three years ago; the best work was done there; the men employed in their coat room were all Jewish. The head machinist was paid by the piece and engaged and paid his own assistants. Until recently one of his assistants was a woman, non-Jewish, who machined linings and earned 3s. a day. The head machinist was paid 11d. a garment and 1d. for extras. The head presser paid the underpresser, and himself received 9d. a coat. The fitter was paid high wages and superintended the work of the tailors; one man was employed to do alterations at 5s. a day. Of the women the buttonholer, a Jewess, was paid 4s. a day; of the six fellers and finishers two were Jewesses, and received 3s. 6d. a day in one case and 12s. for five days in the other, as improver; the others received 18s. for five days, 4s. a day, and 3s. a day in two cases. A machinist was paid 18s. a week for alterations and a shop girl was paid 4s. a week.

The best trousers were made on the premises but they gave out ten times as much as they did inside. Here they employed one presser, a German, and two under pressers, 16 women hand-workers and two women machinists. Of the women one was an English born Jewess; none were foreigners. The hand-workers were paid 1s. a pair, without extras. The actual earnings of the women the week before my visit were 28s. 7½d., 26s. 4d., 25s. 5d., 23s. 4d., 18s. 8d., 17s. 2d., 15s. 5d., 14s. 5d., 14s. 1d., 13s. 2d., 13s., 11s. 2d., 10s. 1d., 10s., 10s., 9s. 2½d., 2s., 2s. (for one day only in the last two cases).

They gave out some trousers to two Jewish men and all the rest to English men and women; one of the women employed several hands. The lowest price paid for the trousers given out was 1s. 4d. a pair; the bulk were 1s. 9d. and the maximum price was 2s. 6d.

The coat out-workers were all Jewish employers, about eight altogether, who on an average took out 50 to 60 coats a week each, but worked for other masters, he believed. The prices paid to them for coats were raised after 1890 :—

Those for stock stitched morning coats were from 2s. 3d. to 3s. 6d.

Those for stock bound morning coats were from 2s. 9d.

Those for stock sack coats were from 1s. 6d. and 1s. 9d. to 2s. 9d.

Those for ordered morning coats were from 3s. 6d. and 3s. 9d. to 4s. 3d. and 4s. 6d.

Those made on the premises went up to 7s. and 7s. 6d.

Although more work was done on the premises this firm yet gave out three times as much work as they did in 1888, owing to increase in business.

Vests were all made outside still, principally by married women who would not work inside, as vests were small and easily carried home. They gave out vests to two Jewish employers, but this was quite a new departure. The firm also gave them out to 15 women, several of whom employ others and come under the Workshops Act; they probably represented about 150 hands altogether. The foreman said that two women working very long hours indeed at home might make five vests a day. The prices were from 1s. 3d. to 1s. 6d. each. The best quality was given to one set of people who probably did them in just as short a time as the others did the cheaper kind. Formerly vests had been bought ready made; but recently there had been a great extension in the amount of " measured " work, and there was therefore little to do at the beginning of the week as the orders came in on Monday and Tuesday for the most part. Stock work could be spread more uniformly over the whole week.

Employer D. said that his firm gave out all their work, making none on the premises. They had no country factories of their own but they gave out work to men who had. Vests were nearly all given out to non-Jewish women ; if very busy they paid 1d. extra all round and the Jewish makers then took some. Trousers were given out (in large quantities to each person) to Gentiles, women principally. Coats were still given out to Jewish masters except the cheaper kind which were sent to the provincial factories referred to above. The class of work done was very much the same as that made in Leeds, and they had probably suffered from competition with Leeds. Their export trade had fallen off since 1888 and with it the demand for the better class of ready-made clothing, and therefore there had been a decided falling off in the amount of wages paid out to the Jewish tailors. They gave out work to about 16 to 18 of these Jewish employers ; only two new ones had been taken on since 1888 and they took the place of two others, one of whom had set up a retail trade and the other had retired from business. The ordinary prices paid were from 2s. 6d. to 3s. for stitched jackets and from 3s. up to 4s. 6d. for morning coats. Dress coats were from 5s. to 8s. The lowest price for lined jackets made by the Jews was 1s. 6d. Coats at a lower price than this were made in the provincial factories with female labour.

From the evidence of the City firms it appears that the competition in the coat trade is not between English non-Jewish men and Jews, but between Jews and English women and girls, the latter of whom take a lower class of work in most cases at present, and are regarded by the wholesale houses as more amenable and less likely to object to innovations than the Jewish men.

The season was at its height when the Jewish employers were visited and gave information and they were exceptionally busy ; but if their statements are correct there are but few Jewish workshops which average four days a week throughout the year and many that only averaged from two to three days a week between Christmas and Easter.

The general slackness of trade is also shown in the numbers receiving relief from the Jewish Board of Guardians, 921 persons describing themselves as tailors, tailors' machinists, or tailors' pressers, and receiving assistance during 1892.

(b.) **West London.**

In the West End the conditions under which tailoring is carried on are entirely different from those prevailing in East London. From the factory inspector's list certain streets were chosen as having a large proportion of foreign tailors, and in these streets 166 workshops were visited, and the nationality of the workers noted. In the following tables the master of the workshop is included in the number of males in the workshop.

CLASSIFICATION of 166 WORKSHOPS in the West End (Soho) District according to NATIONALITY of PERSONS employed.

Classification of Workshops according to Class of Persons Employed.	No. of Work-shops.	Number of Persons Employed.				
		English Males.	Foreign Males.	English Females.	Foreign Females.	Total.
I. English only :						
(a.) English Males	17	26	—	—	—	26
(b.) Females	1	—	—	12	—	12
(c.) „ Males and Females.	56	88	—	101	—	189
Total I. -	77	114	—	113	—	227
II. Foreign only :						
(a.) Foreign Males	19	—	40	—	—	40
(b.) Females	0	—	—	—	0	0
(c.) „ Males and Females.	21	—	35	—	26	61
Total II. -	40	—	75	—	26	101
III. English and Foreign :						
(a.) English and Foreign Males.	1	1	3	—	—	4
(b.) English Males and Foreign Females.	0	0	—	—	0	0
(c.) English Males and Foreign Males, and English Females.	3	10	9	6	—	25
(d.) Foreign Males and English Females.	30	—	73	66	—	139
(e.) Foreign Males and English Females and Foreign Females.	15	—	41	26	21	88
Total III. -	49	11	126	98	21	256
Total I., II., and III.	166	125	201	211	47	584

From the preceding table it is clear that very few foreign women or girls enter the West End tailoring trade. In the 47 foreign females have been included 10 girls, daughters of foreign employers, but English born, and 16 foreign-born wives of foreign employers.

Of the 113 English women and girls in purely English work-shops 26 were wives of the employers.

The nationality and sex of foreigners in West End Tailors' Workshops visited are shown in the following table :—

—	Russian or Polish.	German or Austrian.	Norwegian, Swedish, Danish, or Dutch.	French or Italian.	Of Foreign Extraction, but English born.	Doubtful (but not Russian or Polish).
Males	85	30	32	5	8	32
Females	13	18	2	1	10	3
	98	57	34	6	18	35

Very few of the foreigners, even including the Russians and Poles, seemed to be Jewish.

(c.) **Leeds.**

Number of Jewish Workshops, and of Persons employed in them, in 1888 and 1893.—In 1888 the Superintendent of the Leeds Sanitary Department reported that there were 64 Jewish tailoring workshops in the borough of Leeds in which 2,128 persons were at work at the time of inspection. At the present time there are 98 Jewish tailoring workshops on the register, and from a list supplied by the sanitary inspector it appears that the number of persons found in them when visited and reported upon came to exactly 2,128 in 92 workshops, six work-shops being empty when visited. It does not follow that the number of *Jewish* persons was the same in both cases, and if we take into consideration the increased numbers of girls em-ployed in the Leeds factories since 1888 it seems probable that the number of English girls in the Jewish workshops is less than it was five years ago.

Nor does the number found at work by the sanitary inspector in 1893 represent the full number employed within the week. At the time of my visit to Leeds, in March, the tailoring trade was much depressed and had been so for several months. The employers were only working three, three and a half, or four days a week, and although in several cases the full number of workers was in the room, in others only a small number remained who were finishing off an order, and the slackness everywhere was so marked that for my purposes it was necessary to obtain from the employer the number that made up his full staff during the week.

Of the 98 Jewish workshops on the register I visited 75.

In three of these work was so slack that the employer might be said to have practically stopped working. In the others the number employed on a full day's work came to 1,130 men and boys and 990 women and girls, or 2,120 persons. But in most of these workshops I omitted to ascertain the number of boys and girls engaged in pulling bastings, running errands, &c. If these be taken into account an outside estimate of the numbers employed here would be about 2,250 persons.

In the workshops not visited the total number previously found at work by the sanitary inspector came to 123 men and boys, and 165 women and girls, or 288 persons. The number of persons employed in Jewish tailoring workshops may therefore be estimated at about 2,600.

Numbers and Race of Women and Girls in Jewish Workshops in each Branch.—Particulars of race were obtained in 64 workshops. With but two exceptions the men and boys employed were Jews. But the number of English women was considerable, and in striking contrast with the very small numbers found in London and Manchester. Out of 898 women and girls 518 were Jewesses and 380 were English and not Jewish. Sub-division of labour reaches a pitch in Leeds unknown in London and Manchester, and the table given below shows a marked tendency for certain branches to fall into the hands of Jewesses, and others into those of non-Jewish women. The information tabulated relates to 52 workshops.

RACE and OCCUPATIONS of FEMALES employed in 52 WORKSHOPS in LEEDS.

Buttonholers.		Fellers.		Finishers		Machinists.	
Jewish.	Non-Jewish.	Jewish.	Non-Jewish.	Jewish.	Non-Jewish.	Jewish.	Non-Jewish.
257	42	238	64	15	169	1	113

Classification of Workshops according to Size.—Omitting from consideration workshops in which less than 10 persons were employed, information was given by 44 employers, employing over 1,700 persons, as to the numbers and the daily rates of wages in the various branches of the trade in each workshop. These workshops may be divided into three classes, according to the number employed in them :—

Class of Workshop.	Number employed.	Number of Workshops.	Average Number in each Workshop.
I.	40 and upwards	18	58
II.	25 to 40	14	33
III.	10 to 25	12	18

Omitting bastings pullers and errand boys and girls, the numbers employed in each branch are given in the following table :—

MEN and BOYS.

Class of Workshop.	Numbers employed.			
	Pressers.	Tailors.	Fixers.	Machinists.
I. (employing 40 and over)	107	180	19	268
II. (,, 25 to 40) -	43	67	8	114
III. (,, 10 to 25) -	24	40	2	54
	174	287	29	436
		926		

WOMEN and GIRLS.

Class of Workshop.	Numbers employed.			
	Machinists.	Fellers.	Finishers.	Buttonholers.
I. (employing 40 and over)	55	169	65	133
II. (,, 25 to 40) -	29	88	33	72
III. (,, 10 to 25) -	20	37	21	29
	104	294	119	234
		751		

Wages in each Branch of the Trade.—Owing to the larger numbers employed in Class I., the wages of each person employed in any particular branch were given in comparatively few cases, but the wages earned by the most skilled and the least skilled workers in each branch were, in nearly every case, given with sufficient detail to prove that the few workshops in which the wages of each person were given, were representative of the whole. In Class I., for example, the daily wages of machinists ranged from 7s. and 6s. for best hands to 4s. 6d. to 3s. for lining machinists, down to 2s. 6d. and 2s. for sleeve machinists, in some cases greeners, but more frequently boys of 16 or 17. In Classes II. and III. the maximum paid was slightly lower. Wages of pressers in Class I. rose to 6s. 4d., 6s. 8d., and 7s., but never reached 7s. in Classes II. and III. Buttonholers are always, and fellers often, paid by the piece, and no exact statement can be given of their earnings. The usual rate paid for buttonholes was 5d. a dozen, and earnings varying as widely as the skill of the workers, seemed to range between 5s. and 2s. for a full day's work. With the exception of a few learners, the wages of the fellers, whether on day-work or on piece-work, ranged from 1s. 6d. to 2s. 6d., 2s. to 2s. 6d. being the most common rate. The following table is a summary of the information obtained in cases where full details were given :—

TABLE showing the NUMBERS of PERSONS of various OCCUPATIONS earning the under-mentioned RATES of WAGES per DAY of 10½ hours.

Occupation and Class of Workshop.	Number earning								Total.	Average Wage per Day.
	Under 2s.	2s. to 3s.	3s. to 4s.	4s. to 5s.	5s. to 6s.	6s. to 7s.	7s. to 8s.	8s.		
MEN and BOYS.										*s. d.*
I. Machinists	—	5	3	4	5	9	3	—	29	5 0
II. „	3	8	6	8	8	10	1	—	44	4 2
III. „	1	15	10	5	9	10	1	—	51	4 0
I. Pressers	—	1	10	8	5	9	4	—	37	4 8
II. „	—	2	2	2	6	5	—	—	17	4 8
III. „	—	4	5	—	4	6	—	—	19	4 4
I. Tailors	—	—	—	8	7	3	—	1	19	5 0
II. „	—	1	2	13	8	2	—	—	28	4 5
III. „	—	6	6	9	5	5	—	—	31	4 2
I. Fixers	—	—	—	—	—	5	8	—	13	6 10
II. „	—	—	—	—	—	4	—	—	4	6 6
WOMEN and GIRLS.										
I. Machinists	—	8	8	4	4	2	—	—	26	3 7
II. „	—	6	8	3	2	—	—	—	19	3 3
III. „	3	4	3	3	4	2	—	—	19	3 4
I. Finishers	1	25	—	—	—	—	—	—	26	2 4
II. „	2	19	2	—	—	—	—	—	23	2 2
III. „	1	11	1	—	—	—	—	—	13	2 2

If the average for each class thus obtained be accepted as prevailing in all the workshops in the class, we have the following results :—

TABLE showing the NUMBER and average WAGES per DAY in the following EMPLOYMENTS in LEEDS.

Branch.	Number employed.	Average Wage.
Males.		*s. d.*
Pressers	174	4 7
Tailors	287	4 9
Fixers	29	6 9
Machinists	496	4 8
Females.		
Machinists	104	3 5
Finishers	119	2 3
Fellers	291	2s. to 2s. 1d.

The weekly wages cannot be obtained by multiplying by six. Factory employers and inspectors were agreed that there was an unusual depression in the trade of the Jewish coat makers; with but few exceptions, the average number of days' work in any branch since Christmas seemed to have been from 3 to 3½ days a week.

In six workshops vests were being made. The number of persons employed came to 28 Jews, 20 Jewesses, 30 non-Jewish women and girls, and eight whose race was not distinguished. In one of these workshops the prices paid for boys' and men's vests range from 9d. to 1s. 6d.: in another from 5d. to 1s. 1d., and in a third from 8d. to 1s. 6d., and 2s. 6d. for order work.

Prices paid to Jewish Masters.—All the work done in these 44 workshops was stock work, and the following statements as to the usual class of men's clothing done, and the prices received were made by the Jewish employers:—

(1.) Morning coats, 3s. 6d. to 4s.

(2.)   „   „   2s. 6d. to 3s.

(3.) Men's coats up to 3s. 9d.

(4.) Men's coats, stitched, 2s.: bound, 2s. 6d. Jackets, stitched, 1s. 3d. to 2s. 2d.

(5.) Men's coats, stitched, 2s. 3d.; bound, 2s. 9d.

(6.)   „   „   „   1s. 6d. to 2s. 2d.: bound, 1s. 11d. to 3s. Overcoats, 1s. 9d. to 3s. 3d.

(7.) Men's coats, stitched, 1s. 3d. to 2s.; bound, 1s. 9d. to 2s. 6d.

(8.) Men's coats, bound, 2s. 2d. Morning coats, 3s. 3d. to 3s. 6d.

(9.) Men's coats, stitched, 1s. 2d. to 1s. 6d.; bound, 1s. 8d. to 2s.

(10.) Men's coats, stitched, 1s. to 2s.; bound, 1s. 3d. to 3s. 3d.

(11.)   „   „   „   1s. 9d. to 2s. 3d.: bound, 2s. 6d. to 2s. 9d.

(12.) Men's coats, stitched, 1s. 1d. to 1s. 7d.; bound, 1s. 6d. to 2s. 6d.

(13.) Men's coats, stitched, 1s. 6d. to 2s. 3d.; bound, 2s. to 2s. 9d.

(14.) Men's coats, stitched, 1s. to 1s. 8d.; bound, 1s. 5d. to 2s. 5d. Overcoats, 2s. to 2s. 5d.

(15.) Men's coats, stitched, 1s. 5d. to 1s. 10d.; bound, 1s. 10d. to 2s. Overcoats, 2s. 8d. to 4s.

(16.) Men's coats, bound, up to 3s. 6d.

(17.)   „   stitched, up to 2s. 6d; bound, up to 3s.

(18.)   „   „   „   1s. 4d.; bound, 2s.

(19.)   „   „   „   1s. 9d.; bound, 2s. 6d.

(20.)   „   „   „   1s. 6d. to 3s. and 3s. 6d.

(21.)   „   „   „   1s. 6d. to 2s. 8d.: bound, 2s. 3d. to 3s. 3d. Overcoats, 2s. 6d. to 5s.

(22.) Men's coats stitched, 1s. 10d. to 2s. 3d.; bound, 1s. 11d. and upwards.

(23.) Men's coats, stitched, 1s. 3d. to 2s. 10d.: bound, 1s. 5d. to 3s. 2d.

(24.) Men's coats, stitched, 1s. 6d. to 2s. 10d.; bound, 1s. 9d. to 2s. 6d.

(25.) Men's coats, stitched, 2s. : bound, 2s. 6d.

(26.)   ,,   ,,   ,,   1s. to 2s.

(27.)   ,,   ,,   ,,   1s. to 1s. 6d.; bound, 1s. 8d. to 1s. 11d.

The following general scale of prices obtaining in Leeds was given me by a witness, who, although not an employer, had special opportunities for knowing the facts :—

Morning coats, to measure, double stitched, 4s. 6d. to 5s. 6d.
  ,,   ,,   ,,   . bound, 5s. 6d. to 6s. 6d.
Lounge jackets, to measure, double stitched, 3s. 6d. to 4s. 6d.
Lounge jackets, to measure, bound, 4s. 6d. to 5s. 6d.
Morning coats, stock, 3s. 6d. to 4s. 6d.
Lounge jackets, 2s. 6d. to 3s. 6d.
Common jackets, 1s. 9d. to 2s. 3d.
Common vests, 7d. to 10d.
Common trousers, 8d. to 10d.
Slop, less than "common."

The following prices of work done in different workshops were obtained at the warehouse from which the work was taken out :—

(1.) Men's jackets, stitched, 2s. 4d. to 3s. 6d.; bound, 3s. 2d. to 4s. 2d. and 4s. 10d.
Men's coats, stitched, 3s. 11d. to 4s. 6d.; bound, 4s. 2d. to 6s. 4d. and 6s. 10d.
Boys' jackets, bound, 2s. to 3s. 8d.

(2.) Men's jackets, stitched, 2s. 4d. to 3s. 6d.; bound, 2s. 2d. to 3s.
Boys' jackets, bound, 2s. to 2s. 7d.

(3.) Boys' reefers, stitched, 2s. to 2s. 6d.
Boys' jackets, stitched, 1s. 8d. to 2s. 2d.
Boys' Rugbys, to 1s. 6d.

(4.) Boys' jackets, stitched, 1s. 1d. to 1s. 11d.

(5.) Men's jackets, stitched, 1s. 8d. to 2s. 4d.

(6.) Boys' Cambridges, 1s. 1d. to 1s. 3d.
Boys' Rugbys, 1s. to 1s. 1d.

(7.) (Not Jewish) Men's vests, stitched, 1s. 2d. to 1s. 4d.

(8.) (Not Jewish) Men's vests, 1s.
Boys' vests, 8d. to 10d.

(9.) (Not Jewish) Men's vests, stitched, 1s. 2d. to 1s. 4d.: bound, 1s. 2d. to 2s. and 2s. 4d.
Boys' vests, stitched, 11d. to 1s. 1d.: bound, 11d. to 1s. 10d.

(10.) (Not Jewish) Men's vests, stitched, 1s. 2d. to 1s. 4d.
Boys' vests, stitched, 11d. to 1s. 1d.

According to the Jewish employers this warehouse pays higher prices than most houses in the trade, but expects work in proportion.

The marked depression in their trade is attributed by the Jewish employers to the determination of the English firms to replace Jewish male labour in the workshop by English female labour in the factory. In this belief they seem to be mistaking the will for the deed, and to be over-rating the importance of the action of one firm, which, since the strike of Jewish tailors in 1889, has established a coat workshop under its own management. In this workshop, according to the information given me by the manager of the firm, 150 persons are employed of whom only 17 are Jews and 3 are Jewesses. Three other firms have somewhat similar departments, but the Jews are not entirely superseded in any of them, and it is extremely doubtful whether in the more difficult parts of the better class of stock coats the Jewish male machinist can ever be satisfactorily replaced by the English female machinist. The slackness of trade must be rather attributed to the general depression and amongst special causes, to the prolonged labour disputes in the north of England, which have for the last year considerably diminished the purchasing power of an important section of the customers of Leeds manufacturers. Should the English tailors ever grasp the fact that by sub-division of labour higher earnings might be obtained, even though the rates per garment were lowered, the Jewish employers might suffer severely by their competition, as the possibility of obtaining coats made to order at a moderate price might seriously diminish the demand for Jewish made goods. At present the Jews need only fear the competition with English female labour, cheaper perhaps, but less competent than theirs.

In the Jewish workshop the English machinist seems to be paid on exactly the same terms as the male machinists on the same work, but she is very rarely found doing the most skilled machining, and the Jewish employer, whether rightly or wrongly, considers that he gets the pick of the English women, so far as skill is concerned. In comparing the earnings of the English women with those of the Jewesses, the wages of the Jewish buttonholers must be set off against those of the English machinists, and would seem to be quite as high, so far as it was possible to judge from the statements of some of the buttonholers as to their speed. The average age of the Jewish women and girls to be found in the workshops is decidedly lower than that of the English women and their length of experience is therefore less.

(d.) **Manchester.**

In Manchester I visited the workshops of 61 tailors. In 60 of these the employers were Jewish and made coats and vests, and in one or two instances juvenile suits. The other workshop was directed by an English trouser maker, who employed no Jewish labour, and said that the women he employed generally learnt their trade with German trouser makers. In the Jewish tailors' workshops one man and 19 women were non-Jewish. Out of 161 Jewesses one was married; of the 19 non-Jewish women and girls, nine were married. In 17 of these workshops only stock work was done; in the others order work was done, either with or without stock work in addition. Sub-division was not so minute as in Leeds and organisation in this respect corresponded very closely to the system obtaining in the East London workshops.

The following table classifies the 60 workshops according to size and shows the numbers employed at various occupations :—

Class of Workshop.	Machinists.	Pressers.	Tailors.	Buttonholers.	Fellers and Finishers.	Errand Boys and Girls.	Men and Boys.	Women and Girls.	Workshops.
III.—(10 to 25 persons).	98	56	105	60	67	19	275	130	32
IV A.—(6 to 10 persons).	39	24	41	20	23	6	108	45	20
IV B.—(under 6 persons).	9	4	11	2	3	—	24	5	8
Total - -	146	84	157	82	93	25	407	180	60

Only four machinists were women, of whom one was a Jewess. Finishing is frequently done by the tailors themselves, or by women able to fell, finish, and make buttonholes if required.

Wages.—Piece-work was the rule. In nearly every workshop the head machinist was paid by the piece, but engaged one or more assistants himself, whom he paid by time : 13 machinists were paid day wages by the employer : of the remaining 133 machinists, 77 were assistants engaged and paid by piece-workers : several of these assistants or " seamers " were boys of 15 or 16 years of age. The machinists generally hire the machines and not the employer. The head-pressers were also on piece-work, and engaged their under-pressers on day wages. Buttonholers and fellers were on piecework, in most cases paid by the master of the workshop, but in a few cases where the tailors were on piece-work the buttonholers were engaged and paid by them. In the smaller workshops the tailors were in many cases members of the employer's family, and in some cases they were on piece-work, but in most of the shops the tailors were paid day wages by the employer; and their rate of wages alone admits of comparison with those paid in Leeds.

TABLE showing the NUMBER of TAILORS earning the under-mentioned WAGES per DAY of 10½ HOURS.

Class of Workshop.	Number Earning								Total.	Average Wages per Day.
	Under 2s.	2s. to 3s.	3s. to 4s.	4s. to 5s.	5s. to 6s.	6s. to 7s.	7s. to 8s.	8s. and up-wards.		
III.	2	3	3	8	8	22	5	2	53	5s. 4d.
IVA.	—	1	1	2	1	4	—	—	9	4s. 10d.

So far as could be gathered, the net earnings of the machinists and pressers on piecework were higher than in Leeds, although those of the seamers and under-pressers seemed low. According to one Jewish employer, who had worked in Leeds as well as in Manchester, earnings were less but work easier in Leeds under the daily-wage system than in Manchester under the piece-work system. This statement was confirmed by other evidence.

The rate paid for buttonholes was decidedly lower than that paid in London, the highest in Manchester being 6d. a dozen holes, whereas in London the ordinary rates were 6d. for stock work and 9d. for order work. In London the buttonholer frequently finds her own twist and gimp, which cost her from 1d. to 1½d. in the shilling.

Numbers employed in certain Workshops in 1888 and 1893. —Dr. Tatham, Medical Officer of Health for Manchester, has supplied me with a copy of a Report on 129 Jewish workshops visited in Manchester on April 24th and 26th, 1888. Twenty-seven of the tailors' workshops on this list were amongst those visited by me in the week ending April 29th, 1893. The numbers found at work in 1888 were 161 men, 73 women, 14 young persons, and in 1893 were 199 men, 74 women, 11 young persons. The employer himself is included in both cases. The term young person is used in this report, but probably not in its strict legal sense, and under that heading I have placed the boys and girls employed to run errands and do odd jobs. I made no attempt to find out how many girls or boys under 18 there might be. In Manchester as in London I was left with the impresssion that few Jewish girls in the workshops were under 16 and a middle-aged Jewess was as much a rarity there as in London.

Recent Immigrants working in Tailors' Workshops.—A few particulars with regard to the more recently arrived immigrants whom I found working in tailors' workshops in Manchester are given below :—

Males.

(1.) Underpresser, in England 1½ years.
(2.)   „   „   „   ¼ year.
(3.)   „   „   „   1 year

(4.) Underpresser, in England less than 1 year.
(5.)   ,,   ,,   ,, 1¼ year.
(6.)   ,,   ,,   ,, a few months.
(7.) Machinist (a boy), in England less than 1 year.
(8.)   ,, apprentice, in England 3 months.
(9.) Underpresser,   ,,   ,, less than 1 year.
(10.)   ,,   ,,   ,, 1¼ years.
(11.) Tailor, in England 8 months.
(12.)   ,,   ,,   ,, 1 year; earns 5s. 10d. a day.
(13.) Underpresser, in England less than one year; earns about
    2s. 6d. a day.
(14.) Tailor, in England 2 years.
(15.) Machinist, in England a few months.

Females.

(1.) Feller, in England 1 year; came to her sister and learnt
    the trade.
(2.) Feller, in England a few weeks: earned 5s. 6d. the
    previous week.
(3.) Feller, in England nearly 2 years : to be married shortly.
(4.) Helping fellers, in England 1 week : to be married in a few
    days.
(5.) Feller, in England 8 months ; came to her sisters.
(6.)   ,,   ,,   ,, nearly 2 years.
(7.)   ,,   ,,   ,, 1 year.
(8.)   ,,   ,,   ,, less than 1 year: "not up to much :
earns 4s. to 5s. a week."

All these fellers were paid by the piece.

In the Manchester tailoring trade the women and girls employed
by Jewish employers are themselves Jewish in nearly all cases,
but in no other trade in which Jewesses are employed is this the
case.

(e.) General Summary of Tailoring Trade.

The tailoring trade is the only one in which the majority of
women employed are Jewish, and this is only true of one branch
of it—the coat-making.

Trousers are made almost entirely by non-Jewish women
and girls in factories, workshops, or their own homes. The proportion of men in this branch is small.

Vests are in some cases made in Jewish workshops, but as a
rule they are made by non-Jewish women in their own homes,
in workshops (frequently managed by English women), and in
factories.

Even in the coat department of the ready-made trade the
cheapest classes of coat are made by non-Jewish women and

girls in provincial factories or large workshops such as those of Leeds, Walsall, Colchester, Dudley, and Bristol, in similar large workshops in London, and at their own homes, both in London and the provinces. There are but few instances of Jewesses doing such work at home, but in the large clothing factories or workshops a sprinkling of Jewesses (as in Leeds) can occasionally be found.

Piecework is almost invariably the rule in these branches of the tailoring trade, and even if Jewesses were willing to accept less than non-Jewish girls their numbers are too small to have the least effect on prices.

In the better paid branches of the ready-made coat trade and in the commoner branch of the bespoke coat trade Jewesses are largely employed. In London and Manchester the women in the Jewish coat shops are almost exclusively Jewish, but in Leeds a considerable number are non-Jewish. The comparative number of Jewish and non-Jewish women and girls in coat workshops visited was as follows :—

—	Jewish.	Non-Jewish.
London	211	33
Manchester	161	19
Leeds	518	380

In London in 54 workshops employing 621 persons only eight machinists were women, five of whom were Jewish.

In Manchester in 60 workshops employing 587 persons, four machinists were women, of whom one was Jewish.

In Leeds, in 52 workshops employing about 1,800 persons, 114 machinists were women, of whom only one was Jewish.

In Leeds there was a marked tendency for certain subdivisions of labour to fall into the hands of Jewesses and others into those of non-Jewish women.

The highest wages are earned by buttonholers (nearly all Jewish) and by machinists (all non-Jewish in Leeds). Fellers and finishers earn less wages, but the earnings in the two branches are about the same.

But in comparing the wages of Jewish and non-Jewish women in Jewish coat shops it must be remembered that the average age of the Jewish women is less than that of the non-Jewish women, as Jewesses marry early and give up working more generally than non-Jewish women.

In the ready-made clothing trade in those branches which are not managed by Jewish men the number of women employed is much greater than the number of men. This appears very clearly in the census returns for Leeds a centre which is almost entirely engaged in the ready-made trade. In 1891 in the Leeds tailoring trade there were 4,773 males and 10,916 females as against 2,148 males and 2,740 females in 1881, the trade having increased rapidly during the decade.

In the Jewish workshops the ratio is reversed.

The per-centages of males and females employed in Jewish tailoring workshops of various sizes in different centres are stated in a table on p. 207.

The smaller ratio of males to females in Leeds compared with that of London is principally due to the employment of non-Jewish female machinists in Leeds instead of Jewish males as in London. The higher ratio of males to females in Manchester as compared with London is principally due to the employment of tailors in Manchester on buttonholing and other branches of work usually done by female fellers and finishers in London, the cheaper class of bespoke work being more frequently made in the Manchester workshops visited than in those visited in London.

The evidence of wholesale clothiers in London and Leeds showed that under their system of organisation there was a tendency to employ women to do the work usually done by underpressers in Jewish shops, and that machining was in nearly all cases given over to women and girls. The only obstacle to the displacement by cheaper female labour of about half the Jewish male labour now utilized seemed to be the superiority of Jewish male labour on the better class of ready-made coats.

II.—Cap-making.

(a.) East London.

Nineteen Jewish cap-makers were visited. In 17 of these workshops were employed 89 men and 143 women and girls; in two of the workshops in which were employed 43 women and girls, the number of men was not ascertained. Of the 186 women and girls 83 were Jewish and 103 were non-Jewish. Only one of the men was not Jewish.

The machines used for cap-making are much lighter than those required for tailoring, and this explains the number of Jewesses to be found working them. Out of 136 machinists 46 were men or boys; 90 were women or girls, of whom 37 were Jewish and 53 non-Jewish. Of the 83 needlehands 42 were Jewish and 41 non-Jewish women and girls. Of the cutters, packers, &c. 13 were women, of whom four were Jewesses. The rest of the men were cutters, blockers, pressers, &c.

Of the 103 non-Jewish women and girls six were married. Of the 83 Jewesses only one was married.

All the cap-makers stated that they had less work to do than formerly. They were generally of the opinion that there were fewer workshops in the trade than there used to be; much of

the work that used to be done in them was now done in one
very large cap factory in Whitechapel where female labour,
both Jewish and non-Jewish, was employed; some of the men
employed had been in England less. than one year, but none of
the women had been less than two years in England. All were
paid by the piece, and I could therefore obtain no information
as to total earnings. There seemed to be no question of competition between foreigners and Englishmen, the real change
being the displacement of Jewish men by girls, Jewish and non-
Jewish, in factories working machines with steam-power.

(b.) Manchester.

In Manchester cap-making is almost entirely in the hands of
Jewish employers, but the majority of the girls employed are
non-Jewish. In the 18 workshops visited there were employed
altogether 867 women and girls, of whom 243 were Jewish and
624 non-Jewish. Out of 440 machinists, all female, 98 were
Jewish and 342 non-Jewish. Out of 165 hand workers 120
were Jewish and 45 non-Jewish. Of the remaining 25 Jewesses
and 237 non-Jewish women and girls I did not obtain particulars
of the number in each branch.

The proportion of adult women among the capmakers was
small; there were no married Jewesses and only four married
non-Jewish women. The cap machines are much lighter than the
tailoring machines, and judging from the large number of girls,
both Jewish and non-Jewish, who looked under 16, a considerable
portion of the work must be unskilled.

Piece-work was the rule with one exception. This workshop
was managed by a Jew and was closed on Saturdays, although
only seven out of 22 girls were Jewesses, and only three out of
six men were Jews. The girls only worked five days; one girl
was paid 2s. 6d. a week, the next lowest was 5s.; machinists
ranged as high as 15s. and hand workers earned from 6s. to 9s. 6d.
a week.

At the last-mentioned factory the reason why non-Jewesses
were employed was because Jewesses were not obtainable.
In one factory only seven out of 200 women and girls
were Jewish: here all but the Jewesses worked on Saturday, but the employer, a Jew, said that he would be quite
willing to take on Jewesses notwithstanding that they only
worked five days. Another Jewish employer, employing 25
girls all non-Jewish, gave as his reason for not employing
Jewesses that they were "too noisy and cheeky." Another capmaker, presumably not a Jew, said that he had a "moral
antipathy to employing Jews." Another explained that
" Jewesses do not take to the machine," at which the machinists
have to stand always. Another Jewish capmaker employing
about 300 girls, of whom about 100 were Jewish, said that when
the cap trade was started by Jews in Manchester there were not

enough Jewesses to come into the trade: when they did do machining they were quite as good machinists as the others. Here the works were closed on Saturdays. Another employer who employed 10 Jewesses and 25 non-Jewish women said he worked on Saturdays and therefore preferred non-Jewish girls, but Jewesses did not apply so frequently as others. A capmaker in a small workshop preferred non-Jewish girls because they "listened to one better than Jewesses." Another had been established in the trade for 45 years and had always employed non-Jewish girls, because when he began he could get no Jewesses to come. He was a Jew, and had no prejudices against employing Jewesses. It seemed on the whole fairly clear that capmaking was not sufficiently remunerative to attract Jewesses from the better paid tailoring trade, and that capmakers were therefore obliged to fall back on English labour.

(c.) Summary.

Cap-making in small workshops appears to be dying out and to be replaced by the factory or large workshop system. Although the majority of employers are Jewish the majority of girls employed are non-Jewish. The industry is less remunerative than tailoring, requiring much less skilled adult labour. The proportion of male labour required is very small.

III.—CIGAR-MAKING IN EAST LONDON.

In the cigar trade a considerable number of Jewesses are employed. The secretary of the Women Cigar Makers' Protective Union, who is English and not Jewish said that the Christians and Jewesses worked together quite satisfactorily. The Union prints a quarterly balance sheet: that for the quarter ending April 23rd, 1892, showed an expenditure of 176*l.* and a balance of 122*l.*, with a membership of 620, 145*l.* going for out of work pay at the rate of 6s. per week.

The balance sheet for the quarter ending January 21st, 1893, showed an expenditure of 82*l.* (of which 49*l.* was out-of-work pay), with a balance of 78*l.* and a membership of 709. Although the Union had suffered severely from slackness of work throughout the previous year the membership had nevertheless increased considerably. Several of the members are Jewesses and the treasurer and auditors are Jewish members. The secretary said that there were very few foreign Jewesses in the Union and did not think there were many in the trade.

IV.—WATERPROOF GARMENT-MAKING IN MANCHESTER.

The waterproof trade is now almost entirely carried on in factories or large workshops, the small workshop system having nearly died out. In the largest of these about 100 Jewish and 200 non-Jewish men and boys were employed, and 400 non-Jewish and 16 Jewish women and girls. Of the non-Jewish women 12½ per cent. were married ; one of the 16 Jewesses was married. The factory is open on Saturday, but the Jewesses only work five days.

In a large workshop 57 men and boys, all Jewish were employed in waterproof garment making, and 11 girls, all Jewish but one. Of these, four girls were machining together with three boys, and seven girls were "finishing." Only one girl was under 16 years of age, and none were married. In the week ending April 14th three girls earned 16s., five earned from 12s. to 14s., one earned 10s., one 9s., and one 3s. 6d. The average total weekly wages paid since January were much less than those for the six months from the middle of June 1892 to the middle of December. The average weekly total for these six months was paid in the week ending September 2nd, 1892, when 28 women and girls were employed, several being learners. In this week :—

5 earned	18s.	
1	„	17s.
2	„	15s.
1	„	14s.
4	„	10s. to 12s. 3d.
7	„	7s. to 9s.
8		under 5s.

In the waterproof garment-making department of another firm 10 girls and 20 men were employed : in the season the numbers of both are doubled. All were Jewish.

Altogether it appeared that there were not more than 1,000 persons employed in the waterproof garment-making branch of the india-rubber trade and that of these the proportion of Jewesses was small. Wages seemed fairly high, but the trade in the two firms last referred to was subject to great fluctuations involving the dismissal of hands in the slack season.

V.—MANTLE MAKING.

Both London and Manchester are large centres of the ready-made mantle-making industry and the conditions of production are rather remarkable, a very considerable portion of the mantles being given out and made in workshops managed by women. Those that are not given out are made in the warehouses or (in a few cases) in factories, and here also the majority employed are women and girls. There is considerable scope for sub-division of labour and the rates paid per garment to the outworkers can only be remunerative by the adoption of such a system. It is most difficult to obtain from the women managing these workshops any information as to the rates paid to the girls employed by them. They are engaged on the cheaper class of work, have the reputation of paying very low wages to the girls employed by them, and are of a class inclined to regard a profit of 20s. to 25s. a week as good. In London the domestic workshop is very common, and a very cheap kind of mantle is frequently made throughout by women at their own homes : Bethnal Green, Shoreditch, and Hoxton being the principal centre for this class of work. In the ordered mantle trade of the West End, and in the high class ready-made mantle trade men are employed as cutters, fitters, and pressers, but hitherto they have been but little employed in the medium and low class trade. In Leeds mantles are being made in factories, but in Manchester and London there are only a few houses which use power. England imports cheap mantles from Germany in large quantities, amongst the alleged causes being the family system prevalent in Germany under which the men as well as the women co-operate in the work. During the last five years a few Jewish workshops have been established in East London and Islington and are employed on tailor-made mantles for wholesale City warehouses of a kind hitherto mainly imported from Germany, and Mr. Lakeman states that in some cases although the employer is generally a Polish Jew, the journeyman is found to be German. In these workshops men do the pressing and (generally) the machining. It is as pressers that they are considered superior to women outworkers, and in workshops where power is not used men can generally machine more in the day than women. Regarded as competitors with English women in domestic workshops, the Jewish mantle makers may be regarded as the introducers of a better system of organisation and of a better article. According to the information supplied by three London firms they are in reality making an opening for successful competition with Germany. There are however, two different systems which may prevent the Jewish mantle maker from making head way, one, the factory system, rapidly growing in Leeds, the other, the entrance of English men into the cheap branch of the trade of which at present there is but little sign.

VI.—GENERAL SUMMARY.

The general result of the trade inquiry is to show that the only trade in which Jewesses are employed in large numbers, and, so far as Manchester and London are concerned, almost to the exclusion of non-Jewish women, is the coat-making trade. In the worst paid branches of the ready-made tailoring trade they are not employed at all.

The statements made by English tailors and tailoresses engaged on bespoke work as to the unfair competition of Jewish men and women must be accepted with some caution. As a fact, an Englishman is hardly ever found at work in a Jewish workshop, and many of the English tailors are somewhat slow to understand that with subdivision of labour low rates per garment do not necessarily imply low earnings per day. Those accustomed to the West End system often appear to suppose that the charge of unfair competition made against the Jews and the English wholesale manufacturers is amply proved by showing that the rate paid per garment is much lower than that paid to the English bespoke tailor.

As a matter of fact when it is remembered that there are but few married Jewesses to be found in the Jewish workshops, and that the average age of the Jewesses in the East London tailoring trade is therefore considerably lower than the average age of the West London tailoresses, of whom a large proportion are married, the comparison between their rates of pay is not very unfavourable to the Jewish tailoresses, allowance being made for the difference in the necessary skill.

As an aid to a comparison of the earnings of Jewish tailoresses with the earnings of English women and girls in different trades a few statistics with regard to the latter may be given. The summary of average normal weekly wages of women and girls in certain occupations compiled by the Board of Trade for the Labour Commission gives 12s. 8d. as the average for 151,263 women, and 7s. as the average for 48,772 girls, making for women and girls together an average of 11s. 3d. This includes over 63,000 women in the cotton trade with the high average of 15s. 3d. In a factory in Manchester where 625 women and girls were employed in making corsets, mantles, ready-made shirts, &c., I found the average wage for an ordinary week to be slightly over 10s., and 32·8 per cent. of those employed were over 25 years of age. In Bristol in four clothing factories employing 567 women and girls 53·4 per cent. earned less than 10s. in an ordinary week. In the same town, of 2,593 women and girls employed in various factory industries (including the four factories referred to), 64 per cent. earned less than 12s., and nearly half of these earned less than 8s. In the potteries, of 1,420 women and girls employed in 15 firms, only 14·3 per cent. earned above 12s., although 61·1 per cent. were adults, and 27·4 per cent. were over 25. In a large workroom in North London the average weekly wage of 36 dressmakers was 12s. 8d.; in a similar workroom in West London the average wage of 82 dressmakers was 12s. 3d.

So far as rate of earnings per day only is considered the average rate earned by Jewish girls is higher than that earned on the average by the English women and girls. The average number of days worked per week is probably less; on the other hand, the Jewish tailoress unlike the English factory girl is not obliged to sit in the workshop on the chance that orders may arrive.

If the rate of earnings of Jewish girls be compared with that prevailing in the jam and sweetstuff, rope, and match industries (largely recruited from the Anglo-Irish population) the contrast is entirely in their favour. In 1889 I found that in a jam and sweetstuff factory in East London, out of upwards of 600 women and girls only 6 per cent. earned over 12s. while about 82 per cent. earned less than 10s. Out of more than 1,000 match workers about 12 per cent earned over 12s., and 62 per cent. less than 10s. In a flax mill employing 700 women and girls, in Leeds in 1891, the maximum wages were about 10s. a week, adult women often earning less than 8s. for a week's work. In a rope works in East London in 1892, out of 89 women and girls, 75 earned from 8s. to 10s. In a rope works at Liverpool where two-thirds of those employed were over 18 years of age, 45·5 per cent. earned under 8s., and 37·8 per cent. from 8s. to 12s. It may also be noted here that the proportion of married women in these industries is above the average.

Whereas there seemed to be no tendency amongst Jewesses to under-sell non-Jewish women there is evidently a strong desire amongst wholesale clothiers to replace Jewish male labour by non-Jewish female labour as much as possible, a desire which seemed to be due partly to dislike of the Jews, partly to the greater cheapness of female labour, and partly to the greater self-assertiveness and persistence in making a good bargain displayed by Jewish men as compared with English girls.

If besides losing the lower class of the ready-made trade by this growth of employment of women in provincial factories, the Jewish tailors were threatened on another side by the competition of Englishmen in the manufacture of the better class, on the system taught them by the Jews, the consequences to the Jewish tailoring trade would be most serious. Nothing but the conservatism of the English tailor prevents him from successfully entering into the field opened up by the Jews.

PART IV.—CONCLUDING SUMMARY.

Any useful summary of the results of the present inquiry with respect to the social and economic condition in this country of a certain class of immigrants from Eastern Europe must have reference to the question which of late years has attracted considerable public interest, viz., the desirability and possibility of checking the influx of this class of aliens, or of some portion of them, by legislative enactment. It is not within the functions of this report to express any opinion on the merits of this controversy, or even to sum up the arguments on each side. It may, however, fulfil a useful purpose to indicate how far the facts set forth in previous chapters have a bearing on various aspects of the problem, and serve to some extent to define and narrow the issue.

In the first place the limits of the problem may be more clearly realised after consideration of the results of the statistical investigation embodied in the first report included in this volume, combined with the fact (which is prominently brought out in the course of the report) of the improvement which takes place, after a certain period of residence in this country, in the habits and condition of many of the immigrants, and of the strong tendency towards "assimilation," especially among the children of the immigrants and the second generation of settlers. It thus appears clearly that any social and economic dangers which may be thought to arise out of the influx do not apply equally to the total element which has thus been added to the population, but, in their intensest form, only to that margin of it which has been added during the current and perhaps the previous year, and in a rapidly decreasing ratio to those who have arrived during prior years. It is thus the magnitude of the annual influx of persons arriving for settlement, rather than the total number of this class of immigrants resident in the country which defines at any given time the limits of the problem.

Next, in dealing with the social and economic effects of the continuance of this stream of immigration, there are several points of view from which the subject may be considered, which it is important so far as possible to keep distinct. On the one hand, there is the "internal" question, of the effects of the influx on the immigrants themselves and on the Jewish community generally. On the other hand there is the "external" question, of the effects of the immigration on the welfare of other sections of the population or of the country as a whole.

The latter question again may be yet further analysed. We have to consider the influence of the immigrants on the welfare of (1) other workmen in particular trades, (2) the other inhabitants of particular districts, (3) the public generally.

It may be well to point out how far the various classes of facts detailed in previous sections of the report bear on each of these aspects of the question.

As regards the comparative welfare of the bulk of the immigrants in this country and in those which they have left, there is probably little difference of opinion. Perhaps the most important piece of evidence is the mere fact of the continuance of the influx, and of the extent to which the immigrants come to join their friends who have already settled in this country. The extremely low wages and long hours of work, usually associated with this class of aliens, have been shown to apply chiefly to those who have arrived comparatively lately. All accounts agree as to the "progressive" nature of the foreign Jew, and as to the extent to which the "greener" cheerfully submits to temporary privations in the hope of bettering his condition. Doubtless the attraction of this country to the Russian and Polish Jew is not wholly, or perhaps mainly, economic; the enjoyment of personal liberty and the absence of harassing restrictions having also great weight. But from whatever cause, the mass of the immigrants who come to settle appear to prefer their present to their previous lot, and the Jewish relief organisations by whom they are assisted have often the greatest difficulty in inducing individuals to return to their own country.

So far as the Jewish community generally is concerned the case is different. A section of the immigrants, especially of the newcomers, are a great drain on their funds. It has been explained in the report (pp. 45 and 46) that up to the present time the Jewish poor have been relieved by voluntary agencies, and have not (except rarely) come upon the rates. The amount of relief distributed by the great Jewish organisations is no greater when spread over the total Jewish population than that distributed in indoor, outdoor, and medical relief by boards of guardians in London per head of the London population, and is considerably lower than the amount per head so distributed in some of the poorer districts. It, nevertheless, taxes severely the resources of the voluntary Jewish relief agencies, and many of those who are most closely connected with their administration view the continued influx with anxiety. On the other hand, the strong feeling of race patriotism among the Jews leads them to lay great stress on the preservation of the right of asylum to refugees from political or religious persecution.

It may perhaps be considered that the attitude of members of the Jewish community itself towards the continuance or the restriction of immigration is mainly a question of the internal politics of the community. It is chiefly of public importance in so far as a change in such attitude might conceivably lead to a modification of the present system of relief to the Jewish poor, which might have the effect of throwing some of those now so relieved upon the rates for support. In this case the question of "pauper" aliens might take a new form.

Passing from the internal to the external aspect of the question, we come first to the question of the detrimental effects, if any, of the influx on the non-Jewish workers in certain trades. Such effects might take the form of (1) a displacement of labour: (2) a lowering of wages: (3) the breaking down of agreements between employers and employed with regard to working rules: (4) an interference in disputes by replacing workmen on strike. The question how far any or all of these kinds of interference with native labour have actually taken place is a trade question, which must be resolved by a careful investigation of the conditions of each of the chief industries to which the immigrants resort. The results of such an investigation, so far as concerns the boot and shoe trade, in which the interference is stated to be most marked and most resented, are given in detail in the section beginning on p. 67. The conclusions are summarised at the end of the chapter, and need not be repeated here. Other aspects of the question of trade interference are dealt with in the section beginning on p. 105. Apart from the positive conclusions arrived at, these sections bring out clearly the difficulty and complexity of the task of defining the precise effects of a particular factor like alien immigration on the conditions of industries which (like all the chief trades affected) are in a state of rapid economic transformation, due in the main to other causes. This evolution and the changes which it produces in the internal organisation of these trades, render it also almost impossible to institute useful comparisons between the present rates of wages and those current several years ago.

Turning to the question of the effects produced on the inhabitants of particular districts we have to take into account the local displacement of population, the sanitary condition of the immigrants so far as it affects the remainder of the population of the district, their condition as regards crime, and the burden, if any, which is thrown on the rates by their maintenance as paupers. The data for conclusions on all these points are given in various parts of this report: as regards displacement on pp. 72 and 73, as regards sanitation on pp. 56 to 60, as regards crime on pp. 60 and 61, as regards pauperism on pp. 45 to 56. Opinions may differ as to the degree to which we should take account of other and vaguer causes of like or dislike to the immigrants on the part of the native population of the district, *e.g.*, prejudices of race, religion, or custom. It is sufficient to note here that in some cases such feelings may help to determine, to a greater or less extent, the attitude of the non-Jewish population towards the foreign immigrants, quite apart from any question of economic or social interference.

After exhausting the discussion of the effects of the influx on particular classes we arrive at the far wider and more important question of its effects on the well-being of the general body of the inhabitants of the country. Several of the considerations enumerated above have also weight here, though in different degree. Thus the magnitude or otherwise of the contribution which the immigrants make to the volume of national pauperism and crime is a factor in the question. The extent and rapidity of the tendency towards economic and social "assimilation," discussed on pp. 35 to 45, have to be taken into account. The economic effect of the influx in relation to the volume of national production and the possible extension of foreign trade, is also of importance. When the question, however, is regarded from the point of view of the community as a whole, rather than from that of particular trades, the immigrants must be considered as consumers no less than as producers. The result of their presence in creating a demand for the products of other industries must be taken into account as well as any interference they may exercise as producers with the labour of particular groups of workers. This is a side of the question which should never be lost sight of, though it tends often to pass out of view, because the effect is widely distributed over many trades, whereas the influence of the immigrants as producers is concentrated in a few departments of a few industries.

The above are some of the principal points bearing on foreign immigration, the discussion of which may be facilitated by reference to the data supplied in this report.

So far as they bear on the question of checking immigration they relate almost exclusively to the desirability or otherwise of taking some kind of action, rather than to the expediency or possibility of devising or enforcing particular measures of restriction. If, on considering the evidence, some kind of regulation or restriction should be thought desirable, the further question would arise, how far such action should take the form of the more stringent enforcement of sanitary and other regulations as regards dwellings or workshops, with the view of compelling the newly arrived immigrants to conform to a greater extent to the standard of social and economic conditions customary in this country, or how far it should be directed to stopping the stream of immigration wholly or in part.

Certain parts of the present report may perhaps give some assistance in arriving at a conclusion on this question. So far also as it brings out the characteristic tenacity, persistence, and industry of the foreign Jewish population it suggests the difficulty of deciding by the appearance of the immigrants on arrival the probability or otherwise that they will ultimately prove an undesirable element in the population.

It must, however, be remembered that in deciding such questions as are here raised, there may be a great variety of considerations to be taken into account, many of which it would be out of place to refer to in this report.

APPENDICES

APPENDIX I.

(*a*.)—TABLE showing the TOTAL NUMBER of FOREIGNERS and of RUSSIANS
Districts of LONDON, and tho per-centage they bore to the total popu-

Registration Districts and Sub-Districts.	Total born in Foreign Countries.*			
	Males.	Females.	Total.	Per-cent-age of Popula-tion.
Whitechapel ·	9,729	8,232	17,961	24·12
Spitalfields ·	2,624	2,408	5,032	22·41
Mile End New Town	3,210	2,729	5,939	33·16
Whitechapel Church	2,749	2,331	5,080	25·03
Goodman's Fields ·	835	647	1,482	22·21
Aldgate	311	117	428	6·01
St. George-in-the-East ·	4,229	3,204	7,433	16·23
St. George's North · ·	4,102	3,182	7,284	19·30
St. John, St. George-in-the-East ·	127	22	149	1·85
Stepney · · · · ·	899	294	1,193	2·08
Shadwell · · ·	241	75	316	3·08
Ratcliff · ·	125	54	179	1·20
Limehouse · · ·	533	165	·698	2·17
Mile End Old Town · ·	3,176	2,521	5,607	5·30
Mile End Old Town Western	2,601	2,092	4,693	12·14
Mile End Old Town Eastern	575	429	1,004	1·46
Poplar · · ·	1,423	495	1,918	1·15
Bow · · · ·	195	107	302	·75
Bromley · · ·	353	175	528	·75
Poplar · · ·	875	213	1,088	1·93
Shoreditch · · ·	1,104	551	1,655	1·33
Shoreditch South · ·	363	174	537	2·67
Hoxton New Town · ·	347	163	510	1·74
Hoxton Old Town · ·	187	78	265	·93
Haggerston · · ·	207	136	343	·74
Bethnal Green · ·	1,057	739	1,796	1·39
Bethnal Green North · ·	242	153	395	·77
Bethnal Green South · ·	557	416	973	2·91
Bethnal Green East · ·	258	170	428	·97
Hackney · · · ·	1,725	1,198	2,923	1·27
Stoke Newington · ·	257	202	459	1·48
Stamford Hill · ·	93	81	174	·98
West Hackney · ·	424	292	716	1·68
Hackney · · ·	641	433	1,074	1·11
South Hackney · ·	310	190	500	1·20
Totals for above Districts ·	23,342	17,234	40,576	3·34

* Excluding persons born in these countries.

TO PART I.

APPENDIX I.

and RUSSIAN POLES residing in certain Registration Districts and Sub-
lation of those Districts or Sub-Districts, according to the Census of 1891.

Number born in Russia.*			Number born in Russian Poland.*			Total Number born in Russia and Russian Poland.*			
Males.	Females.	Total.	Males.	Females.	Total.	Males.	Females.	Total.	Per-cent-age of Popula-tion.
3,497	2,870	6,367	3,760	3,411	7,171	7,257	6,281	13,538	18·18
905	740	1,645	955	960	1,915	1,860	1,700	3,560	15·85
1,339	1,127	2,466	1,532	1,319	2,851	2,871	2,446	5,317	29·69
996	804	1,800	1,025	946	1,971	2,021	1,750	3,771	18·58
217	168	385	235	176	411	452	344	796	11·93
40	31	71	13	10	23	53	41	94	1·32
1,116	808	1,924	1,632	1,417	3,049	2,748	2,225	4,973	10·86
1,113	807	1,920	1,632	1,414	3,046	2,745	2,221	4,966	13·16
3	1	4		3	3	3	4	7	·03
23	9	32	29	17	46	52	26	78	·14
7	2	9	9	2	11	16	4	20	·20
7	2	9	3	4	7	10	6	16	·11
9	5	14	17	11	28	26	16	42	·13
726	562	1,288	1,142	1,010	2,152	1,868	1,572	3,440	3·20
687	535	1,222	1,057	945	2,002	1,744	1,480	3,224	8·34
39	27	66	85	65	150	124	92	216	·31
67	7	74	18	16	34	85	23	108	·06
12	5	17	2	2	4	14	7	21	·05
12	2	14	8	4	12	20	6	26	·04
43	—	43	8	10	18	51	10	61	·11
42	26	68	64	32	96	106	58	164	·13
18	14	32	36	21	57	54	35	89	·44
11	3	14	6	1	7	17	4	21	·07
6	4	10	14	3	17	20	7	27	·10
7	5	12	8	7	15	15	12	27	·06
271	189	460	271	239	510	542	428	970	·75
36	26	62	30	20	50	66	46	112	·22
215	150	365	205	189	394	420	339	759	2·27
20	13	33	36	30	66	56	43	99	·22
147	98	245	85	65	150	232	163	395	·17
13	11	24	6	3	9	19	14	33	·11
1	4	5	2	—	2	3	4	7	·04
35	22	57	22	18	40	57	40	97	·23
48	28	76	24	22	45	71	50	121	·13
50	33	83	32	22	54	82	55	137	·33
8,889	7,559	10,458	7,001	6,207	13,208	12,890	10,776	23,666	2·54

who were returned as " British Subjects."

Appendix I.—*cont.*

(b.)—Table showing the Total Number of Foreigners and of Russians and Russian Poles residing in each of the Registration Sub-districts, or portions thereof, that form any part of the Urban Sanitary District of Manchester, and the per-centage they bore to the total population of those Sub-districts or portions, according to the Census of 1891.

Registration Districts and Sub-districts.	Total born in Foreign Countries.*				Number born in Russia.*			Number born in Russian Poland.*			Total Number born in Russia and Russian Poland.*			
	M.	F.	To-tal.	Per-centage of Population.	M.	F.	To-tal.	M.	F.	To-tal.	M.	F.	To-tal.	Per-centage of Population.
Chorlton :														
†Didsbury -	21	22	43	2·54	—	1	1	—	—	—	—	1	1	·06
†Ardwick -	154	178	332	·35	—	3	3	3	3	6	3	6	9	·01
Chorlton-upon-Medlock }	607	353	960	1·61	26	6	32	10	15	25	36	21	57	·10
†Hulme -	123	100	223	·31	1	4	5	4	2	6	5	6	11	·02
Manchester :														
Ancoats	162	104	266	·58	4	3	7	3	2	5	7	5	12	·03
Central	1,054	822	1,876	4·98	556	501	1,057	222	177	399	778	678	1,456	3·83
St. George -	418	255	673	1·10	98	60	158	117	63	180	215	123	338	·55
Prestwich :														
Newton -	82	76	158	·24	5	1	6	5	4	9	10	5	15	·02
Cheetham -	2,307	2,016	4,323	10·82	1,131	977	2,108	531	536	1,067	1,662	1,513	3,175	7·95
†Failsworth and Blackley - }	36	32	68	·33	—	2	2	2	1	3	2	3	5	·02
Ashton-under-Lyne :														
†Audenshaw -	9	10	19	·57	—	—	—	1	—	1	1	—	1	·03
Total (U.S.D. of Manchester) }	5,073	3,968	8,941	1·77	1,821	1,558	3,379	898	803	1,701	2,719	2,361	5,080	1·01

* Excluding persons born in these countries who were returned as "British subjects."
† The figures given relate to that portion of the Registration Sub-district only which lies within the boundaries of the Urban Sanitary District of Manchester.

Appendix I.—*cont.*

(c.)—TABLE showing the TOTAL NUMBER number of FOREIGNERS and of RUSSIANS and RUSSIAN POLES residing in each of the Registration Sub-districts, or portions thereof, that form any part of the Urban Sanitary District of LEEDS, and the per-centage they bore to the total population of those Sub-districts or portions, according to the Census of 1891.

Registration Districts and Sub-districts.	Total born in Foreign Countries.*				Number born in Russia.*			Number born in Russian Poland.*			Total Number born in Russia and Russian Poland.*			
	M.	F.	Total.	Percentage of Population.	M.	F.	Total.	M.	F.	Total.	M.	F.	Total.	Percentage of Population.
Hunslet:														
†Hunslet and Whitkirk	38	30	68	·12	—	1	1	—	—	—	—	1	1	—
Holbeck:														
†Holbeck	13	15	28	·12	2	2	4	—	—	—	2	2	4	·02
Bramley:														
Bramley	7	8	15	·10	—	1	1	—	—	—	—	1	1	·01
Wortley	31	31	62	·13	1	1	2	—	—	—	1	1	2	—
Leeds:														
S. E. Leeds	61	32	93	·28	6	4	10	6	3	9	12	7	19	·06
N. Leeds	2,198	2,121	4,619	7·62	1,527	1,271	2,798	642	574	1,216	2,169	1,845	4,014	6·62
W. Leeds	498	374	872	1·01	170	120	290	110	79	189	280	199	479	·57
Kirkstall	48	59	107	·36	3	2	5	1	—	1	4	2	6	·02
†Chapeltown	26	37	63	·16	6	3	9	3	2	5	9	5	14	·10
Total (U.S.D. of Leeds)	3,820	2,707	5,927	1·61	1,715	1,405	3,120	762	658	1,420	2,477	2,063	4,540	1·24

* Excluding persons born in these countries who were returned as " British subjects."
† The figures given relate to that portion of the Registration Sub-district only which lies within the boundaries of the Urban Sanitary District of Leeds.

APPENDIX II.

List of 92 Trades in which 430 apprentices (apprenticed by the Industrial Committee of the Jewish Board of Guardians) were employed at the end of the year 1893.

Trade.	No. of Appren- tices.	Trade.	No. of Appren- tices.
		Brought forward -	178
Furnishing and Wood- working Trades.		*Building Trades*	
Cabinet makers (various) -	49	Marble masons - -	7
Upholsterers - -	22	Gasfitters and plumbers -	6
Wood carvers - -	22	Carpenters and joiners -	5
French polishers - -	16	Signboard and glass writers -	5
Ivory and hardwood turners and carvers - -	8	Builders' plumbers and de- corators - - -	2
Carvers and gilders - -	4	Fret lead glaziers - -	2
Overmantel makers - -	3		
Bamboo furniture makers -	2		
Box and packing case maker	1	*Clothing Trades.*	
Cane and invalid chair maker	1		
Clock dial silverer and lac- querer - - -	1	Bootmakers and clickers -	45
Fret cutter - - -	1	Clothiers' cutters - -	15
Furniture japanner - -	1	Dressmakers - -	5
Glass beveller and silverer -	1	Tailors and measure cutters -	3
Marquetrie cutter - -	1	Mantle maker - -	1
Photographic frame maker -	1		
Pianoforte case maker -	1	*Printing and Bookbinding Trades.*	
Metal Trades.		Compositors and printers -	20
		Bookbinders - -	6
Engineers - - -	11	Lithographic artists and designers - - -	5
Copper, iron and tin plate workers - - -	6	Wood engravers - -	4
Bicycle and tricycle makers -	5	Gold blockers - -	3
Art metal workers - -	4	Lithographic printers -	3
Metal platers and polishers -	2	Account-book binders -	2
Metal plate workers -	2	Book and card edge gilders -	2
Brass finisher - -	1	Compositor and reporter -	1
Cutler - - -	1	Machine ruler - -	1
Enamelled copper letter maker - - -	1	Zinco engraver - -	1
Lathe and tool maker -	1		
Scale and weighing machine maker - - -	1	*Jewellery and Precious Metal Workers.*	
Scientific Instrument Makers.		Watchmakers - -	20
		Diamond setters - -	6
Electricians - - -	2	Silver chasers and embossers	5
Scientific instrument makers	2	Diamond mounters and jewellers - - -	3
Dental instrument maker -	1	Jewellers (working) -	3
Optician - - -	1	Electro-platers and metal polishers - - -	2
Photographic apparatus maker - - -	1	Silversmiths - -	2
Telegraphic engineer and electrician - -	1	Gold and silver caster -	1
Carried forward -	178	Carried forward -	364

Appendix II.—*cont.*

Trade.	No. of Apprentices.	Trade.	No. of Apprentices.
Brought forward -	364	Brought forward	389
Lapidary and jewel cutter -	1	*Miscellaneous.*	
Nickel plater - -	1		
		Mounters (general) - -	12
Leather and Hair Workers.		Pianoforte tuners and polishers - - -	6
Harness-makers and saddlers	7	Engravers - - -	5
Bag and portmanteau makers	3	Ticket and show card writers	5
Fancy leather workers	3	Organ makers - -	2
Brush makers - -	2	Dentist (mechanical) -	1
Whip makers - -	2	Die sinker - - -	1
Chamois leather dresser -	1	Die sinker and seal engraver	1
Portmanteau and trunk maker - - -	1	Figure carver and modeller -	1
		Glass decorator and embosser	1
		Lamp maker - -	1
Coach and Carriage Builders.		Naturalist - - -	1
		Pencil maker - -	1
Coach and cart painters -	2	Slate enameller - -	1
Coachsmith - - -	1	Stained glass artist - -	1
Wheelwright - -	1	Weaver of upholsterers' trimmings -	1
Carried forward -	389	Total number of apprentices at end of 1893 -	430

APPENDIX III.

RETURN giving particulars of PRISONERS of RUSSIAN and POLISH NATION-
ALITY who were in Convict and Local Prisons on the 10th January
1894.

(*Abbreviations:*—P.S. = Penal Servitude ; H.L. = Hard Labour.)

Prison where confined.	Name of Prisoner.	Date of Conviction.	Place of Conviction.	Offence.	Sentence.
Parkhurst (Convict)	Roman Marwig.	14.11.92	Cent. Crim. Court.	Feloniously throwing corrosive fluid with intent to do grievous bodily harm.	5 years' P.S.
	Joseph Kopelewitz.	9.1.93	,,	Feloniously administering a stupefying drug with intent to enable him to commit an indictable offence.	10 years' P.S.
	Solomon Barmash.	1.5.93	,,	Forging and uttering an order and warrant for payment of 583l. with intent to defraud.	7 years' P.S.
	Maurice Robinowitz.	1.5.93		Forging and uttering an order and warrant for payment of 583l. with intent to defraud.	5 years' P.S.
	Lazarus Joans	23.5.93	North London Sessions,Clerkenwell.	Breaking and¹ entering dwelling-house and stealing there in 2 books.	5 years' P.S. and 2 years' police supervision.
Portsmouth (Convict)	Israel Fulman	24.3.90	Cent. Crim. Court.	Forgery	5 years' P.S.
	David Bock	3.5.90	Manchester Assizes.	Arson	7 years' P.S.
	Solomon Balleski.	19.5.90	Cent. Crim. Court.	Obtaining money by false pretences.	5 years' P.S.
	David J. Balcon.	8.9.90	,,	Receiving stolen goods.	5 years' P.S.
	Judith Geis	24.11.90		Warehouse breaking and stealing shawls, &c.	7 years' P.S.
	Samuel Israel	15.11.92	Northampton Assizes.	Burglary and larceny	3 years' P.S. and remanet 348 days.
	Lewis Wilkins	7.3.92	Cent. Crim. Court.	Larceny in dwelling-house.	3 years' P.S.
	Samuel Bloomstein.	15.11.92	Northampton Assizes.	Burglary	3 years' P.S.
Birmingham	John Kelisher	28.12.93	Birmingham Police Court.	Neglect of family	21 days' H.L.
Cardiff	Franz Gronquest.	29.6.93	Cardiff Boro' Quarter Sessions.	Maliciously wounding	9 cal. mons. H.L.
Holloway	Rose Push	6.12.93	Marlborough Street Police Court.	Stealing 5l. note	2 cal. mons. H.L.
Hull	Hyman Kaufman.	13.12.93	Hull Police Court.	Non-payment of arrears of bastardy order.	Pay 82s. 6d. or 30 days.

Appendix III.—cont.

Prison where confined.	Name of Prisoner.	Date of Conviction.	Place of Conviction.	Offence.	Sentence.
Leeds	Julius Stein	23.10.93	Leeds Sessions.	Stealing the sum of 50l. from his master at Leeds.	12 cal. mons. H.L.
	Marks Trevor	8.1.94		Stealing an overcoat at Leeds.	2 cal. mons. H.L.
	Bernard Wine	8.1.94		Warehouse-breaking and stealing at Leeds.	5 cal. mons. H.L.
Lewes	Solomon Mark alias Mendal Lofer.	4.8.93	Sussex Assizes.	Three charges of burglary.	6 cal. mons. H.L.
	Abraham Rockets alias Rogeszenski, or Roser.	4.8.93	„	„	
Liverpool	Charles Julius	14.11.93	Liverpool Assizes.	Wounding with intent to do grievous bodily harm.	4 cal. mons. H.L.
	Thomas Zerms	14.11.93	„	„	3 cal. mons. H.L.
	Martin Ucokski.	14.11.93	„	„	6 cal. mons. H.L.
	John Winstyn	14.11.93	Liverpool County Sessions.	Stealing seven shirts	3 cal. mons. H.L.
	Dominick Lueschwick.	20.12.93	Liscard Petty Sessions.	Assault	1 cal. mon. H.L.
	Elizabeth Schaizzi.	8.1.94 (Date of committal).	Liverpool City Sessions.	Stealing a watch	Awaiting trial.
	Peter Smith	8.1.94 (Date of committal).	„	„	
Newcastle	John Snicker	5.1.94 (Date of committal).	Newcastle City Police Court.	Wilful damage	On remand.
Pentonville	Gershon Abraham.	1.5.93	Cent. Crim. Court.	Conspiracy to defraud	12 cal. mons.
	Levy Woolf	17.7.93	Mansion House Police Court.	Stealing sateen	6 cal. mons.
	Mendal Silverman.	24.7.93	Cent. Crim. Court.	Abduction to carnally know.	18 cal. mons.
	Patk. Muczvewski.	11.9.93	„	Burglary	12 cal. mons.
	Lewis Cowen	8.11.93	Worship Street Police Court.	Stealing two talysons	3 cal. mons.
	Simon Nolbt	20.12.93	Guildhall Police Court.	Assault	1 cal. mon.
	Jacob Shyman	21.12.93	Worship Street Police Court.	Stealing chocolate	6 weeks.
	George Brandt	23.12.93	„	Stealing money	1 cal. mon.
	Isaac Long	3.1.94	„	R.V. Frequenting	6 weeks.
	Barnet Donn	8.1.94	Guildhall Police Court.	Assault Police	1 cal. mon.

Appendix III.—*cont.*

Prison where confined.	Name of Prisoner.	Date of Conviction.	Place of Conviction.	Offence.	Sentence.
Pentonville—*cont.*	Isaac Marks -	9.1.94	Guildhall Police Court.	R.V. Frequenting	1 cal. mon.
	Harris Marks	13.11.93	Cent. Crim. Court.	Possessing counterfeit coin.	18 cal. mons.
	Max Landau -	3.11.93	Thames Police Court.	Found in house and assault.	6 cal. mons.
	Hyman Benjamin.	3.1.94	Worship Street Police Court.	R.V. Frequenting -	6 weeks.
Reading -	Annie Lazarus	19.10.93	New Windsor Boro' Petty Sessions.	Stealing a purse containing a postal order for 15s. and 7d. in money.	3 cal. mons. H.L.
Strangeways	Maurice Schindler.	3.8.93	Manchester City Sessions.	Fraud	6 cal. mons. H.L.
	Morris Mendelshonn.	1.1.94	Manchester Police Court.	Breach of the peace	Sureties, or 1 cal. mon.
	Levi Jacobs -	5.1.94	,,	Non - payment of money.	Pay 68s. or 14 days' imprisonment.
	Charles Weisnor. *alias* William Buelski.	9.1.94	,,	Assault -	Pay 23s. or 7 days' H.L.
	Louis Selamberg.	9.1.94 (Date of remand.)	,,	Fraudulent bankrupt	Remanded till 16.1.94.
Wandsworth	Andrew Franceskoom.	10.10.93	South London Sessions, Newington.	Incorrigible rogue -	12 cal. mons. H.L.
	Nathan Bloom	29.12.93	Thames Police Court.	Unlawful possession	1 cal. mon. H.L.
Wormwood Scrubs.	Arthur Kohn	23.10.93	North London Sessions.	Feloniously receiving stolen property.	4 cal. mons. H.L.
	Emanuel Klinberg.	6.11.93	,,	Stealing a suit of clothes, &c.	5 cal. mons. H.L.
	Isaac Frakman.	13.11.93	Cent. Crim. Court.	Diminishing three sovereigns with intent to pass them so diminished.	3 years' P.S.
	Mike Woolf -	20.11.93	North London Sessions.	Stealing a quantity of sarcenet of his master.	9 cal. mons. H.L.

APPENDICES TO PART II.

Occupations of Russians and Poles in East London, Leeds, and Manchester.

APPENDICES

APPENDIX IV.

(a.)—TABLE showing the OCCUPATIONS of RUSSIANS and RUSSIAN POLES in LONDON according to

Occupations.	HACKNEY.											
	Stoke Newington.		Stamford Hill.		West Hackney.		Hackney.		South Hackney.		Totals.	
	M.	F.	M.	F.	M.	F.	M.	F.	M.	F.	M.	F.
Building trades	—	—	—	—	—	—	2	—	—	—	2	—
Engineering and metal trades.	—	—	—	—	1	—	2	—	—	—	3	—
Textile trades	—	—	—	—	—	—	—	—	—	—	—	—
Printing trades	1	—	—	—	3	—	—	—	3	—	7	—
Clothing trades:—												
Boot and shoe makers	—	—	—	—	1	—	25	6	26	1	52	7
Slipper makers	—	—	—	—	—	1	1	—	1	—	2	—
Tailors and tailoresses	—	—	—	—	4	1	1	2	7	1	12	4
Cap makers	—	—	—	—	2	1	1	—	1	—	4	1
Furriers	—	—	—	—	3	1	1	—	1	—	5	1
Dress and mantle makers.	—	2	—	—	2	4	—	1	—	1	2	8
Others	—	—	—	—	3	—	1	—	—	—	4	—
Cabinetmakers and woodworkers.	—	—	—	—	4	—	5	—	2	—	11	—
Food and drink preparation trades:—												
Bakers, confectioners, &c.	—	—	—	—	—	—	—	—	—	—	—	—
Butchers	—	—	—	—	1	—	—	—	2	—	3	—
Others	—	—	—	—	—	—	—	—	—	—	—	—
Watchmakers, &c. (jewellers).	4	—	—	—	—	—	3	—	5	—	12	—
Miscellaneous skilled occupations.	1	—	—	—	—	—	3	1	1	—	5	1
Seamen	—	—	—	—	—	—	2	—	—	—	2	—
General labourers, carmen, and railway workers.	—	—	—	—	—	—	—	—	—	—	—	—
Clerks and warehousemen	1	—	—	—	—	—	3	—	—	—	4	—
Retail tradesmen and shop assistants.	—	—	—	—	2	—	—	2	3	—	5	2
Hawkers, &c.	—	—	—	—	1	—	—	—	—	—	1	—
Hairdressers	1	—	—	—	1	—	4	—	2	—	8	—
Cigar makers, &c.	—	—	1	—	2	—	1	—	2	1	6	1
Stick makers, &c. (umbrellas).	2	—	1	—	2	—	1	—	—	—	6	—
Rag sorters, &c. (merchants).	—	—	—	—	—	—	—	—	—	—	—	—
Domestic servants, waiters, &c.	—	1	—	1	—	3	—	1	—	1	—	7
Scholars	—	—	1	—	5	2	1	1	2	—	9	3
Miscellaneous	5	—	.	.	18	—	11	—	6	—	40	—
Unspecified	4	11	—	3	2	27	—	34	18	50	24	125
Own means	—	—	—	—	—	1	3	2	—	—	3	3
Total number of Russians and Poles	19	14	3	4	57	40	71	50	82	55	232	163

TO PART II.

APPENDIX IV.

the under-mentioned Registration Districts and Sub-Districts of the Census of 1891.

SHOREDITCH.										Occupations.
Shoreditch South.		Hoxton New Town.		Hoxton Old Town.		Hagger-stone.		Totals.		
M.	F.	M.	F.	M.	F.	M.	F.	M.	F.	
2	—	—	—	—	—	—	—	2	—	Building trades.
—	—	1	—	1	—	—	—	2	—	Engineering and metal trades.
—	—	—	—	—	—	—	—	—	—	Textile trades.
—	—	—	—	—	—	—	—	—	—	Printing trades.
										Clothing trades :—
3	—	1	—	—	—	2	—	6	—	Boot and shoe makers.
—	—	—	—	1	—	—	—	1	-	Slipper makers.
17	1	—	—	1	1	4	2	22	4	Tailors and tailoresses.
—	1	—	—	—	—	1	—	1	1	Cap makers.
1	—	1	—	—	—	1	—	3	—	Furriers.
—	—	—	—	—	—	—	—	—	—	Dress and mantle makers.
1	—	—	—	—	—	—	—	1	—	Others.
7	1	—	—	—	—	1	—	8	1	Cabinetmakers and wood-workers.
										Food and drink preparation trades :—
—	—	1	—	—	—	1	—	2	—	Bakers, confectioners, &c.
—	—	—	—	1	—	—	—	1	—	Butchers.
—	—	—	—	—	—	—	—	—	—	Others.
2	—	—	—	2	—	1	—	5	—	Watchmakers, &c. (jewellers).
1	—	1	—	1	—	—	—	3	—	Miscellaneous skilled occupations.
—	—	—	—	—	—	—	—	—	—	Seamen.
—	—	—	—	—	—	—	—	—	—	General labourers, carmen, and railway workers.
—	—	—	—	—	—	—	—	—	—	Clerks and warehousemen.
—	1	—	—	1	2	2	1	6	4	Retail tradesmen and shop assistants.
—	—	2	—	—	—	—	—	2	-	Hawkers, &c.
9	—	2	—	3	—	2	—	16	—	Hairdressers.
1	—	—	—	—	—	—	—	1	—	Cigar makers, &c.
—	—	6	—	2	—	—	—	8	—	Stick makers, &c. (umbrellas).
—	—	—	—	—	—	—	—	—	—	Rag sorters, &c. (merchants).
—	3	—	—	—	—	—	—	—	3	Domestic servants, waiters, &c.
4	6	—	—	2	—	—	—	6	6	Scholars.
4	—	2	—	2	—	—	—	8	—	Miscellaneous.
2	22	—	4	—	1	—	9	2	39	Unspecified.
—	—	—	—	—	—	—	—	—	—	Own means.
54	35	17	4	20	7	15	12	106	58	Total number of Russians and Poles.

Appendix IV.—*cont.*

(a.)—TABLE showing the OCCUPATIONS of RUSSIANS AND RUSSIAN POLES in LONDON according to the

Occupations.	Bethnal Green North. M.	F.	Bethnal Green South. M.	F.	Bethnal Green East. M.	F.	Totals. M.	F.	Spital-fields. M.	F.
Building trades	1	—	3	—	1	—	5	—	58	—
Engineering and metal trades.	2	—	—	—	—	—	2	—	9	—
Textile trades	—	—	—	—	3	—	3	—	—	—
Printing trades	1	—	1	—	2	—	4	—	8	—
Clothing trades:—										
Boot and shoe makers	9	1	58	1	3	—	70	2	240	2
Slipper makers	—	—	3	—	—	—	3	—	14	—
Tailors and tailoresses	6	2	127	35	12	6	145	43	568	205
Cap makers	1	2	2	1	1	—	4	3	42	16
Furriers	1	—	8	3	—	—	9	3	55	19
Dress and mantle makers	—	—	—	7	—	—	—	7	23	33
Others	4	—	4	—	3	1	11	1	7	18
Cabinetmakers and wood-workers.	17	—	97	—	2	1	116	1	108	1
Food and drink preparation trades:—										
Bakers, confectioners, &c.	—	—	3	—	—	—	3	—	17	1
Butchers	1	—	—	—	1	—	2	—	16	3
Others	—	—	1	—	—	—	1	—	1	—
Watchmakers, &c. (jewellers).	—	—	—	—	3	—	3	—	17	—
Miscellaneous skilled occupations.	5	—	7	—	2	—	14	—	32	—
Seamen	—	—	—	—	—	—	—	—	—	—
General labourers, carmen, and railway workers.	—	—	—	—	—	—	—	—	3	—
Clerks and warehousemen	—	—	—	—	—	—	—	—	5	—
Retail tradesmen and shop assistants.	2	1	5	4	2	—	9	5	82	34
Hawkers, &c.	—	—	3	—	—	—	3	—	32	7
Hairdressers	5	—	8	—	5	—	18	—	11	—
Cigar makers, &c.	—	—	7	2	—	—	7	2	29	20
Stick makers, &c. (umbrellas).	3	—	9	1	2	—	14	1	19	—
Rag sorters, &c. (merchants).	—	—	3	—	—	1	3	1	11	1
Domestic servants, waiters, &c.	—	2	—	7	—	2	—	11	3	65
Scholars	—	1	7	11	6	4	13	16	136	131
Miscellaneous	4	—	18	1	3	—	25	1	133	17
Unspecified	4	37	46	266	4	28	54	331	176	1,115
Own means	—	—	—	—	1	—	1	—	5	12
Total number of Russians and Poles	66	46	420	339	56	43	542	428	1,860	1,700

Appendix IV.—cont.

the under-mentioned Registration Districts and Sub-Districts of Census of 1891—continued.

WHITECHAPEL.

Mile End New Town.		White- chapel Church.		Goodman's Fields.		Aldgate.		Totals.		Occupations.
M.	F.	M.	F.	M.	F.	M.	F.	M.	F.	
60	—	61	—	12	—	—	—	191	—	Building trades.
20	—	14	—	6	—	1	—	50	—	Engineering and metal trades.
—	—	2	—	—	—	—	—	2	—	Textile trades.
7	—	8	—	3	—	—	—	26	—	Printing trades.
										Clothing trades:—
115	10	249	6	27	—	1	—	902	18	Boot and shoe makers.
25	2	22	2	7	—	—	—	68	4	Slipper makers.
1,691	331	653	185	119	10	15	4	2,476	765	Tailors and tailoresses.
72	24	70	15	9	5	3	1	196	56	Cap makers.
43	25	45	27	16	4	—	1	159	76	Furriers.
23	36	16	35	3	8	—	—	65	112	Dress and mantle makers.
8	24	10	13	4	—	—	—	29	55	Others.
250	2	70	2	9	—	—	—	437	5	Cabinetmakers and woodworkers.
										Food and drink preparation trades :—
16	1	22	—	11	—	1	—	67	2	Bakers, confectioners, &c.
17	—	27	5	8	—	1	—	69	8	Butchers.
1	—	7	2	2	—	—	—	11	2	Others.
15	—	32	—	6	—	2	—	72	—	Watchmakers, &c. (jewellers).
29	1	37	1	12	—	3	—	113	2	Miscellaneous skilled occupations.
—	—	1	—	—	—	8	—	9	—	Seamen.
4	—	1	—	—	—	—	—	8	—	General labourers, carmen, and railway workers.
3	—	4	—	1	—	—	—	13	—	Clerks and warehousemen.
83	37	63	20	19	3	2	1	249	95	Retail tradesmen and shop assistants.
15	3	35	1	6	—	2	—	123	11	Hawkers, &c.
15	—	22	—	5	—	3	—	56	—	Hairdressers.
50	23	86	35	17	6	—	—	162	84	Cigar makers, &c.
36	—	39	1	6	—	2	—	102	1	Stick makers, &c. (umbrellas).
6	—	2	—	—	—	—	—	19	1	Rag sorters, &c. (merchants).
8	79	5	68	1	22	—	1	20	235	Domestic servants, waiters, &c.
290	310	132	143	26	17	2	11	586	612	Scholars.
121	9	141	12	14	7	6	—	445	45	Miscellaneous.
135	1,511	168	1,165	39	228	1	22	517	4,044	Unspecified.
5	18	4	12	1	6	—	—	15	48	Own means.
2,871	2,446	2,021	1,750	452	344	53	41	7,257	6,281	{ Total number of Russians and Poles.

Appendix IV.—*cont.*

(*a.*)—TABLE showing the OCCUPATIONS of RUSSIANS and RUSSIAN POLES in LONDON according to the

Occupation.	ST. GEORGE-IN-THE-EAST.						STEPNEY.							
	St. George's North.		St. John St. George-in-the-East.		Totals.		Shadwell.		Ratcliffe.		Limehouse.		Totals.	
	M.	F.	M.	F.	M.	F.	M.	F.	M.	F.	M.	F.	M.	F.
Building trades	61	—	—	—	61	—	—	—	1	—	2	—	3	—
Engineering and metal trades.	12	—	—	—	12	—	—	—	1	..	—	—	1	—
Textile trades	—	—	—	—	..	—	—	—	..	—	—	—	—	—
Printing trades	5	—	—	—	5	—	—	—	..	—	—	—	—	..
Clothing trades:—														
Boot and shoe makers.	343	3	—	—	343	3	4	..	1	—	—	—	5	..
Slipper makers	63	4	—	—	63	4	—	—	—	—	—	—	—	—
Tailors and tailoresses	1,042	264	—	1	1,042	265	5	1	—	1	6	4	11	6
Cap makers	68	16	—	—	68	16	—	..	1	—	—	—	1	—
Furriers	61	25	—	—	61	25	1	..	—	—	1	—	2	—
Dress and mantle makers.	21	39	—	1	21	40	—	—	—	2	—	—	—	2
Others	11	15	—	1	11	16	—	—	—	—	3	2	3	2
Cabinetmakers and woodworkers.	53	2	—	—	53	2	—	—	—	—	3	—	3	—
Food and drink preparation trades:—														
Bakers, confectioners, &c.	43	1	—	—	43	1	—	—	..	..	..	..	..	—
Butchers	11	—	—	—	11	—	—	—	—	—	—	—	—	—
Others	28	2	—	—	23	2	—	—	—	—	—	—	..	..
Watchmakers, &c. (jewellers).	20	—	—	—	20	—	—	—	—	—	1	—	1	—
Miscellaneous skilled occupations.	22	1	—	—	22	1	..	—	—	—	—	—	..	—
Seamen	15	—	3	—	18	—	1	—	—	—	1	—	2	—
General labourers, carmen, and railway workers.	1	—	—	—	1	—	—	—	—	—	—	—	—	—
Clerks and warehousemen.	3	1	—	—	3	1	—	—	—	—	—	—	—	—
Retail tradesmen and shop assistants.	49	20	—	—	49	20	—	—	1	—	1	—	2	—
Hawkers, &c.	36	2	—	—	36	2	—	—	1	—	—	—	1	—
Hairdressers	29	—	—	—	29	—	1	—	3	—	1	1	5	1
Cigar makers, &c.	31	11	—	—	31	11	1	—	—	—	1	—	2	—
Stick makers, &c. (umbrellas).	43	—	—	—	43	—	1	—	—	—	—	—	1	—
Rag sorters, &c. (merchants).	7	1	—	—	7	1	—	—	1	—	—	—	1	—
Domestic servants, waiters, &c.	5	52	—	1	5	53	—	—	—	—	—	1	—	1
Scholars	41	16	—	—	41	16	—	—	—	—	2	1	2	1
Miscellaneous	129	12	—	—	129	12	2	—	1	—	—	1	3	1
Unspecified	487	1,711	—	—	487	1,711	—	3	—	3	3	6	3	12
Own means	10	23	—	—	10	23	—	—	—	—	—	—	—	—
Total number of Russians and Poles	2,745	2,221	3	4	2,748	2,225	16	4	10	6	26	16	52	26

Appendix IV.—cont.

the under-mentioned Registration Districts and Sub-Districts of Census of 1891—continued.

MILE END OLD TOWN.						POPLAR.								
Mile End Old Town Western.		Mile End Old Town Eastern.		Totals.		Bow.		Bromley.		Poplar.		Totals.		Occupation.
M.	F.	M.	F.	M.	F.	M.	F.	M.	F.	M.	F.	M.	F.	
32	—	—	—	33	—	—	—	—	—	2	—	2	—	Building trades.
9	1	—	—	9	1	1	—	—	—	—	—	1	—	Engineering and metal trades.
—	—	—	—	2	—	—	—	—	—	—	—	—	—	Textile trades.
2	—	—	—	12	—	—	—	—	—	—	—	—	—	Printing trades.
														Clothing trades:—
165	1	15	—	180	1	—	—	1	—	1	—	2	—	Boot and shoe makers.
27	—	—	—	27	—	—	—	—	—	—	—	—	—	Slipper makers.
91	201	26	6	717	207	—	—	1	1	2	1	6	2	Tailors and tailoresses.
43	9	3	—	46	9	—	—	—	—	—	—	—	—	Cap makers.
44	18	1	1	45	19	—	—	1	—	—	—	1	—	Furriers.
29	21	—	3	21	24	—	—	—	—	—	—	—	—	Dress and mantle makers.
10	4	3	4	13	8	—	—	1	—	1	—	2	—	Others.
47	—	3	—	50	—	—	—	1	—	2	—	3	—	Cabinet makers and woodworkers.
														Food and drink preparation trades:—
22	2	1	—	23	2	—	—	—	—	—	—	—	—	Bakers, confectioners, &c.
7	1	2	—	9	1	—	—	—	—	—	—	—	—	Butchers.
9	2	1	—	10	2	—	—	—	—	—	—	—	—	Others.
16	—	2	—	18	—	1	—	—	—	1	—	2	—	Watchmakers, &c. (jewellers).
9	—	4	—	13	—	1	—	2	—	1	—	4	—	Miscellaneous skilled occupations.
1	—	2	—	3	—	1	—	3	—	31	—	35	—	Seamen.
2	—	—	—	2	—	—	—	—	—	1	—	1	—	General labourers, carmen, and railway workers.
2	—	—	—	2	—	—	—	—	—	1	—	1	—	Clerks and warehousemen.
49	8	3	1	52	9	1	—	2	—	—	—	3	—	Retail tradesmen and shop assistants.
19	—	—	—	19	—	—	—	—	—	—	—	—	—	Hawkers, &c.
14	1	18	—	32	1	—	—	—	—	1	—	1	—	Hairdressers.
36	14	6	1	42	15	—	—	—	—	—	—	—	—	Cigar makers, &c..
16	—	7	—	23	—	—	—	1	—	—	—	1	—	Stick makers, &c. (umbrellas).
7	1	—	—	7	1	—	—	—	—	—	—	—	—	Rag sorters &c. (merchants).
2	34	—	3	2	37	—	1	—	—	1	—	—	2	Domestic servants, waiters, &c.
80	57	2	2	82	89	—	1	—	1	—	—	1	1	Scholars.
129	11	10	1	139	12	4	—	3	—	5	1	12	1	Miscellaneous.
214	1,055	13	65	227	1,120	5	5	1	5	1	7	7	17	Unspecified.
8	9	—	5	8	14	—	—	—	—	—	—	—	—	Own means.
1,744	1,480	124	92	1,868	1,572	14	7	20	6	51	10	85	23	{ Total number of Russians and Poles.

Appendix IV.—*cont.*

(*b.*)—SUMMARY of foregoing TABLE (*a.*) showing the OCCUPATIONS of RUSSIANS and RUSSIAN POLES in EAST LONDON and HACKNEY according to the Census of 1891.

Occupations.	Grand Totals for East London and Hackney.		
	Males.	Females.	Males and Females.
Building trades	299	—	299
Engineering and metal trades	80	1	81
Textile trades	7	—	7
Printing trades	54	—	54
Clothing trades :—			
Boot and shoemakers	1,560	31	1,591
Slipper makers	164	8	172
Tailors and tailoresses	4,431	1,296	5,727
Cap makers	320	86	406
Furriers	285	124	409
Dress and mantle makers	109	193	302
Others	74	82	156
Cabinet makers and wood workers	681	9	690
Food and drink preparation trades:—			
Bakers, confectioners, &c.	138	5	143
Butchers	95	9	104
Others	45	6	51
Watchmakers, &c. (jewellers)	133	—	133
Miscellaneous skilled occupations	174	4	178
Seamen	69	—	69
General labourers, carmen, and railway workers	12	—	12
Clerks and warehousemen	23	1	24
Retail tradesmen and shop assistants	375	135	510
Hawkers, &c.	185	13	198
Hairdressers	165	2	167
Cigar makers	251	113	364
Stick makers, &c. (umbrellas)	198	2	200
Rag sorters, &c. (merchants)	37	4	41
Domestic servants, waiters, &c.	27	349	376
Scholars	740	744	1,484
Miscellaneous	801	72	873
Unspecified	1,321	7,399	8,720
Own means	37	88	125
Total number of Russians and Poles	12,890	10,776	23,666

Appendix IV.—cont.

(c.)—TABLE showing the OCCUPATIONS of RUSSIANS and RUSSIAN POLES in the URBAN SANITARY DISTRICT of MANCHESTER, according to the Census of 1891.

Occupations.	Russians.		Russian Poles.		Total of Russians and Russian Poles.		
	Males.	Females.	Males.	Females.	Males.	Females.	Males and Females.
Building trades	76	—	37	—	113	—	113
Engineering and metal trades	10	—	—	—	10	—	10
Textile trades	2	—	—	—	2	—	2
Printing trades	1	1	—	—	1	1	2
Clothing trades :—							
Boot and shoe makers	37	2	28	—	65	2	67
Slipper makers	91	2	73	5	164	7	171
Tailors and tailoresses	567	170	303	83	870	253	1,123
Cap makers	85	111	47	38	132	149	281
Furriers	3	2	—	—	3	2	5
Dress and mantle makers	6	32	1	14	7	46	53
Others*	123	24	86	14	209	38	247
Cabinet makers and woodworkers†	105	—	34	—	139	—	139
Food and drink preparation trades :—							
Bakers, confectioners, &c.	11	—	12	—	23	—	23
Butchers	7	1	6	—	13	1	14
Others	4	—	4	1	8	1	9
Watchmakers, &c. (jewellers)	36	—	12	. .	48	—	48
Miscellaneous skilled occupations	16	—	7	2	23	2	25
General labourers, carmen, and railway workers.	—	—	5	—	5	—	5
Clerks and warehousemen	5	—	—	—	5	—	5
Retail tradesmen, shop assistants, &c.‡	65	20	32	11	97	31	128
Hawkers, &c.§	171	4	67	—	238	4	242
Hairdressers	1	—	3	—	4	—	4
Cigar makers, &c.	21	12	1	3	22	15	37
Stick makers, &c. (umbrellas)	27	2	8	—	35	2	37
Rag sorters, &c. (merchants)	13	3	3	—	16	3	19
Domestic servants, waiters, &c.	—	38	—	12	—	50	50
Scholars	87	75	28	28	115	103	218
Miscellaneous	79	8	34	3	113	11	124
Unspecified	167	1,034	66	577	233	1,611	1,844
Own means	5	17	1	12	6	29	35
Total in U.S.D. of Manchester	1,821	1,558	898	803	2,719	2,361	5,080

* Nearly all waterproof garment makers.
† Including a few upholsterers.
‡ Excluding clothes and furniture dealers.
§ All people describing themselves as travellers, hawkers, costers, &c. The bulk of them are jewellery or drapery travellers.

Appendix IV.—*cont.*

(*d.*)—TABLE showing the OCCUPATIONS of RUSSIANS and RUSSIAN POLES in the URBAN SANITARY DISTRICT of LEEDS, according to the Census of 1891.

Occupations.	Russians.		Russian Poles.		Total of Russians and Russian Poles.		
	Males.	Females.	Males.	Females.	Males.	Females.	Males and Females.
Building trades	37	—	13	—	50	—	50
Engineering and metal trades	5	—	1	1	6	1	7
Textile trades	—	—	—	—	—	—	—
Printing trades	1	—	1	—	2	—	2
Clothing trades:— Boot and shoe makers	93	3	45	4	138	7	145
Slipper makers	142	8	33	2	175	10	185
Tailors and tailoresses	997	317	438	130	1,435	447	1,882
Cap makers	3	—	3	1	6	1	7
Furriers	—	—	—	—	—	—	—
Dress and mantle makers	4	14	5	5	9	19	28
Others	4	7	—	1	4	8	12
Cabinet makers and woodworkers	6	—	4	—	10	—	10
Food and drink preparation trades:— Bakers, confectioners, &c.	11	—	15	—	26	—	26
Butchers	4	—	5	—	9	—	9
Others	—	—	—	1	—	1	1
Watchmakers, &c. (jewellers)	8	—	9	1	17	1	18
Miscellaneous skilled occupations	2	—	3	—	5	—	5
General labourers, carmen, and railway workers.	1	—	1	—	2	—	2
Clerks and warehousemen	3	—	—	1	3	1	4
Retail tradesmen, shop assistants, &c.*	20	9	28	10	57	19	76
Hawkers, &c.†	54	2	33	—	87	2	89
Hairdressers	2	—	2	—	4	—	4
Cigar makers, &c.	3	11	4	—	7	11	18
Stickmakers, &c. (umbrellas)	—	—	—	—	—	—	—
Rag sorters, &c. (merchants)	3	—	6	—	9	—	9
Domestic servants, waiters, &c.	4	14	—	10	4	24	28
Scholars	108	95	25	27	133	122	255
Miscellaneous	57	15	31	5	88	20	108
Unspecified	129	901	55	452	184	1,353	1,537
Own means	5	9	2	7	7	16	23
Total in U.S.D. of Leeds	1,715	1,405	762	658	2,477	2,063	4,540

* Excluding clothes and furniture dealers.
† All people describing themselves as travellers, hawkers, or costers. The bulk of them are jewellery, drapery, or boot and shoe travellers.

APPENDICES TO PART II.

Boot and Shoe Trade.

APPENDIX V.

BOOT AND SHOE TRADE.

TABLE showing NUMBERS and NATURE of OCCUPATION of INDOOR and OUT-
DOOR WORKERS employed by 70 EMPLOYERS in the LONDON BOOT and
SHOE TRADE who have furnished RETURNS.

A.—*Firms working under 1st Class Statement.*

Index No. of Firm.	Numbers employed.						Total Out-doors.	Occupations of Outdoor Workers.
	Indoors.							
	Clickers and Rough Stuff Cutters.	Ma-chinists.	Lasters.	Finishers.	Others.	Total.		
1	8	21	9	13	3	54	3	Hand-sewn men.
2	20	—	18	17	7	62	106 {	4 machinists. 102 hand-sewn men.
3	8	28	26	16	7	85	—	
4	4	30	23	20	2	79	—	
5	4	—	6	8	2	20	8 {	3 machinists. 5 hand-sewn men.
6	4	12	8	8	3	35	—	
7	· 6	40	16	16	5	83	1	Unspecified
Total	54	131	106	98	29	418	118	—

B.—*Firms working under 2nd Class Statement.*

Index No. of Firm.	Clickers and Rough Stuff Cutters.	Ma-chinists.	Lasters.	Finishers.	Others.	Total.	Total Out-doors.	Occupations of Outdoor Workers.
8	10	8	20	18	9	65	6	Sew-round men.
9	4	—	—	—	2	6	—	
10	6	18	14	12	3	53	—	
11	4	—	4	4	—	12	30	{Hand-sewn men.
12	—	—	13	9	—	22	—	
13	5	—	11	10	2	28	11 {	3 machinists. 8 hand-sewn men.
14	5	16	10	9	1	41	—	
Total	34	42	72	62	17	227	47	—

Appendix V.—cont.

C.—*Firms working under Uniform Statement (sometimes known as the 3rd Class Statement).*

Index No. of Firm.	Numbers employed.							Occupations of Outdoor Workers.
	Indoors.						Total Outdoors.	
	Clickers and Rough Stuff Cutters.	Machinists.	Lasters.	Finishers.	Others.	Total.		
15	4	—	2	20	11	37	9 {	7 machinists. 2 hand-sewn men.
16	15	5	19	14	2	55	13 {	6 machinists. 3 lasters. 4 finishers.
17	3	—	5	5	—	13	2 {	1 machinist. 1 finisher.
18	6	—	15	14	2	37	8 {	7 machinists. 1 sole sewer.
19	6	21	14	ͺ	5	51	5 {	4 hand-sewn men. 1 sole sewer.
20	9	3	21	19	2	54	1	Finisher.
21	8	—	7	8	2	25	3	Machinists.
22	3	1	6	5	—	15	1	Machinist.
23	4	—	11	8	4	27	—	
24	7	—	20	19	2	48	8	Machinists.
25	2	—	—	—	—	2	15 {	3 machinists. 6 finishers. 5 hand-sewn men. 1 sole sewer.
26	2	—	4	3	—	9	2	Machinists.
27	7	—	20	18	2	47	6	Machinists.
28	8	—	24	20	3	55	20	Machinists.
29	4	5	6	4	3	22	—	
30	5	—	8	6	1	20	3	Machinists.
31	4	1	18	8	2	33	—	
32	2	4	6	4	1	17	—	
33	8	—	21	15	—	44	12 {	7 machinists. 2 lasters. 2 finishers. 1 sole sewer.
34	4	—	5	5	1	15	4 {	3 machinists. 1 laster.
35	8	—	1	7	6	22	—	
36	6	6	—	13	10	35	3 {	2 machinists. 1 sole sewer.
37	8	—	22	22	18	70	9 {	1 blocker. 7 machinists. 1 sew round.
38	8	—	12	15	1	36	6 {	5 machinists. 1 sole sewer.
39	7	—	23	15	2	47	7 {	6 machinists. 1 finisher.
40	1	—	4	4	1	10	3 {	2 machinists. 1 sew round.

Appendix V.—cont.

C.—*Firms working under Uniform Statement*—continued.

Index No. of Firm.	Numbers employed.						Total Out-doors.	Occupations of Outdoor Workers.
	Indoors.							
	Clickers and Rough Stuff Cutters.	Ma-chinists.	Lasters.	Finishers.	Others.	Total.		
41	1	—	4	4	*41	50	†	Machinists.
42	4	4	5	4	2	19	—	
43	10	—	38	32	2	82	15 {	12 machinists. 2 finishers. 1 laster.
44	4	—	10	10	1	25	3	Machinists.
45	4	—	8	8	1	21	5	Machinists.
46	1	4	3	2	—	10	1	Finisher.
47	10	28	20	23	4	85	—	
48	3	—	6	6	—	15	5 {	4 machinists. 1 sole sewer.
49	10	20	6	12	32	80	44 {	4 machinists. 35 nursery sewers. 3 hand-sewn men. 2 finishers.
50	2	—	5	4	1	12	—	
51	22	23	49	20	7	121	5	Machinists.
52	3	—	10	9	—	22	4	Machinists.
53	3	—	8	3	—	14	4 {	3 machinists. 1 hand-sewn man.
54	2	—	7	4	—	13	3 {	2 machinists. 1 sole sewer.
55	1	—	4	2	—	7	1	Machinist.
56	3	—	2	2	—	7	3 {	2 machinists. 1 sole sewer.
57	5	3	12	8	—	28	1	Finisher.
58	3	3	5	3	1	15	—	
59	2	4	5	4	1	16	—	
60	6	4	9	7	6	32	4	Machinists.
61	—	2	3	2	—	7	—	
62	18	—	33	30	8	89	11 {	8 machinists. 3 finishers.
63	11	16	24	16	5	72	—	
64	3	—	7	4	—	14	3	Machinists.
Total	280	157	577	498	193	1,705	252	

* Including 40 hand-sewn men.
† Number unspecified.

Appendix V.—cont.

D.—Firms working under Special " Shop-Statements."

Index No. of Firm.	Numbers employed.						Total Outdoors.	Occupations of Outdoor Workers.
	Indoors.							
	Clickers and Rough Stuff Cutters.	Machinists.	Lasters.	Finishers.	Others.	Total.		
65	2	10	7	6	1	26	3	Unspecified.
66	5	7	16	10	1	39	—	
67	155	4	243	168	98	468	200 {	2 lasters. 11 finishers. 187 hand-sewn men.
68	3	—	6	5	3	17	3	Machinists.
69	—	—	10	6	2	18	6 {	1 machinist. 5 hand-sewn men.
70	8	—	17	15	2	42	15	Machinists.
Total	173	21	299	210	107	810	227	

E.—Summary.

Class of Statement.	Number of Firms.	Numbers employed.						Total Outdoors.
		Indoors.						
		Clickers and Rough Stuff Cutters.	Machinists.	Lasters.	Finishers.	Others.	Total.	
1st class	7	54	131	106	98	29	418	118
2nd ,,	7	34	42	72	62	17	227	47
Uniform	50	280	157	577	498	133	1,705	252
Special Shop Statements	6	173	21	299	210	107	810	227
Total	70	541	351	1,054	868	346	3,160	644
Average per firm		8	5	15	12	5	45	9
Percentage which the number employed in each department forms of the total number of indoor workers		17·1	11·1	33·3	27·5	10·9	100·0	—

F.—Summary of Occupations of " Outdoor workers " employed by the above firms.

Occupations.	Number.
Sew-round and hand-sewn hands	398
Machinists	188
Finishers	35
Sole sewers	9
Lasters	9
Blocker	1
Unspecified	4
Total	644

APPENDIX VI.

MACHINERY and SUB-DIVISION of LABOUR in the BOOT and SHOE TRADE as carried on in FACTORIES.

The following statement gives a list of processes through which an ordinary boot or shoe passes before completion, in the "Wheatsheaf" Boot and Shoe Works at Leicester of the Co-operative Wholesale Society. employing about 2,000 operatives. The particulars given below have been supplied to the Department by the Manager of the Works :—

[NOTE:—*Processes marked with an asterisk* (*) *are done by hand and cannot be done by machinery. All other processes are done by machinery.*]

LIST OF PROCESSES THROUGH WHICH AN ORDINARY BOOT OR SHOE HAS TO GO.

Clicking Department.

*1. Cut patterns.
    (a.) Standard.   (d.) Toe-cap.
    (b.) Back or leg.   (e.) Lining.
    (c.) Vamp or golosh.
*2. Give order out to clicker.
*3. Give patterns out to clicker.
*4. Give material out to clicker.
*5. Clicking, i.e., cut material up to patterns mentioned in No. 1.
 6. Skiving.
 7. Blocking (if an elastic side boot).
*8. Rounding after blocking.
*9. Gouging vamps.
10. Punching caps, vamps, &c.
11. Crimping.
*12. Marking linings, sizes, &c.
13. Scolloping button bits.
*14. Marking facings (if laced boots).
*15. Sorting the material into the different qualities after it is cut.
16. Gilt blocking. (Putting trade mark, &c. in gold on lining, &c.)
*17. Tying up work ready for the upper closing room.

Upper Closing Room.

18. Make linings (i.e.. machine together down the back).
19. Machine toe linings on to back linings.
*20. Ink edges.
*21. Staying (putting supports on back of quarter to prevent buttons
    from tearing the quarter).
22. Closing back seams.
23. Rubbing back seams down.
24. Silking back seams.
25. Beading button piece by machine.
26. Machining round button-piece.
*27. Trimming button-piece.
28. Working button holes.
*29. Pulling ends of silk through and fastening same between button-
    piece and button-piece lining.
30. Barring holes.
31. Machining button-piece on to quarter.
*32. Rubbing front seam down.
33. Silking front seam.
34. Stitching buttons on (by hand and machine).
35. Turning in edge of vamp by machine.
*36. Fitting linings to quarters.
37. Machining round.

Appendix VI.—*cont.*

38. Embroidering.
39. Machining vamps on.
*40. Cleaning off.
*41. Covering.

Preparing Bottom Stuff.

*42. Cutting patterns.
    (*a*.) Out-soles.   (*d*.) Stiffenings.
    (*b*.) In-soles.   (*e*.) Lifts for heels.
    (*c*.) Middle-soles.
*43. Welting leather.
*44. Rounding the leather (taking belly and shoulder off the side).
45. Rolling the leather.
46. Cutting soles.
47. Cutting top-pieces.
48. Cutting middle-soles, &c.
49. Cutting lifts for heels.
50. Levelling.
51. Skiving.
52. Stiffening blocking.
53. Channelling if sewn; if rivet, pricking soles.
*54. Sorting.
55. Stamping size and shape.
*56. Tying up.
57. Building heels.
58. Pressing heels.
59. Top-piecing heels.

Making.

60. Feathering in-sole.
61. Skiving middle-sole.
62. Fitting shank.
*63. Cementing soles, middle-sole and shank together.
64. Moulding out-sole and in-sole.
65. Channel opening.
*66. Pulling upper over.
*67. Put in, stiffening, puff and side lining.
68. Lasting.
69. Tack sole on and sprig seat.
*70. Take last out.
71. Sew (*i.e.*, sewing outsole, middle-sole, upper and in-sole together).
*72. Put on last again.
73. Close channel and hammer button out.
74. Attach heel.
75. Slug heel.

Finishing.

76. Ploughing.
77. Trimming edge.
78. Trimming waist.
79. Paring heel.
80. Taking seat out.
*81. Paring heel corners and jointing heel.
82. Scouring heels.
*83. Inking.
84. Heel burnishing.
85. Seat wheeling.
86. Edge setting.
*87. Stitch wheeling.
88. Bottom scouring.

Appendix VI.—*cont.*

89. Scouring waist.
*90. Damping down.
*91. Strip marking.
92. Strip burnishing.
*93. Top ironing.
*94. Making fiddle waists.
*95. Rubbing off.
*96. Socking.

Stock Room.

97. Treeing.
*98. Cleaning and dressing.
*99. Boxing.
*100. Packing.

SEW-ROUND GOODS.

The only difference between these goods and ordinary machine-sewn or riveted goods is in the processes which are as follow :—

*1. Turn upper lining outside (a sew round is made inside out).
2. Channel sole on the flesh side, not on grain side as in machine sewn.
3. Plough sole.
*4. Fasten sole on last, grain side to the last.
*5. Last upper over.
6. Sew sole and upper together.
*7. Trim upper off level with channel of sole.
*8. Turn upper right side out (up to this point it has been inside or lining outside).
9. Hammer bottom out.
*10. Attach heel.
*11. Put pad in.

Ready for finishing.

APPENDIX VII.

RECOGNISED RATES OF WAGES IN THE LONDON BOOT AND SHOE TRADE.

Uniform Statement of Wages in Home Trade.

The following is a copy of the Uniform Statement of Wages for Lasters and Finishers compiled in 1890 by the Board of Conciliation and Arbitration, and applicable to all firms other than those governed by the First and Second Class Statements.

WOMEN'S WORK.

To come into Operation on and after Monday, March 23, 1891.

Description of Standard Women's Boot (size 4).—Button or balmoral; 1½ in. military heel; puff toe; 7 in. at back seam of leg; machine-sewn, channels down; or brass rivets; pumps or welts; finished round strip or black waist.

Appendix VII.—cont.

Classification of Material.

Class.	A	B	C	D	E	F	G	H
	d.	d.	d.	d.	d.	d.	d.	d.
Price per pair { Laster.	11	10	9	8	7	6	5½	5
Price per pair { Finisher.	10	9	8	7	6	5	5	1½
Material.								
1. Glove kid	1st	—	2nd	—	—	—	—	—
2. Glacé kid	1st	—	2nd	3rd	—	—	—	—
3. Patent calf	1st	—	2nd	3rd	—	—	—	—
4. Wax calf	—	1st	2nd	—	3rd	—	—	—
5. Real French straight grain and levant morocco	—	1st	—	2nd	—	—	—	—
6. Glove and glacé lamb	—	1st	—	2nd	—	—	—	—
7. Seal levant	—	1st	—	2nd	—	—	—	—
8. Calf kid	—	—	1st	2nd	3rd	4th	—	—
9. Glacé goat and dongola	—	—	1st	—	2nd	3rd	—	—
10. Cordovan (including bellies and shanks)	—	—	1st	—	2nd	3rd	—	—
11. Levant and straight grain goat	—	—	1st	—	2nd	3rd	—	—
12. Soft alum mock kid	—	—	—	1st	2nd	3rd	—	—
13. Stuffs	—	—	—	1st	—	2nd	—	3rd
14. Satin hide and kid	—	—	—	1st	2nd	3rd	—	—
15. Glove hide	—	—	—	1st	2nd	3rd	—	—
16. Glacé and straight grain sheep	—	—	—	1st	2nd	3rd	4th	—
17. All patents (except patent calf)	—	—	—	1st	2nd	3rd	—	—
18. Mock kid	—	—	—	—	1st	2nd	—	3rd
19. Grain	—	—	—	—	1st	2nd	3rd	—
20. Levant kip and hide	—	—	—	—	1st	2nd	3rd	—
21. Sheep levant	—	—	—	—	1st	2nd	—	3rd

Notes on Classification of Material.

The Board of Conciliation and Arbitration will adopt standard samples in the various classes.

Combinations of Material.

1. Goods to come under this definition must comprise at least a "high vamp" of a different material to that in the quarters.

2. The material in the "leg" or "quarter" to determine the class.

3. When a material which is classed on the statement as better than that in the "leg" or "quarter" is used in combination therewith, the price to be fixed midway between that of the "leg" or "quarter" class and the class next above in the better material introduced.

Example.—A woman's 2nd soft alum mock kid, with real glove, "high vamps" would be 8d. to laster, this being the price midway between "E" class in soft alum mock kid and "C" class in glove kid (this latter being the class next above).

Appendix VII.—*cont.*

Deductions (from Standard and not accumulative).

—	Per Pair. Laster.	Per Pair. Finisher.
	d.	*d.*
Leg, 6 in. and under, except side springs	½	½
Side springs and shoes	½	½
Top piece heel ($\frac{7}{8}$ in.), when finished	½	½
Do. split lift and top piece only (½ in.) when finished	¾	¾
Spring heel	1	1
Finished Square to heel	—	½
Cut-down waist. F G and H classes only	—	½
Heeling by machinery and no split lifts. A class	2½	—
B "	2¼	—
C "	2	—
D "	1¾	—
E "	1½	—
F and G classes	1¼	—
H class	1	—
Breasting military heels	—	—
Breasting and paring military heels ready for papering	—	—
Paring edges (waist and foreparts)	—	—
Socking	—	—
Channels up A B C classes	1	—
D E "	¾	—
F G H "	½	—
Foreparts not made out	—	½
Bottoms and waists not made out	—	1

Extras (on Standard and not accumulative).

—	Per Pair. Laster.	Per Pair. Finisher.
	d.	*d.*
Leg :—Height above 7 in.	½	½
Height above 7½ in.	1	1
Foreparts :—Coloured welts	—	1
Bevel edge, painted any colour	—	1
Fair stitched	2	1
do. when pricked up by fudge	2	1½
do. do. hand	2	3
Nailing toe and joint, nails found by laster	1	½
Nailing toe and joint (two rows), nails found by laster	2	1
Sewn cork welts ($\frac{1}{8}$ in.)	1	—
do. clumps, inserted and finished split edge, when cut out or fitted up by employer	2	4
do. round or bevel edge, when cut out or fitted up by employer	2	5
do. pin points (one row)	3	—
do. do. (one and a half rows	4½	—
do. do. (two rows)	6	—
Square edge clumps over $\frac{5}{16}$ in. when finished, A to D classes	1	1
do. pin points	—	1

Appendix VII.—*cont.*

—	Per Pair. Laster.	Per Pair. Finisher.
	d.	*d.*
Fiddle foreparts	—	½
Bordered foreparts	—	1
Half wide welts, up to $\frac{3}{16}$ in. when finished	1	1
Wide welts, over $\frac{3}{16}$ in when finished	2	2
Bevel edge clumbs, not split	—	3
Marked up dull foreparts	—	½
Bunking foreparts	—	1
Real spike toe	½	—
Waist:—Fiddle waist, including breast and top piece	—	1
Brown waist on common work, as per standard sample	—	½
Flexura waist, fitted when given out	1	2
Do. when fitted by laster	2	2
Bunking waist	—	¼
Peak strip waist	—	½
Upper:—Patent vamps (except house boots), extra to finisher on A to D classes only	½	½
Toe caps on vamped work. A to E classes only	½	—
Brogue wing vamps	½	—
Fur or lamb's wool lining	1	½
All goloshed work in leather	½	—
Patent goloshed work	—	½
Whole goloshed in leather. A to E classes only	—	½
Soilable colours, outsides (except sheep and other common material) to be shopped clean	1	1
Soilable colours, outsides (sheep and other common materials) to be shopped clean	½	½
Leather linings on boots only		—
Leather linings (persians and light basils) on boots only E to H classes	¼	—
Heels:—Over 1½ in.	½	½
Over 1¾ in.	1	1
Over 2 in.	2	2
French heel (beyond military heel) up to 1¾ in. when finished	1	1
Wurtemberg leather lifts	12	6
Cased heel	10	4
Mock Wurtemberg	3	3
Tips filled in. A to E classes	1	—
Do. F to H classes	½	—
Tips or plates got up by finisher	—	1
(Plates carry no extras to lasters.)		
Sundries:—Heel pins (when not bespoke)	½	—
Fitting (when not bespoke)	½	—
Eights size and over (except felt and house boots and slippers). A to E classes	1	1
Eights size and over (except felt and house boots and slippers). F to H classes	½	½
Lasting on wooden lasts	4	—
Bracing	3	—
Rounding bottom stuff	2	—
Sample pairs, when given out as such	1	1
Measures or bespoke	1	1

Appendix VII.—*cont.*

GIRLS' WORK.

TO COME INTO OPERATION ON AND AFTER MONDAY, MAY 4, 1891.

Description of Standard Girls' Boots.—Button or balmoral: up to 1 in. military heel; puff toe; 5½ in. at back seam of leg on size 11; machine-sewn, channels down, or brass rivets; pumps or welts; finished round strip or black waist.

Combinations of material.

In girls' work to be subject to the same rules as in women's work.

Deductions (from standard and not accumulative).

—	Per Pair. Laster.	Per Pair. Finisher.
	d.	*d.*
Sizes, 7's to 10's	½	½
Legs, 47 in. and under (except side springs)	½	¼
Top-piece heel, under ½ in. when finished	¼	¼
Heeling by machinery and no split lifts: A to C classes, 11's to 1's; 11*d.* per doz. from laster	—	—
Heeling by machinery and no split lifts: " 7's to 10's; 10*d.* per doz. from laster	—	—
Heeling by machinery and no split lifts: D to H classes, 11's to 1's; 9*d.* per doz. from laster	—	—
Heeling by machinery and no split lifts: " 7's to 10's; 8*d.* per doz. from laster	—	—
Breasting military heels	—	—
Breasting and paring military heels ready for papering	—	—
Paring edges (waist and foreparts)	—	—
Socking	—	—
Channels up: A to F classes	½	—
Channels up: G and H classes	¼	—

All other deductions one-half those on women's work.

Classification of Material.

Class.	A	B	C	D	E	F	G	H
Price per pair. 11's to 1's.	*d.*	*d.*	*d.*	*d.*	*d.*	*d.*	*d.*	*d.*
Laster	7¾	7¼	6¾	6¼	5¾	5¼	4¾	4¼
Finisher	7¼	6¾	6¼	5¾	5¼	4¾	4¼	3¾
Material.								
1. Glove kid	1st	—	2nd	—	—	—	—	—
2. Glacé kid	1st	—	2nd	3rd	—	—	—	—
3. Patent calf	1st	—	2nd	3rd	—	—	—	—
4. Wax calf	—	1st	2nd	—	3rd	—	—	—
5. Real French straight grain and levant morocco	—	1st	—	2nd	—	—	—	—
6. Glove and glacé lamb	—	1st	—	2nd	—	—	—	—
7. Seal levant	—	1st	—	2nd	—	—	—	—
8. Calf kid	—	—	1st	2nd	3rd	4th	—	—
9. Glacé goat and dongola	—	—	1st	—	2nd	3rd	—	—
10. Cordovan (including bellies and shanks)	—	—	1st	—	2nd	3rd	—	—

Appendix VII.—cont.

Class.	A	B	C	D	E	F	G	H
Price per pair. 11's to 1's. { Laster Finisher	d. 7¾ 7¼	d. 7¼ 6¼	d. 6¾ 6¼	d. 6¼ 5¾	d. 5¾ 5¼	d. 5¼ 4¾	d. 4¾ 4¼	d. 4¼ 3¾
Material.								
11. Levant and straight grain goat -	—	—	1st	—	2nd	3rd	—	—
12. Soft alum mock kid	—	—	—	1st	2nd	3rd	—	—
13. Stuffs - - -	—	—	—	1st	—	2nd	—	3rd
14. Satin hide and kip -	—	—	—	1st	2nd	3rd	—	—
15. Glove hide - -	—	—	—	1st	2nd	3rd	—	—
16. Glacé and straight-grain sheep -	—	—	—	1st	2nd	3rd	4th	—
17. All patents (except patent calf) -	—	—	—	1st	2nd	3rd	—	—
18. Mock kid - -	—	—	—	—	1st	2nd	—	3rd
19. Grain - - -	—	—	—	—	1st	2nd	3rd	—
20. Levant kip and hide	—	—	—	—	1st	2nd	3rd	—
21. Sheep levant - -	—	—	—	—	1st	2nd	—	3rd

Extras (on standard and not accumulative).

	Per Pair.	
	Laster.	Finisher.
	d.	d.
Leg:—Height above 5½ in. - - - -	½	½
Height above 6½ in. - - - -	1	1
Heels:—Over 1 in. - - - -	½	½

All other extras one-half those on women's work.

Notes.

1. No deductions or extras to be claimed beyond those mentioned in the foregoing lists. Any items not provided for in this statement, unless otherwise agreed upon, to be decided by the Board of Conciliation and Arbitration.

2. No alteration of the classification of materials to be made, except at least three months' notice be given in writing, to the Board of Conciliation and Arbitration.

3. Any alteration in classification of materials shall take effect either on January 1 or July 1 in any year, but the first notice of alteration shall not take effect until January 1, 1892.

4. Notice of an alteration in classification of material by the Board of Conciliation and Arbitration shall be given to the trade either on May 1 or November 1.

Signed for the Board of Conciliation and Arbitration.

Chairman.
Vice-Chairman.
London, March 24. 1891. *Secretary.*

At a Meeting of the Board of Conciliation and Arbitration in June, 1892, the following provisions were adopted as applying to 4's and 6's children's work :—

A and B classes, 1½d. deduction from Girl's Standard for 11's to 1's.

C to E classes, 1¼d. deduction from Girl's Standard for 11's to 1's.

F to H classes, 1d. deduction from Girl's Standard for 11's to 1's.

It was also decided that the foregoing should come into operation on and after the 11th of July, 1892.

APPENDIX VIII.

FORM of PERMIT granted by the London Board of Conciliation and Arbitration to Lasters and Finishers to work at home.

BOARD OF CONCILIATION AND ARBITRATION.

PERMIT.

Issued to Mr.
of
Employed by
of   *at*
Distance
Age
Complaint
Date

The bearer, Mr.   of   , a Laster or Finisher, in the employ of M   of   is permitted under Rule No. *one* or *three* of the Rules applying to Shopping of Work ; *to work at home on the grounds of age or ill-health* ; or *to shop his work to and from the employer's factory and the workshop at*

Dated this   day of   189   .

..........................., ..., *Chairman.*
            Secretary, ..., *Vice-chairman.*
30, Finsbury Pavement,   159, Hackney Road, E.
London, E.C.

Issued by......................

NOTE.—A new permit must be applied for upon leaving the employer whose name is mentioned above.

Rules to apply to the Shopping of Work when Shops are not on the Employer's Factory.

1. That no women be allowed to shop work except in the cases where the men are permitted to work at home.
2. That all persons allowed to shop work as provided in Rules 1 and 3 must obtain a permit from the Board of Conciliation and Arbitration signed by the chairman, vice-chairman, and secretary.
3. That no workman be expected to shop work at a greater distance than 100 yards from his workshop unless with the sanction of the Board of Conciliation and Arbitration.
4. That all employers must put up a notice stating the exact shop-time for each workman. A workman presenting himself at the time fixed be not detained longer than necessary beyond his time.
5. That all work required to be shopped other than at shop-time be sent for by the employer. That shopping only be done once a day.
6. That should any dispute arise in carrying out these rules notice to be given to the Board of Conciliation and Arbitration who will at once investigate and report.
7. That the operation of Rules 2, 3, and 5 be subject to revision in 12 months from 1st May 1890.

APPENDIX IX.

PARTICULARS OF CERTAIN EAST LONDON BOOT AND SHOE WORKSHOPS.

The following Tables give, in tabular form certain particulars obtained by personal visits during the early part of 1894 to the under-mentioned Workshops in Whitechapel, Mile End Old Town, and St. George's-in-the-East, engaged in various branches of the Boot, Shoe, and Slipper Trade.

I.—MANUFACTURERS AND "CHAMBER MASTERS."

Trade and Index No. of Workshop.	Clicking and Rough Stuff cutting.	Machining.	Lasting.	Finishing.	Others.	Men.	Lads.	Women and Girls.	Nature.	No. of Outworkers.	Occupier.	Employees.	Sanitary and general Condition of Workshop.	Statement of Occupier or Workmen as to Prices, Earnings, and Hours.	General Remarks.
BOOT AND SHOE MANUFACTURERS. (1)	31	12	33	36	7	89	4	14	Machining and "sew rounds," and one laster with special "permit."	—	Yes.	Yes (men); women non-Jewish.	Sanitary accommodation bad. Workshops airy.	Working on "uniform statement." For full work good lasters will earn 35s. to 40s., knifers 35s. to 50s., and finishers 30s. to 52s. in a week.	No "greeners." Finishers and lasters mostly foreign. Prefers indoor system, but thinks it more expensive than outdoor.
(2)	3	—	7	—	1	11	—	—	Finishing and machining.	—	Yes.	Yes.	Fair.	Lasters 4s. 6d. per dozen, finishers 3s. 6d.	Complains of bad trade and "Union intimidation."
(3)	2	—	7	2	—	11	—	—	Machining and some finishing.	—	Yes.	—	Fair.	·	Occupier has had two or three strikes. Is a contractor for a firm in North London.

Appendix IX.—continued.

Particulars of East London Boot and Shoe Workshops—continued.

I.—MANUFACTURERS AND "CHAMBER MASTERS."

Trade and Index No. of Workshop.	Clothing and Rough Stuff cutting.	Machining.	Lasting.	Finishing.	Others.	Men.	Lads.	Women and Girls.	Nature.	No. of Outworkers.	Occupiers.	Employees.	Sanitary and general Condition of Workshop.	Statement of Occupier or Workmen as to Prices, Earnings, and Hours.	General Remarks.
	Number employed at time of Visit on Premises in					Total on Premises.			Work given out.		Whether Jewish.				
(4)	1	1	10	{(4)}	—	5	—	1	·	—	Yes.	—	·	Lasters 3s. 6d. per dozen, finishers 3s. 3d.	Occupier does sticking; wife machines; four men do lasting. Complains of importation of German uppers made of "lasting" which are given out to foreigners. Also complains of Leicester and Northampton firms getting work done in domestic workshops with whole families working.
(5)	7	4*	4	2	4†	20	5	—	Machining of uppers.	—	Yes.	Men mostly English.	Bad.	No information	Is introducing machinery wherever possible. Denounces union regulations.
(6)	21	—	4	3	—	8	1	—	Machining	—	Yes.	Yes. "Greeners" only in country 12 months.	Bad. Workshop dirty.	No information (occupier out).	—
(7)	3	—	6	4	—	11	2	—	Machining	—	Yes.	—	Workshop dilapidated.	No information	Makes (1) for "factors"; (2) for export, (3) for retail shops. Trade very bad.

* Sole-sewing machines.　† Heeling machines.

Appendix IX.—continued.

Particulars of East London Boot and Shoe Workshops—continued.

I.—MANUFACTURERS AND "CHAMBER MASTERS."

Trade and Index No. of Workshop.	Clicking and Rough Stuff cutting.	Machining.	Lasting.	Finishing.	Others.	Men.	Lads.	Women and Girls.	Nature.	No. of Outworkers.	Occupier.	Employees.	Sanitary and general Condition of Workshop.	Statement of Occupier or Workmen as to Prices, Earnings, and Hours.	General Remarks.
(8)	See Remarks.					3	—	—	—	—	No.	No.	—	States that they can earn "comfortable living" by working 10 hours a day.	Man and two sons, making boots right out. Each can turn his hand to any branch of trade. Complains of Jewish labour cutting down prices.
(9)	—	—	4	—	—	6	—	—	Machining and finishing.	—	Yes.	No.	Very clean and plenty of room.	No information as to prices. Hours 8–8, Saturdays, 8–1.	Complains of bad trade, "greeners", machinery, and strikes.
(10)	—	1	3	—	21	21	1	1	Finishing and some lasting.	—	No.	No.	—	No trustworthy information.	Remainder of hands, four lasters, three finishers, and sole sewer, absent from work (day being Monday).
(11)	—	—	—	—	—	8	1	3	All lasting, finishing and machining.	4	Yes.	Yes (men).	Shop and back room used as workshop. Not overcrowded.	—	Makes for retail shops.
(12)	7*	—	—	—	—	8	4	—	—	—	Yes.	—	Fair.	trade from the strike of 1890 for indoor workshops, but lasting and finishing shops are now standing empty and all the work is given out. Says he does not get two days' work a week all the year round.	[occupiers] of the strike, and dates decline of his provided workshops. He ...

* Clicking rough stuff and heel cutting, &c.

Appendix IX.—continued.

Particulars of East London Boot and Shoe Workshops—continued.

I.—MANUFACTURERS AND "CHAMBER MASTERS."

Trade and Index No. of Workshop.	Number employed at time of Visit on Premises in					Total on Premises.			Work given out.		Whether Jewish.		Sanitary and general Condition of Workshop.	Statement of Occupier or Workmen as to Prices, Earnings, and Hours.	General Remarks.
	Checking and Rough Stuff cutting.	Machining.	Lasting.	Finishing.	Others.	Men.	Lads.	Women and Girls.	Nature.	No. of Outworkers.	Occupier.	Employees.			
(13)	6	—	See Remarks.			2	—	—	.	—	Yes.	Yes.	.	-	Domestic workshop in bed-room and living room combined. Occupier stated to be deaf and dumb; said to make boots throughout for customers.
(14)	4	—	20	10	4	37	2	1	Machining .	—	„	„	One workshop, overcrowded.	-	
(15)	4	—	4	4	2	12	1	1	Machining, "saw round," and some finishing.	—	Yes.	„	.	-	Sells to retail shops.
(16)	1	—	4	4	1	16	—	—	Machining .	1	Yes.	Yes.	.	They can turn out four dozen a day when busy. These are sold at 24s. a dozen, out of which 9s. goes in wages, 13s. 6d. in material, grindery, and all other expenses except rent, leaving 1s. 6d. a dozen profit to occupier, i.e., a profit of 6s. a day, out of which 12s. a week goes in rent. Of the finishers, one is a greener and can finish six dozen a week; the others can do nine dozen.	Knifer at present is only coming for about two hours a day. One of finishers is a greener. Sells to retail shops.

Particulars of East London Boot and Shoe Workshops—*continued.*

1.—MANUFACTURERS AND "CHAMBER MASTERS."

Trade and Index No. of Workshop.	Number employed at time of Visit on Premises in					Total on Premises.			Work given out.		Whether Jewish		Sanitary and general Condition of Workshop.	Statement of Occupier or Workmen as to Prices, Earnings, and Hours.
	Clicking and Rough Stuff cutting.	Machining.	Last-ing.	Fin-ish-ing.	Others.	Men.	Lads.	Women and Girls.	Nature.	No. of Out-work-ers.	Occu-pier.	Em-ployees.		
(17)	5	—	9	7	5	35	1	1	Machining	—	Yes.	Yes.	Some rooms over-crowded.	-
(18)	2	—	—	—	—	2	—	—	Finishing and machining.	?	Yes.	Yes.	Good workshop at back of yard.	-
(19)	14	—	17	5	6	41	1	4	Machining, and some lasting and finishing.	4 or 5 (for lasting and finish-ing.)	Yes.	Yes.	17 lasters in underground cellar with room for 10 or less.	States that four finishers can finish eight dozen to a gross a day.
(20)	3	9	10	7	—	20	—	9	One out-worker with "permit."	—	No.	No.	Satis-factory.	A union house. Works on the uniform statement.

Appendix IX.—continued.

Particulars of East London Boot and Shoe Workshops—continued.

I.—Manufacturers and "Chamber Masters."

Trade and Index No. of Workshop	Clicking and Rough Stuff Cutting.	Machining.	Lasting.	Finishing.	Others.	Men.	Lads.	Women and Girls.	Nature.	No. of Out-workers.	Occupier.	Employees.	Sanitary and general Condition of Workshop.	Statement of Occupier or Workmen as to Prices, Earnings, and Hours.	General Remarks.
(21)	2?	(See Remarks.)	—	—	—	2?	—	—	—	—	No.	No.	Good.	·	Visited in slack time. A month previously had five men and four women. Expected soon to be busy again. (This is a "ticketed" shop, occupier having formerly been a member of the union and now stated to be paying less than statement.)
(22)	—	—	—	(14)	—	8	—	—	Stated to be none.	—	?	?	Good.	·	Makes boots throughout for a firm, but claims not to be an out-worker.
(23)	?	—	—	—	—	15	—	—	Machining ·	—	—	—	·	·	·
(24)	1	1	5	3	—	7	—	3	·	—	—	—	Work carried on in ordinary rooms of houses.	·	Work carried on in two houses. Complains of bad trade. Works for a firm in Hackney. (? Out-workers.)

Appendix IX.—continued.

Particulars of East London Boot and Shoe Workshops—continued.

II.—OUTWORKERS.

Branch of Trade and Index No. of Workshop.	Number employed when visited.			Whether Jewish or not.	Whether working for a Jewish Employer.	Statement of Occupier as to Price received per Dozen Pairs.	Statement of Occupier as to Number of Pairs done in a Day; or as to Daily Earnings.	Statement of Occupier as to Hours worked per Day.	Remarks.
	Men.	Lads.	Women and Girls.						
LASTERS. (1)	5	—	—	Yes.	Yes.	—	—	—	Underground cellar workshop, overcrowded.
(2)	3	1	—	Yes.	Yes.	—	—	—	—
(3)	1	—	—	Yes.	Yes.	—	—	—	Was outworker before the strike. Then left London for provincial town; now hearing that outwork is reviving in London has come back; workshop in back yard.
(4)	2	1	—	Yes.	Yes.	—	—	—	Fair sanitary condition.
(5)	1	2	1 (fitting up.)	Yes.	No.	3s. 3d. lasting with channeling; 3s. 6d. without.	2½ doz.	12 hours.	Workshop very dirty and insanitary.
(6)	2	—	—	Yes.	Yes.	2s. 6d.	5 to 6 doz.	8 a.m. to 9 p.m.	Underground workshop; insanitary.
(7)	2	—	—	—	Yes.	2s. 6d.	2 doz.	13 hours.	Women's lace and button kid boots. Sanitary condition fair.

Appendix IX.—continued.

Particulars of East London Boot and Shoe Workshops—continued.

II.—OUTWORKERS.

Branch of Trade, and Index No. of Workshop.	Number employed when visited.			Whether Jewish or not.	Whether working for a Jewish Employer.	Statement of Occupier as to Price reserved per Dozen Pairs.	Statement of Occupier as to Number of Pairs done in a Day; or as to Daily Earnings.	Statement of Occupier as to Hours worked per Day.	Remarks.
	Men.	Lads.	Women and Girls.						
LASTERS—cont. (8)	2	1	—	—	No.	—	—	8 a.m. to 9 p.m. (Monday to Friday). 8 a.m. to 4 p.m. (Saturday).	Lasting women's boots, uppers imported from Germany ready machined, made of "lasting." Underground workshop in fair condition.
(9)	3	—	—	Yes.	Yes.	—	—	—	Refuse in backyard. Take out lasting, then return the boots, which are given out again to be finished.
LASTERS AND FINISHERS. (10)	5	—	1	Yes.	Yes.	—	—	—	Good workshop at back of yard. Man denies being outworker, claiming that he buys the uppers from a firm and then sells the boots, either to that firm or to others, probably, however, this is only an evasion of the agreement.
(11)	7	—	—	—	Yes.	—	—	—	Five men working in a wretched tumble-down shed with stone floor behind house, heated by coke with only sufficient cubic space for two at most. Stench very bad. Shop has since been condemned by local sanitary authority.
FINISHERS. (12)	5	—	—	Yes.	Yes.	3s. 6d.	6 doz.	6 a.m. to 8 p.m. summer, 9 to 6 in slack time.	Formerly one of a team of "finishers." Then after agreement worked indoors at finishing; now has come out as a "knifer" with a team of finishers, alleging that he was displaced by finishing machinery (see p. 79).

Appendix IX.—continued.
Particulars of East London Boot and Shoe Workshops—continued.
II.—OUTWORKERS.

Branch of Trade and Index No. of Work-shop.	Number employed when visited.			Whether Jewish, or not.	Whether working for a Jewish Employer.	Statement of Occupier as to Price received per Dozen Pairs.	Statement of Occupier as to Number of Pairs done in a Day; or as to Limit Earning.	Statement of Occupier as to Hours worked per Day.	Remarks.
	Men.	Lads.	Women and Girls.						
FINISHERS—cont. (13)	1	—	—	Yes.	Yes.	—	Earns 4s. a day.	9 to 6.	Domestic workshop. When busy occupier employs another man.
(14)	6	—	—	Yes.	Yes.	2s. to 2s. 6d.	Knifer earns 4s. (net), Finisher 4s. 9d.	7 a.m. to 10 p.m.	Workshop over-crowded. Two of the employes are "greeners," having been only two months in England. The others range from 2½ to 7 years in England. State that price for same work was 4s. only two years ago.
MACHINISTS. (15)	5	1	?	—	Yes.	—	—	—	Workshop over-crowded and very dirty. Five men and one woman machinist, one boy and one girl pasting and fitting.
(16)	2?	—	1	—	Yes. (Woman non-Jewish.)	—	—	—	Outworker for several firms. This is a case of an associated workshop. The machinists occupy part of a large workshop at top of house, part of which is also occupied by two other groups of workers—purse making and cutting uppers for slippers.
(17)	4	—	1	Yes.	Yes.	5s. a gross.	5 gross for 6 machines, i.e., 10 doz. per machine.	—	When fully employed there are six machinists and three "table hands." The machines work as a "team," subdividing the machining of the uppers into three or four parts. One machine alone can do six dozen a day, but working in a team they can produce at rate of 10 dozen.

M 2

Appendix IX.—continued.

Particulars of East London Boot and Shoe Workshops—continued.

II.—OUTWORKERS.

Branch of Trade, and Index No. of Workshop.	Number employed when visited.			Whether Jewish or not.	Whether working for a Jewish Employer.	Statement of Occupier as to Price received per Dozen Pairs.	Statement of Occupier as to Number of Pairs done in a Day; or as to Daily Earnings.	Statement of Occupier as to Hours worked per Day.	Remarks.
	Men.	Lads.	Women and Girls.						
MACHINISTS—*cont.*									
(18)	2	—	—	(*See* last col.)	Yes.	—	—	—	Outworker for several people in a small way in district.
(19)	2	1	1	Yes.	Yes.	—	—	—	Men at machines, lad and girl at table pasting, &c.; overcrowded.
(20)	1	1	2	—	Yes.	—	—	—	Trade said to be very slack.
(21)	3	1	—	Yes.	Yes.	—	—	—	Outworker for several small men. One man apparently a "greener," another had been in England two years.
(22)	—	—	15	—	No.	—	—	—	Machining uppers and linings. Over-crowded (room only for 10).
(23)	6	—	—	(*See* last col.)	Yes.	—	—	—	Sole sewer and perforator for the trade. Insanitary; most of men English.
SEW ROUND.									
(24)	3	—	—	Yes.	Yes.	—	—	—	Underground room, very untidy and dirty. Occupier had been six years in England, two men, two years each, and one, three months.
(25)	2	—	—	Yes.	Yes.	3s.	—	—	Six months before four men and two women had been found working. Dirty, dilapidated room. Work done in living room. Takes out uppers already closed from shop, and does "sew round" and finishing processes.

Appendix IX.—continued.

Particulars of East London Boot and Shoe Workshops—continued.

II. OUTWORKERS.

Number employed when visited.			Whether Jewish or not.	Whether working for a Jewish Employer.	Statement of Occupier as to Price received per Dozen Pairs.	Statement of Occupier as to Number of Pairs done in a Day; or as to Daily Earnings.	Statement of Occupier as to Hours worked per Day.	Remarks.
Men.	Lads.	Women and Girls.						
1	—	—	Yes.	Yes.	2s. 6d.	—	14 hours.	Domestic workshop, family work, sleep, and live in one room. Buckskin slippers. Room in filthy condition, and occupants apparently half-starved.
1	—	—	Yes.	No.	2s. 6d.	—	14 hours.	Domestic workshop. Man complains of Jewish competition, and alleges that prices have been cut down to half during last 10 years. Irregularly employed. Workroom very dirty.
1	1	?	Yes.	No.	3s. 6d.	3 doz. (working full time).	Not over 12 hours.	Felt slippers, "sew-rounds." Complains of Jewish competition, and states that he used to get 5s. for same class of work 12 to 14 years ago. Very slack; hardly any work. Family employed.
1	1	—	Yes.	Yes.	—	—	—	Sew-round; trade very slack. In slack season he turns to finishing (indoors).
1	1	—	Yes.	Yes.	—	—	—	When visited a month previously, six men working.
2	2	—	Yes (two shops).	No.	6s. reduced to 5s. in slack times 10s. a dozen for men's court slippers.	6 doz. working from 8 a.m. to 11 p.m.	—	Very dull. Only working two hours the day when visited. One man said he was looking out for a good finishing indoors. Working in front room of house. Fairly high quality of work.

Appendix IX.—continued.

Particulars of East London Boot and Shoe Workshops—continued.

III. SLIPPER MAKERS.

Trade and Index No. of Workshop.	Number employed on Premises.			Work given out.		Whether Jewish.		Remarks.
	Men.	Lads.	Women and Girls.	Nature.	Number of Outworkers.	Occupier.	Employees.	
SLIPPER MANUFACTURERS.								
(1)	7	—	2	Machining.	2	Yes.	Yes.	Occupier states that man can earn 30s. in busy, and 12s. to 15s. in slack season. Making and finishing done on premises.
(2)	6 to 8*	—	—	None.	—	Yes.	Yes.	Manufactures slippers throughout to sell to retail shops. This is slack season, and no work was going on.
(3)	2	—	—	Machining and sew-round.	3	Yes.	Yes.	Employs three men when busy.

* When busy. None working when visited.

APPENDIX X.

TRADE DISPUTES IN LONDON BOOT AND SHOE TRADE.

TABLE showing particulars of TRADE DISPUTES in the LONDON BOOT AND SHOE TRADE reported to the BOARD OF TRADE as occurring between May 1890 and April 1894.

District.	Class of Operatives affected.	No. of Establishments affected.	No. of Persons affected.	Date of Commencement and Termination.	Cause or Object.	Result.
				1890.	1890.	
London, E.C.	Bootmakers	3	—	June · · · June · · ·	For advance in wages · · ·	Successful.
London (chiefly E. and E.C.).	Handsewn shoemakers (Higher class sew-round).	54	600	September (lasted about 3 weeks)	For uniform statement of wages based on advance.	Strike was followed by formation of Conciliation Board and an advance of about 12½ per cent.
London, W.	Boot and shoe makers.	2	33	September 11 · September 30	For advance in wages · · ·	One firm granted advance. Others unsuccessful; then resumed on old terms.
				1891.	1891.	
London, E.	Clickers, &c.	1	11	February 7 · April 18	Against excessive employment of boys	Unsuccessful. Hands replaced.
London, E.	Riveters and finishers.	3	About 80	March · April ·	Against refusal of employers to agree to full terms of advanced price list or statement which had been generally accepted.	Successful. Employers accepted statement.
London, E.	Finishers	1	100	April · May ·	Struck work in defiance of Union while question of revised statement was under consideration.	Work resumed in obedience to ballot.

Appendix X.—continued.

Trade Disputes in London Boot and Shoe Trade—continued.

District.	Class of Operatives affected.	No. of Establishments affected.	No. of Persons affected.	Date of Commencement and Termination.	Cause or Object.	Result.
London, S.E.	Lasters and finishers.	1	120	Commencement 1891. August 24; Termination 1891. August 28	Against dismissal of certain colleagues.	Work resumed unconditionally, the Union disapproving the strike.
London	Boot and shoe operatives.	1	46	October 4; October 31	Against alleged delay of Conciliation Board in settling prices.	Men resumed on understanding that grievances should be immediately dealt with by Conciliation Board.
London	Do. (lock out)	150	10,000	October 31; November 5	In consequence of above strike	Lock-out withdrawn on settlement of strike.
London, S.E.	Boot and shoe operatives.	1	60	1892. May 21; 1892. May	Alleged refusal of employer to pay "list" prices or to classify the work on accepted scale.	Unsuccessful. Hands replaced.
London, E.	Clickers and rough stuff cutters.	1	47	1893. August 15; 1893. August 22	Against discharge of four clickers for refusal to accept reduced statement of prices.	Unsuccessful. Hands replaced.
London, E.	Boot and shoe operatives.	1	50	June 17; July 1	For reduction in hours	Successful.
London, E.	Boot and shoe operatives.	1	20 to 50	September 2; January 6, 1894	Against refusal to pay according to London statement.	Unsuccessful. Hands replaced.
London, E.	Boot and shoe operatives.	1	42	September 26; November 7, 1893	Against refusal to pay according to London statement	Successful.

APPENDICES TO PART II.

Boot and Shoe Trade, Exports and Imports.

APPENDIX XI.

(a.)—TABLE showing QUANTITIES and VALUES of BOOTS and SHOES EXPORTED
from 1873 to

Countries to which Exported.	1873.		1874.		1875.		1876.	
	Quantity.	Value.	Quantity.	Value.	Quantity.	Value.	Quantity.	Value.
FOREIGN COUNTRIES.	Dozen Pairs.	£	Dozen Pairs.	£	Dozen Pairs.	£	Dozen Pairs.	£
Holland	—	—	1,853	6,894	—	—	—	—
Belgium	—	—	2,027	7,306	—	—	—	—
France	2,160	9,503	—	—	—	—	—	—
Turkey Proper	2,062	7,336	—	—	—	—	—	—
Egypt	6,335	21,772	4,401	12,739	4,670	13,844	4,898	14,466
Foreign West Indies	3,733	13,391	2,458	10,952	5,092	15,399	—	..
Central America	—	—	—	—	3,804	15,911	—	—
United States of Columbia	17,963	63,635	10,038	39,601	2,843	11,030	—	—
Peru	17,479	55,064	5,238	15,545	8,821	28,397	—	—
Chili	8,730	33,135	4,419	13,225	7,606	20,003	8,773	19,585
Brazil	39,430	144,452	31,320	126,364	37,720	144,791	30,620	116,486
Uruguay	11,674	48,894	4,280	9,327	6,210	11,171	—	—
Argentine Republic	41,626	132,350	18,722	74,753	34,014	101,639	—	—
Total to Foreign Countries	151,192	511,422	84,786	315,134	110,780	358,575	44,291	150,537
BRITISH POSSESSIONS.								
Channel Islands	5,837	24,583	7,983	39,023	5,214	22,918	5,313	23,867
British Possessions in South Africa	77,023	239,815	75,487	247,891	94,153	314,688	97,242	312,164
Bombay and Scinde	2,609	10,941	3,305	12,200	5,823	21,500	—	—
Madras	906	3,394	468	2,477	—	—	—	—
Bengal and Burmah	2,740	12,664	2,315	10,648	2,558	11,297	—	—
Ceylon	—	—	1,330	6,070	—	—	—	—
Australia	226,063	677,488	180,744	556,903	185,688	603,251	193,002	611,873
British North America	13,362	49,042	8,394	28,644	7,124	26,373	—	—
British West Indies and British Guiana	31,475	97,817	31,394	113,552	28,753	88,789	35,302	106,624
Total to British Possessions	360,015	1,135,143	311,430	1,010,934	329,313	1,088,811	331,039	1,057,229
To other Countries (not stated whether British or Foreign)	16,487	61,321	13,898	48,234	22,747	69,881	67,963	196,309
Grand Total exported from the United Kingdom	527,694	1,707,886	410,114	1,374,302	462,840	1,517,267	443,293	1,404,075

APPENDIX XI.

from the UNITED KINGDOM to the under-mentioned COUNTRIES in each YEAR 1893 inclusive.

	1877.		1878.		1879.		1880.		1881.		1882.	
	Quantity.	Value.	Quantity.	Value.	Quantity.	Value.	Quantity.	Value.	Quantity.	Value.	Quantity.	Value.
	Dozen Pairs.	£	Dozen Pairs.	£	Dozen Pairs. 6,489	£ 13,749	Dozen Pairs. 6,542	£ 15,169	Dozen Pairs. 9,036	£ 17,576	Dozen Pairs. 10,701	£ 17,587
	—	—	—	—	—	—	—	—	—	—	4,690	17,171
	—	—	—	—	—	—	—	—	—	—	—	—
	—	—	—	—	—	—	—	—	—	—	—	—
	—	—	—	—	—	—	—	—	—	—	—	—
	—	—	—	—	3,000	11,600	1,864	6,913	2,894	9,110	2,179	7,450
	—	—	—	—	3,010	10,360	3,036	9,969	4,319	16,031	3,365	13,176
	—	—	—	—	—	—	—	—	—	—	—	—
	—	—	—	—	—	—	—	—	6,071	8,570	6,040	11,531
	30,605	107,284	30,118	112,233	32,170	111,140	37,983	130,664	48,919	175,750	40,683	163,361
	—	—	—	—	—	—	—	—	—	—	—	—
	—	—	—	—	9,590	21,410	12,680	27,300	14,875	35,624	16,672	44,396
	30,605	107,284	30,118	112,233	54,200	168,230	62,114	188,905	86,714	262,661	90,333	275,602
	8,111	30,691	7,789	26,856	8,530	31,000	5,077	16,669	6,207	20,600	5,550	17,343
	77,612	244,978	93,885	302,161	114,211	361,422	132,715	417,680	154,492	490,695	153,810	503,963
	—	—	—	—	4,741	17,031	8,966	27,793	13,594	44,348	14,268	49,399
	—	—	—	—	—	—	—	—	—	—	—	—
	—	—	—	—	—	—	4,099	15,517	5,050	20,081	8,114	29,867
	—	—	—	—	—	—	—	—	—	—	—	—
	207,626	651,757	190,407	576,140	188,096	545,874	140,493	429,709	233,714	599,215	287,049	788,750
	—	—	—	—	—	—	—	—	3,420	9,461	8,497	16,485
	30,696	90,112	25,182	82,391	34,050	97,890	36,111	104,130	27,400	77,437	10,307	112,582
	324,048	997,848	326,263	987,378	349,628	1,054,177	327,461	1,010,302	444,396	1,252,828	519,265	1,511,881
	81,513	331,346	73,802	216,130	29,516	88,846	30,614	88,013	83,115	67,541	21,806	74,994
	436,166	1,336,478	430,273	1,315,731	433,374	1,311,293	420,189	1,282,221	554,255	1,583,230	634,401	1,862,477

Appendix XI.—continued.

(a.)—TABLE showing QUANTITIES and VALUES

Country to which Exported.	1883. Quantity.	1883. Value.	1884. Quantity.	1884. Value.	1885. Quantity.	1885. Value.	1886. Quantity.	1886. Value.
FOREIGN COUNTRIES.	Dozen Pairs.	£	Dozen Pairs.	£	Dozen Pairs.	£	Dozen Pairs.	£
Germany	—	—	—	—	—	—	—	—
Holland	10,019	16,692	12,588	21,632	11,809	19,591	8,935	17,898
Belgium	—	—	—	—	4,169	11,777	3,683	10,985
France	—	—	—	—	—	—	7,484	32,589
Egypt	6,081	17,997	3,834	10,578	3,646	13,217	5,483	21,543
U. S. of America, Atlantic	—	—	—	—	—	—	—	—
South America:— Brazil	46,152	171,892	40,024	148,217	39,667	140,588	48,450	157,058
Argentine Republic	21,023	46,125	12,519	37,252	22,842	47,523	13,901	26,939
Other Countries	10,769	26,874	9,423	29,952	6,145	19,903	4,974	17,676
Other Foreign Countries	—	—	—	—	13,055	42,663	12,330	40,898
Total to Foreign Countries	94,074	282,020	78,408	241,561	101,333	294,248	105,240	325,036
BRITISH POSSESSIONS. Channel Islands	7,677	19,542	8,934	22,469	5,856	16,191	7,597	20,525
British Possessions in South Africa	100,141	311,520	101,110	317,836	84,623	239,405	83,152	241,143
British East Indies:— Bombay and Scinde	17,906	58,720	12,513	44,451	13,412	45,662	15,386	49,019
Bengal and Burmah	8,896	31,331	10,565	33,805	9,804	32,263	10,938	34,344
Other	—	—	—	—	—	—	—	—
Australasia:— West Australia	210454	648,418	247,351	743,844	—	—	—	—
South Australia					31,681	85,886	19,263	58,733
Victoria					29,643	87,072	29,679	86,189
New South Wales					108,263	459,312	139,017	356,677
Queensland					17,816	46,623	18,703	50,351
Tasmania					7,001	20,902	11,051	33,902
New Zealand					46,350	152,105	39,733	123,619
Other Colonies					1,857	5,423	2,939	9,661
British North America	2,797	11,070	2,935	11,514	3,094	13,542	3,167	12,995
British West Indies and British Guiana.	38,092	106,371	41,997	118,190	30,919	82,301	35,824	91,130
Other British Possessions	—	—	—	—	7,907	27,927	8,648	27,156
Total to British Possessions	394,963	1,180,992	425,405	1,255,803	458,976	1,333,083	425,117	1,223,166
To other Countries (not stated whether British or Foreign)	24,097	79,060	22,731	80,080	—	—	—	—
Grand Total exported from the United Kingdom	513,134	1,542,072	526,544	1,577,444	560,309	1,627,331	530,357	1,548,202

Appendix XI.—*continued.*

of Boots and Shoes EXPORTED, &c.—*continued.*

	1887.		1888.		1889.		1890.		1891.		1892.		1893.
Quantity.	Value.	Quantity.	Value.	Quantity.	Value.	Quantity.	Value.	Quantity.	Value.	Quantity.	Value.	Quantity.	
Dozen Pairs.	£	Dozen Pairs.	£	Dozen Pairs.	£	Dozen Pairs.	£	Dozen Pairs.	£	Dozen Pairs.	£	Dozen Pairs.	
2,418	6,313	2,913	8,316	2,383	6,321	2,049	6,103	1,873	5,813	2,716	7,556	2,971	
11,112	21,517	8,926	17,616	9,801	17,635	8,858	19,282	7,109	13,872	7,251	15,172	9,807	
2,983	8,272	3,348	8,670	3,748	9,875	2,928	7,747	3,934	9,618	2,886	7,771	4,136	
4,824	21,029	5,015	22,981	4,439	19,738	3,360	15,379	2,511	10,753	1,891	7,518	1,424	
4,291	15,247	3,163	14,370	5,265	18,287	5,847	21,092	3,055	12,421	4,482	15,105	5,181	
1,316	9,651	707	6,674	986	7,491	703	5,533	410	3,248	607	4,681	505	
53,084	188,650	52,160	188,769	51,745	182,998	68,464	231,648	62,596	211,281	37,445	130,315	53,332	
15,863	30,613	20,169	39,747	23,075	54,152	8,466	22,205	1,228	5,369	681	2,762	1,019	
9,851	25,930	10,725	25,262	9,233	21,872	10,051	23,978	8,222	22,197	17,310	40,531	18,683	
11,303	37,382	9,707	31,418	9,571	29,747	9,447	29,129	10,121	31,633	9,272	28,930	10,659	
117,438	**361,885**	**117,233**	**356,706**	**122,176**	**367,496**	**120,173**	**385,287**	**101,719**	**327,402**	**84,541**	**259,645**	**108,324**	
9,841	26,091	9,026	24,481	8,920	21,524	9,868	23,461	10,921	26,395	12,330	28,777	12,776	
120,624	358,088	132,629	377,271	174,730	499,885	186,610	513,076	182,138	488,491	189,769	499,790	219,019	
16,388	54,929	11,231	36,446	12,780	37,997	14,642	46,481	13,396	38,685	10,190	29,801	13,190	
15,301	44,487	11,847	34,573	14,448	41,726	13,847	40,042	18,586	53,625	14,683	42,697	17,592	
—	—	—	—	—	—	—	—	1,679	5,111	4,585	13,812	3,554	
—	—	5,396	17,063	5,105	15,611	5,804	18,611	6,454	19,689	9,459	27,936	7,648	
20,329	51,951	19,801	47,806	17,336	41,909	13,367	31,288	14,616	36,453	13,752	32,649	13,833	
30,897	84,589	18,583	118,296	43,701	101,033	38,967	98,890	16,072	121,764	27,289	62,543	21,501	
135,060	376,817	102,741	319,589	138,378	339,566	148,884	382,887	166,237	481,451	138,030	383,126	129,828	
26,512	74,770	34,058	98,474	26,374	64,463	20,785	53,811	24,054	64,263	20,290	69,083	17,360	
5,908	18,980	6,134	18,874	7,561	19,836	10,881	29,333	11,462	31,887	8,901	21,017	7,744	
39,096	132,816	39,685	117,819	33,372	93,580	37,887	100,131	46,398	119,507	47,225	115,276	44,010	
1,508	15,841	7	16	61	113	8	27	74	160	106	382	90	
3,713	12,611	3,856	12,107	4,162	13,635	3,864	10,988	3,248	10,517	3,500	18,052	4,806	
19,765	118,951	18,503	111,212	46,371	104,169	60,516	136,963	49,651	108,816	58,389	129,821	65,026	
8,027	21,379	9,071	26,030	10,131	28,413	10,115	27,666	9,212	26,767	5,882	17,987	6,355	
485,278	**1,384,037**	**544,674**	**1,446,020**	**543,733**	**1,421,846**	**575,629**	**1,513,003**	**604,798**	**1,581,924**	**575,370**	**1,440,176**	**584,725,1**	
—	—	—	—	—	—	—	—	—	—	—	—	—	
602,716	**1,745,922**	**661,907**	**1,802,726**	**665,909**	**1,789,342**	**695,802**	**1,896,290**	**706,517**	**1,909,326**	**659,911**	**1,699,821**	**693,049**	1

Appendix XI.—*continued.*

(b.)—TABLE showing QUANTITIES and VALUES of BOOTS and SHOES IMPORTED
from 1873 to

Country from which Imported.	1873. Quantity.	1873. Value.	1874. Quantity.	1874. Value.	1875. Quantity.	1875. Value.	1876. Quantity.	1876. Value.
FOREIGN COUNTRIES.	Dozen Pairs.	£	Dozen Pairs.	£	Dozen Pairs.	£	Dozen Pairs.	£
Germany	7,780	29,803	6,222	23,891	9,040	34,371	18,432	66,151
Holland	5,769	26,190	3,922	17,575	3,320	14,481	3,073	13,724
Belgium	—	—	—	—	—	—	8,217	21,645
France	24,962	83,908	29,940	96,414	67,274	180,464	75,632	213,795
United States of America	—	—	—	—	—	—	—	—
Total from Foreign Countries	38,520	141,403	40,084	139,880	80,534	229,116	105,354	315,316
BRITISH POSSESSIONS.								
British North America	—	—	—	—	—	—	—	—
Other British Possessions	—	—	—	—	—	—	—	—
Total from British Possessions	—	—	—	—	—	—	—	—
From other Countries (not stated whether British or Foreign)	1,784	5,328	4,658	13,990	4,199	10,884	4,542	13,163
Grand Total imported into the United Kingdom	40,304	146,731	44,742	153,870	84,733	240,000	109,896	328,479

into the UNITED KINGDOM from the under-mentioned COUNTRIES in each YEAR 1893 inclusive.

	1877.		1878.		1879.		1880.		1881.		1882.
	Quantity.	Value.	Quantity.	Value.	Quantity.	Value.	Quantity.	Value.	Quantity.	Value.	Quantity.	Value.
	Dozen Pairs.	£	Dozen Pairs.	£	Dozen Pairs.	£	Dozen Pairs.	£	Dozen Pairs.	£	Dozen Pairs.	£
	11,794	30,376	14,785	37,546	—	—	12,864	38,887	16,901	73,760	25,244	69,801
	3,540	9,476	13,262	38,230	46,903	166,612	16,092	63,608	23,085	84,771	28,075	108,350
	8,089	19,966	2,144	7,925	4,799	16,170	—	—	—	—	9,506	25,258
	60,025	239,633	65,758	268,793	67,823	275,325	59,649	261,293	41,100	216,475	43,089	229,632
	5,939	15,963	1,879	6,178	2,827	5,927	—	—	—	—	—	—
	93,293	333,436	99,828	362,962	122,352	464,034	89,205	363,281	81,725	377,006	106,574	428,151
	5,818	14,058	2,642	6,352	3,053	9,446	2,821	7,694	2,049	4,818	—	—
	—	—	—	—	—	—	—	—	—	—	—	—
	5,818	14,058	2,642	6,352	3,053	9,446	2,821	7,694	2,049	4,818	—	—
	285	1,292	220	833	2,000	6,018	3,161	10,603	2,677	8,938	3,385	9,149
	99,396	348,786	102,690	370,147	127,504	479,498	95,487	381,579	86,451	390,756	109,959	437,300

Appendix XI.—*continued.*

(*b.*)—TABLE showing QUANTITIES and VALUES

Country from which Imported.	1883.		1884.		1885.		1886.	
	Quan-tity.	Value.	Quan-tity.	Value.	Quan-tity.	Value.	Quan-tity.	Value.
FOREIGN COUNTRIES.	Dozen Pairs.	£	Dozen Pairs.	£	Dozen Pairs.	£	Dozen Pairs.	£
Germany	3,766	10,478	957	3,509	2,703	6,073	7,469	15,153
Holland	23,321	85,585	15,539	50,481	15,974	57,993	15,080	51,886
Belgium	38,203	81.453	48,761	98,619	43,303	92,936	52,008	122,018
France	53,437	233,038	44,632	196,327	39,706	187,147	26,991	137,959
United States	331	1,400	—	—	—	—	—	—
Other Foreign Countries	—	—	—	—	163	587	210	690
Total from Foreign Countries	119,058	411,689	109,889	348,636	101,849	344,736	102,958	327,648
BRITISH POSSESSIONS.								
British North America	3,080	6,706	—	—	461	1,177	255	582
Australasia: New South Wales	29	100	—	—	—	—	—	—
Channel Islands	464	2,317	—	—	277	489	287	440
Other British Possessions	—	—	—	—	195	532	41	174
Total from British Possessions	3,573	9,133	—	—	933	2,148	583	1,196
From other Countries (not stated whether British or Foreign)	427	398	1,515	3,931	—	—	—	—
Grand Total imported into the United Kingdom	123,058	421,214	111,204	352,567	102,782	346,884	103,541	328,844

Appendix XI.—*continued*.

of Boots and Shoes IMPORTED. &c.—*continued*.

	1887.		1888.		1889.		1890.		1891.		1892.		1893.
	Quantity.	Value.	Quantity.	Value.	Quantity.	Value.	Quantity.	Value.	Quantity.	Value.	Quantity.	Value.	Quantity.	Value.
	Dozen Pairs.	£	Dozen Pairs.	£	Dozen Pairs.	£	Dozen Pairs.	£	Dozen Pairs.	£	Dozen Pairs.	£	Dozen Pairs.	£
	3,150	9,047	2,324	7,979	1,774	6,926	3,437	13,017	3,485	10,865	4,842	16,695	4,751	15,767
	10,302	44,950	15,680	50,522	14,120	48,540	8,015	25,573	9,201	30,649	14,434	46,009	23,501	75,702
	92,176	211,473	81,730	179,939	50,184	119,886	56,713	136,948	61,347	136,503	63,995	149,766	60,551	132,212
	33,662	175,921	27,815	147,466	28,343	159,311	29,644	153,178	26,700	144,307	34,166	158,487	31,134	145,255
	—	—	1,360	5,097	1,832	5,386	183	542	—	—	—	—	2,068	5,822
	441	1,505	125	419	71	415	123	414	875	4,577	395	1,489	84	297
	140,251	431,578	129,043	387,342	96,336	338,707	98,145	329,792	101,308	320,993	118,002	372,046	122,116	376,829
	528	1,123	742	2,191	3,788	11,985	1,312	4,262	680	1,592	311	622	71	195
	—	—	—	—	—	—	—	—	—	—	—	—	9	3
	134	262	—	—	—	—	—	—	—	—	—	—	—	9
	32	56	195	293	71	64	156	457	85	161	73	150	13	28
	694	1,441	937	2,484	3,859	12,140	1,468	3,219	774	1,753	384	772	103	227
	—	—	—	—	—	—	—	—	—	—	—	—	—	—
	140,945	433,019	129,980	389,826	100,195	350,856	99,613	333,011	102,082	322,746	118,386	372,818	122,219	379,056

Appendix XI.—*continued.*

(c).—TABLE showing QUANTITIES and VALUES of BOOTS and SHOES (of British and Irish Produce) EXPORTED from the PORT of LONDON during each of the YEARS from 1879 to 1893 inclusive.

Years.				Quantity.	Value.	Average Price Per Dozen Pairs.		
				Dozen Pairs.	£	£	s.	d.
1879 -	-	-	-	264,680	793,813	3	0	0
1880 -	-	-	-	233,534	729,641	3	2	6
1881 -	-	-	-	339,953	935,162	2	15	0
1882 -	-	-	-	413,061	1,192,691	2	17	9
1883 -	-	-	-	313,577	944,077	3	0	3
1884 -	-	-	-	337,806	1,005,573	2	19	6
1885 -	-	-	-	387,260	1,126,677	2	18	2
1886 -	-	-	-	347,449	1,011,640	2	18	3
1887 -	-	-	-	370,325	1,075,200	2	18	1
1888 -	-	-	-	432,407	1,148,665	2	13	2
1889 -	-	-	-	405,104	1,070,915	2	12	10
1890 -	-	-	-	431,154	1,149,921	2	13	4
1891 -	-	-	-	474,017	1,259,005	2	13	1
1892 -	-	-	-	429,914	1,078,145	2	10	2
1893 -	-	-	-	427,374	997,518	2	6	8

APPENDICES TO PART III.

APPENDICES TO PART III.

APPENDIX XII.

DETAILED TABLE showing RESULTS of INQUIRY as to CASES of IMMIGRANT WOMEN who landed in LONDON during a certain PERIOD of 1892.

Index No. of Immigrant.	Relative or Friend alleged to be in London.	Money alleged to be in Immigrant's Possession.	Result of Inquiry.
1. Man and wife	Friend	2 marks	Not known at address given. A Jewess, formerly a lodger there, *may* have been the friend whose address was given.
2. ,,	,,	45 marks	The address given proved to be that of a barber; the friend whose name was given is a customer of the barber. The latter knew No. 2, and said that he was getting on all right as a bootmaker, and his wife was with him and did not go out to work.
3. Man and daughter	,,	50 marks	The man, a tailor, and his daughter, age 13, stayed for six months at the address given. The girl is now in service as a nurserymaid.
6. Woman and child	Friends	20 marks	This woman went to friends at the address given, and is now living in the house of another member of her friends' family. She is very poor and not strong enough to do anything herself; her father came to England some time before, and supports her and her child.
7. German girl	—	—	Called herself a domestic servant, and gave no address.
8. Man and wife	Friend	240 marks	Address insufficient.
9. Woman and son, a shoe-maker.	Daughter	14 marks	The address given proved to be a common lodging-house for men. Nothing known of her.
10. Sempstress	Father	—	The girl joined her father, who, however, is not in London now. She learnt cigarette making, and can now earn about 8s. a week, but was then out of work through slackness. She lives with her mother.
11. Woman and five children.	Husband	—	All the people at the address given were newcomers, and knew nothing of their predecessors.
12. Man, brother, and sister.	—	—	Were sent to the United States by the Jewish Board of Guardians.
13. Single woman	Sister	20 marks	The sister was living at the address given. Said that No. 13 came over to her *fiancé*, who was in England, and was married at once.
14. ,, ,,	—	—	Was sent on to her brother in the United States by the Jewish Board of Guardians.
15. Married woman	Husband	10 marks	The persons living at the address given were newcomers and knew nothing of her.

Appendix XII.--cont.

Index No. of Immigrant.	Relative or Friend alleged to be in London.	Money alleged to be in Immigrant's Possession.	Result of Inquiry.
16. Austrian	Husband	13⁴ marks	No address given.
18. Married woman			She found her husband, but he refused to live with her. She does a little washing and cleaning, and is very poor.
19. Single woman	Sister	—	A girl at the address given said that No. 19 came there last May to a married sister who was lodging there. They moved afterwards. The married sister does not work; No. 19 makes button-holes.
20. „ „		6 marks	Occupiers at the address knew her. She went by a different name in England, but they were sure it was the same person. She came to a married sister as stated, lives with her still and goes out to work; her sister does not work. Statement afterwards verified.
22. Married woman and boy.	Husband	—	Saw No. 22; pretended to know nothing about No. 23 until the other lodgers began to speak about her, and then said she was her sister, and was now a button-holer earning about 10s. a week at the most. She professed to know nothing of No. 24 who was said to be her cousin.
23. Single woman	—	—	
24.	—	—	
25. Woman and child	Children	—	Occupier at address given said she was No. 25's daughter. No. 25 is living with a son at Peckham, and her husband (occupier's father) has now come over, and is getting on all right. No. 25 does not work.
26. Single woman	—	1 mark	Was taken to the Girls' Home and afterwards to her sister in London.
27. Married woman	Husband	—	Not known at address given.
29. „	—	—	Occupier at address given knew nothing of her.
30. Man and wife	—	5 marks	No Jews living at address given.
31. Married woman	Husband	—	Newcomers at the address given knew nothing of her.
35. „ „	—	—	The office keeper at the address given had no such name on his books. A Jew had lived there until March, and the woman might have stayed at his rooms for a time without the knowledge of the office-keeper.
36. „ „	„	116 marks	No such person known by the office-keeper at the address given.
38. Man and woman	—	—	In the alien list the woman was entered as the wife of the man, who was said to be drunk at the time, and to have made a statement that he was going to the United States, and had 200 marks. In the books of the Girls' Home is the name of a woman with the same first name (a peculiar one), who was brought there from the same ship, but did not stay the night, and was presumably called for by friends.
39. Widow	—	1 mark	Stated by the secretary of the Poor Jews' Shelter to have been sent on to United States.
40. Single woman (German)	—	35 marks	Gave no address and was not taken to the Girls' Home.

Appendix XII.—*cont.*

Index No. of Immigrant.	Relative or Friend alleged to be in London.	Money alleged to be in Immigrant's Possession.	Result of Inquiry.
41. Man, wife, and child	—	5 marks	Saw the man's wife at the address given; said her husband got work at once as a tailor. The three live in one small room, very clean, for which they pay 4s. a week.
42. Man and wife	Son	5 marks	Occupier at address given was a friend and knew them; said the man lived with his son, and his wife lived with a married daughter: she does not work for her living.
44. Widow	,,	6 marks	Saw an old woman who came *two* years ago to join her son, and had the same first name as No. 44; said no one had come to the house since. Probably No. 44 had given an account of this woman instead of an account of herself.
45. Man, wife, and two adult sons.	—	2 marks	Gave no address.
47. Single woman	Uncle	—	Address was that of a restaurant with lodgings for men only.
48. ,, ,,	—	10 marks	Not known at address given. Was taken to the Girls' Home when she landed; was there three days and then went into service; paid what she owed to the Home afterwards.
51. ,, ,,	Parents	—	Was taken to the Girls' Home, and then to her parents. Has not been to the Home since.
52. ,, ,,	—	—	No. 51 and No. 52 said they were sisters and both were taken to their alleged parents. But No. 52 was brought back, turning out to be no relation. A situation in service was found for her next day, to which she went.
53. ,, ,,	Mother	—	Was taken to the Girls' Home, and then to a married sister.
55. Widow	Daughter	10 marks	Not known at address given.
56. Married woman and child.	Husband	18 marks	Occupier at address given knew her. Said she joined her husband, a tin smith; does not go out to work.
57. Widow and four children.	—	3 marks	Not known at address given.
58. Married woman and three children.	—	—	Was sent on to New York by the Jewish Board of Guardians to join her husband.
59. Man and wife	Brother	26 marks	Saw the wife at address given. Said her husband was a cap-maker, as in Poland. She herself does not work.
60.⎱ 61.⎰ Widow, daughter, and two children.	Daughter	26 marks	Address was that of a public-house; nothing was known of them.
62. Widow	,,	—	Occupier at address given gave me No. 62's present address. Saw the woman herself, who said she was living with her children, who supported her.
64. Married woman and two children.	Husband	2 marks	The house of which the address was given is now part of the premises of a large shopkeeper, of whom it was useless to make inquiries.
65. Single woman	Brother	20 marks	Saw the brother at the address given. He said that his sister came over unexpectedly on a visit, and he sent her back again.

Appendix XII.—*cont.*

Index No. of Immigrant.	Relative or Friend alleged to be in London.	Money alleged to be in Immigrant's Possession.	Result of Inquiry.
66. Man and sister-in-law, and her child.	—	82 marks	The woman still lives at the address given. Her brother who was there when they came supported her for a few weeks, and now she earns her living as a nurse.
68. Single woman	Sister	1 mark	Married woman at the address given said her sister came to see her in May and was now in Colney Hatch; she had been in England before and had come back again. But her sister's name bore no resemblance to that of No. 68. The agent of the Girls' Home, however, stated that he took No. 68 to her sister at this address in May.
69. Married woman	Husband	8 marks	Gave no address.
71. Man and wife	—	1 mark	Received relief from the Jewish Board of Guardians some time after arrival.
72. Single woman	—	—	Saw her sister-in-law at the address given. Said that the girl is working for her brother as a fur sewer in the city, and lodges with a friend.
73. „ „ (German).	—	—	The agent of the Girls' Home took her to the office of the employer who had engaged her as domestic servant before she came over. She came to the Home recently to get another situation.
76. Single woman	—	150 marks	Address given was that of a shop, kept by her brother, who said that she came to live with him and went out to work as a button-holer for a short time. She is married now and only keeps house.
77. Man and wife	Uncle	25 marks	Not known by occupiers at address given. Some one did come there last year and went back again to Poland.
78. Married woman and two children.	Husband, a tailor.	—	Found a woman with the same surname at address given, but with different first name. Her husband is a tailor, but she has lived there two years and knew nothing of the woman I was inquiring about.
79. Married woman and child.	Husband	25 roubles	Occupier at address given said that the man had letters sent to his house and called for them. Occupier knew him years ago in Poland. The man's wife came over last year and joined him. Occupier knew they lived at Bow, but did not know their address.
81. Man and mother	—	50 marks	All gave the same address, but occupier said no strangers had been to the house at all during the last year. No. 102 who came over in the same ship did not know where they lived, but saw the sister now and then and knew she was a tailoress.
82. Sister	—	—	
83. Married woman	Son	100 marks	
84. Man and wife	—	—	Occupier had only been at address given six months, and knew nothing of his predecessors. (The man had lived in London eight years and had then gone back to Poland.)
86. Married woman	Husband	—	Not known at address given.
87. „ „ „	„	—	Husband of 87 met them when they landed.
88. and mother and children	—	—	

Appendix XII.—*cont.*

Index No. of Immigrant.	Relative or Friend alleged to be in London.	Money alleged to be in Immigrant's Possession.	Result of Inquiry.
89. Man and wife and } 90. Sister and three children • }	—	20 marks •	Not known at address given.
91. Man and sister •	—	3 marks •	,, ,,
92. Single woman	Sister; had lost address.	—	A girl entered in the books of the Girls' Home by a different name was met on board this ship. She had lost her sister's address. Her relatives were found, and she was taken to them. The girl was undoubtedly the same. Probably she had given the Customs agent her sister's name instead of her own.
93. Married woman •	Daughter •	—	Not known at address given.
94. ,, ,, and children.	Seeking husband.	3 roubles	Applied for and received assistance from the Jewish Board of Guardians.
95. Man and sister •	Friend •	30 marks•	Saw the sister. She lived with her cousin, and did nothing for three months. Then she got work at a capmakers in a small Jewish workshop where she machines linings. She is 20 years old and earns only 6s, a week as at first.
96. Woman • •	—	—	No address given.
98. Married woman •	Husband •	4 marks •	The occupiers at address given said that a woman with the same first name (Sprenza) came there from Poland in 1893 to join her husband, a hawker; her other name bore no resemblance to the one given me.
99. Married woman and two children.	Husband •	—	There are two houses with the same number as in the address given. One of these was a stationer's shop. Occupiers in both cases were quite sure no such person had ever come there. Possibly letters were sent to the stationer and called for by the husband who may have met the woman on board.
102. Single woman •	Brother •	3 marks •	Saw her at address given. Strong and good looking. Is living in her brother's house and works for him. Fairly well-to-do.
103. Man and daughter •	—	5 marks •	Incorrect address.
104. Woman and brother	Father •	—	Occupier at address given knew them. The woman lives with her father, and earns her living as a monthly nurse.
105. Woman • •	—	—	Gave same address as 104, but was not known there.
106. Married woman and two children.	Husband •	4 marks •	Address given was that of a general shop. Occupier said the woman came over last year and found that her husband was living with another woman. She is very poor, and comes in occasionally to ask if they can find her some washing or cleaning to do.
107. Married woman •	Children •	6 marks •	Residents of three houses in the street remembered some one whom they called Blumberg (the first name of No. 107 was Blume) who came last July to the address given, and lived with her children there. They had moved to a neighbouring street and her children still support her.

Appendix XII.—*cont.*

Index No. of Immigrant.	Relative or Friend alleged to be in London.	Money alleged to be in Immigrant's Possession.	Result of Inquiry.
108. Man and wife and 109. daughter	—	—	Occupiers at address given knew about them. They had moved now. The man is a tailor; his wife does nothing, and his daughter goes out to work somewhere, but they did not know where.
110. Woman	Sister	—	Address unintelligible.
111. Single woman	Parents	—	Incorrect address. Was taken to the Girls' Home and then to her brother's house.
112. Married woman and child.	Husband	150 marks	Was not at address given. Found out about her from the keeper of a grocer's shop who knew her in Poland. She came over to find her husband. He had heard that she had divorced him (which was not true), and had married again: he was living somewhere in the Commercial Road; he was a very respectable man, but too poor to do anything for his first wife. She is lame, and hardly able to work; she lodges with a girl who makes wigs; she gets orders occasionally for her and has a small commission on them; but on the whole she lives on the charity of neighbours.
113. Man, wife, and children.	—	200 marks	No address given.
114. Man, wife 115. daughter, and son.	Son	—	Their son, a well-dressed young man, came to meet them.
116. Married woman	Husband	—	Not known at address given.

APPENDIX XIII.

TABLE showing PARTICULARS of UNMARRIED FOREIGN GIRLS brought to the JEWISH HOME FOR GIRLS on landing.

Date of Landing.	Index No.	Remarks.
July 1892	118	Had lost address of relatives; was taken to the Home; stayed two days, and was then taken to her relatives.
	92	See foregoing list of immigrants.
,,	111	,,
,,	120	Was found employment at dressmaking; lived at the Home and went out to work. At the end of one month went to America to join her brother who sent her the ticket to go. Still owes 26s. for board.
,,	121	Situation found for her as domestic servant. Was saving up money to go to America. Paid up her debts to the Home.

Appendix XIII.—*cont.*

Date of Landing.	Index No.	Remarks.
July 1892	122	Had a cousin in London who refused to receive her. At the end of a week she found friends, and obtained work as a tailoress (her occupation in Poland); paid the 5s. due to the Home three months afterwards.
„	123	Was a tailoress in Poland. Situation as domestic servant found for her at the end of a week; paid the 5s. due to the Home three weeks afterwards.
„	124	Could not find her friends when she landed. Was taken to the Home; her friends came the same day and took her away.
„	125	Came with her married sister on the way to America. Her married sister went; but there was not enough money for her. She went into service and paid her debt to the Home within three weeks.
„	126	Lost address of relatives; did not find them until a month afterwards; went out as a dressmaker in the meantime. Was engaged to be married when she came. Relatives were very respectable. She is now married.
„	127	A German, not Jewish, but accustomed to live with Jewish people. A situation was found for her. She owed 7s. to the Home, and paid it a fortnight after. Is in the same place still and visits the Home.
„	128	Went to a situation as domestic servant the day after her arrival.
„	129	Parents were sent to Siberia. She came to England. Stayed in the Home till January 1893, and then started as a dressmaker on her own account and is doing well. Had worked at a dressmaker's in the meantime, earning from 8s. to 10s. a week.
„	130	At the Home for four days; then went to relatives; did not pay what she owed. "Those who go to relatives rarely do."
„	131	Had an address of a brother in Essex. One of her brothers came to the Home and sent her to the other brother in Essex.
August 1892	132	Came with her father, who had lost the address of his friends. Her father came for her five days afterwards.
„	133	Had lost her brother's address; found him two days afterwards. Is a dressmaker.
„	134, 135, and 136.	Three sisters; came with No. 137 who had a cousin in London. They took a room and lived together; two of them found work at a glove shop and the third as a button-holer.
„	137	Had a cousin in London. Stayed 11 days at the Home, and then found work at an umbrella maker's, and paid her account. Is a good hand and learnt the trade in Poland. Is still at the same place.
„	138	Was on the way to America; a man took her ship ticket and money and got her in his power. He said she was his wife; she resisted him and came to the Home. Was given money to go to United States and put in charge of the guard.
„	139	Address and purse stolen; went into service.
September 1892	140	A Christian girl; was taken to the Travellers' Aid Society.
October 1892	141	A German; came over to a situation and was taken to it.
December 1892	142	Came from Germany; travelled first class. Was brought to the Home by the agent for the Poor Jews' Shelter. Was sent on to the United States by the Jewish Board of Guardians.

APPENDIX XIV.

STATEMENT showing the NUMBER of MACHINES used, and the NUMBER of PERSONS employed in certain JEWISH WORK-SHOPS in various districts of EAST LONDON.

The information given in this Table was kindly furnished by the COLLECTORS of the "SINGER MANUFACTURING COMPANY."

GENERAL SUMMARY for COMMERCIAL ROAD, MILE END ROAD, ALDGATE, and WHITECHAPEL DISTRICTS.

—	Workshops on the List of Factory Inspector and known to Collectors.	Workshops in which Number of Machines was known.	Number of Machines.	Workshops in which Number of Persons was known approximately.	Number of Persons approximately.
Fur and Waterproof -	9	4	5	4	35
Dress - -	24	20	31	17	65
Caps -	27	21	154	22	317
Mantles - -	33	32	138	31	303
Vests and Juvenile Suits.	12	11	16	9	94
Trousers	32	27	64	26	248
Total -	137	115	438	109	1,062
Coats and General:					
Stock - -	169	165	574	150	1,265
Order - -	156	134	339	147	848
Doubtful -	47	36	71	29	225 (100 in one workshop.)
Total	372	335	984	326	2,338
Grand Total -	509	470	1,422	435	3,400

ADDENDUM to above Table, showing the AVERAGE NUMBER of MACHINES and PERSONS per WORKSHOP, and of PERSONS per MACHINE.

—	Average Number of Machines to a Workshop.	Average Number of Persons to a Workshop.	Average Number of Persons to a Machine.
Caps - -	7·3	14·4	2·0
Mantles - -	4·3	9·8	2·3
Trousers - -	2·4	9·5	4·0
Coats and General:			
Stock -	3·5 } 2·9	8·4 } 7·1	2·4 } 2·5
Order -	2·2 }	5·8 }	3·6 }

Appendix XIV.—*cont.*

STATEMENT showing the NUMBER of MACHINES used, and the NUMBER of PERSONS employed in certain JEWISH WORK-SHOPS in various Districts of EAST LONDON.

(1.) COMMERCIAL ROAD DISTRICT.

—	Workshops on the List of Factory Inspector and known to Collectors.	Workshops in which Number of Machines was known.	Number of Machines.	Workshops in which Number of Persons was known approximately.	Number of Persons approximately.
Fur and Waterproof -	2	2	3	2	28
Dress - - -	9	9	14	6	25
Caps -	10	7	46	8	104
Mantles - -	13	13	64	13	145
Vests and Juvenile Suits.	8	8	37	7	76
Trousers -	24	20	48	19	213
Total -	66	59	212	55	591
Coats and General:					
Stock -	48	47	209	44	557
Order -	75	73	171	69	489
Doubtful - -	19	11	25	6	145 (100 in one workshop.)
Total - -	142	131	405	119	1,191
Grand Total -	208	190	617	174	1,782

ADDENDUM to above Table, showing the AVERAGE NUMBER of MACHINES and PERSONS per WORKSHOP, and of PERSONS per MACHINE.

—	Average Number of Machines to a Workshop.	Average Number of Persons to a Workshop.	Average Number of Persons to a Machine.
Caps - - - -	6·6	13·0	2·0
Mantles - - -	4·9	11·2	2·3
Vests and Juvenile Suits -	4·6	10·9	2·3
Trousers (19 Order, 3 Stock, 2 Doubtful).	2·4	11·2	4·7
Coats:			
Stock - - -	4·4 } 3·2	12·7 } 9·3	2·8 } 2·9
Order - -	2·3 }	7·1 }	3·0 }

STATEMENT showing the NUMBER of MACHINES used, and the NUMBER of PERSONS employed in certain JEWISH WORK-SHOPS in various Districts of EAST LONDON.

(2.) MILE END ROAD DISTRICT.

—	Workshops on the List of Factory Inspector and known to Collectors.	Workshops in which Number of Machines was known.	Number of Machines.	Workshops in which Number of Persons was known approximately.	Number of Persons approximately.
Fur	5	1	1	1	4
Dress	9	5	6	5	10
Caps	4	3	8	4	67
Mantles	14	11	12	13	87
Vests and Juvenile Suits.	2	1	3	1	8
Trousers	2	1	3	1	5
Total	36	25	63	25	181
Coats and General:					
Stock	27	24	84	16	120
Order	52	52	104	50	232
Doubtful	6	4	11	5	33
Total	85	80	199	71	385
Grand Total	121	105	262	96	566

ADDENDUM to above Table, showing the AVERAGE NUMBER of MACHINES and PERSONS per WORKSHOP, and of PERSONS per MACHINE.

—	Average Number of Machines to a Workshop.	Average Number of Persons to a Workshop.	Average Number of Persons to a Machine.
Caps	2·7	16·75	6·3
Mantles	3·0	9·7	2·2
Coats:			
Stock	3·5 } 2·5	7·5 } 5·3	2·1 } 2·2
Order	2·0 }	4·6 }	2·3 }

Appendix XIV.—*cont.*

STATEMENT showing the NUMBER of MACHINES used and the NUMBER of PERSONS employed in certain JEWISH WORK-SHOPS in various Districts of EAST LONDON.

(3.) ALDGATE and WHITECHAPEL DISTRICT.

—	Workshops on the List of Factory Inspector and known to Collectors.	Workshops in which Number of Machines was known.	Number of Machines.	Workshops in which Number of Persons was known approximately.	Number of Persons approximately.
Fur · · ·	2	1	1	1	3
Dress · · ·	6	6	11	6	30
Caps · · ·	13	11	100	10	146
Mantles · ·	6	5	32	5	71
Vests and Juvenile Suits.	2	2	6	1	10
Trousers · ·	6	6	13	6	30
Total · ·	35	31	163	29	290
Coats and General :					
Stock ·	94	94	281	90	588
Order · ·	29	29	64	28	127
Doubtful · ·	22	21	35	18	47
Total · ·	145	144	380	136	762
Grand Total ·	180	175	543	165	1,052

ADDENDUM to above Table, showing the AVERAGE NUMBER of MACHINES and PERSONS per WORKSHOP, and of PERSONS per MACHINE.

—	Average Number of Machines to a Workshop.	Average Number of Persons to a Workshop.	Average Number of Persons to a Machine.
Caps · · · ·	9·1	14·6	1·6
Mantles ·	6·4	14·2	2·2
Trousers · · ·	2·2	5·0	2·3
Coats and General :			
Stock · · · ·	3·0 } 2·8	6·5 } 6·1	2·2 } 2·2
Order · · · ·	2·2 }	4·5 }	2·1 }

APPENDIX XV.

TABLE showing for certain JEWISH TAILORING WORKSHOPS of various Classes* in Leeds, London, and Manchester, the Per-centage that the Number employed at each Occupation was of the Total, distinguishing Males from Females.

Locality and Class* of Workshop.	Males.			Females.				Total Number on which Percentages are based.†
	Pressers.	Tailors.	Machinists.	Machinists.	Buttonholers.	Fellers.	Finishers.	
Leeds:								
Class I. -	10·7	20·0	26·9	5·5	13·4	17·0	6·5	996
„ II. -	9·5	16·5	25·1	6·4	15·8	19·4	7·3	454
„ III. -	10·6	18·5	23·8	8·8	12·8	16·3	9·2	227
All Classes	10·4	18·8	26·0	6·2	14·0	17·5	7·1	1,677
London:								
Class III. -	14·0	22·5	24·1	1·3	12·7	25·4		386
„ IVa. -	12·1	21·5	27·6	—	12·1	26·7		116
„ IVb. -	13·7	37·3	25·5	—	15·7	7·8		51
All Classes -	13·6	23·7	25·0	·9	12·8	24·0		553
Manchester:								
Class III. -	14·5	27·2	24·6	·8	15·5	17·4		386
„ IVa. -	16·3	27·9	25·9	·7	13·6	15·6		147
„ IVb. -	13·8	37·9	31·0	—	6·9	10·4		29
All Classes -	14·9	27·9	25·3	·7	14·6	16·6		562
Leeds -	55·2			44·8				1,677
London -	62·2			37·8				553
Manchester -	68·1			31·9				562

* Class I. includes workshops in which the number employed was 40 or above; Class II., 25 to 40; Class III., 10 to 25; Class IVa., 6 to 10; and Class IVb., under 6 persons.
† Errand boys and errand girls are not included.

APPENDIX XVI.

TABLE showing the VALUE of APPAREL and SLOP CLOTHING EXPORTED
Year, from 1873

Countries to which Exported.	1873. Value.	1874. Value.	1875. Value.	1876. Value.
FOREIGN COUNTRIES.	£	£	£	£
Germany	27,535	30,661	32,862	33,877
Holland	—	—	—	—
Belgium	64,236	65,723	59,296	61,000
France	38,460	34,997	39,860	51,550
Egypt	53,712	—	111,760	—
United States of America	178,533	182,957	94,349	74,017
South America:				
Chili	90,844	47,827	34,467	31,687
Brazil	35,100	19,206	38,260	32,046
Republic of Columbia	61,530	45,103	—	—
Argentine Republic	236,612	100,167	71,433	27,220
Other Countries	98,552	35,839	—	—
Other Foreign Countries	—	68,179	—	—
Total to Foreign Countries	**900,114**	**660,659**	**482,236**	**311,397**
BRITISH POSSESSIONS.				
Channel Islands	—	—	—	—
British Possessions in South Africa	458,114	427,528	523,340	529,280
India, Ceylon, Straits Settlements, and British East Indies.	78,069	104,105	95,464	86,658
Australasia:				
West Australia				
South Australia				
Victoria	1,419,720	1,411,283	1,461,630	1,467,009
New South Wales				
Queensland				
Tasmania				
New Zealand	—	—	—	—
Other Colonies	—	—	—	—
British North America	245,955	284,814	289,268	233,321
British West Indies and British Guiana	98,503	98,096	84,476	101,951
Other British Possessions	—	—	—	—
Total to British Possessions	**2,300,939**	**2,325,829**	**2,454,187**	**2,418,219**
To other Countries (not stated whether British or Foreign).	236,357	214,365	248,902	232,437
Grand Total Exported from the United Kingdom	**3,437,410**	**3,200,853**	**3,185,325**	**2,962,053**

APPENDIX XVI.

from the United Kingdom to the under-mentioned Countries in each
to 1893 inclusive.

1877.	1878.	1879.	1880.	1881.	1882.
Value.	Value.	Value.	Value.	Value.	Value.
£	£	£	£	£	£
25,784	25,970	21,540	14,962	14,078	21,559
—	—	19,940	18,792	15,900	15,743
49,072	54,080	52,030	62,535	56,802	58,389
54,469	81,218	128,860	145,794	111,194	95,702
—	—	—	7,780	—	—
51,052	50,555	64,720	68,702	64,337	58,579
20,072	12,093	—	15,030	13,923	22,243
29,781	27,382	23,040	23,751	16,216	17,112
—	—	22,740	27,071	22,155	18,514
—	24,050	30,530	27,246	11,180	12,840
—	—	—	10,150	11,237	14,267
—	—	42,690	45,194	58,243	42,363
230,230	**284,348**	**405,000**	**463,747**	**461,565**	**407,371**
—	—	15,840	4,206	11,738	11,518
431,361	628,332	890,890	917,101	1,034,714	1,083,021
82,518	71,800	94,651	95,527	109,644	106,676
1,536,158	1,626,741	1,417,510	1,364,861	1,702,694	2,120,354
—	—	—	—	—	—
203,018	189,046	134,700	156,197	179,472	200,866
80,041	87,195	95,770	95,185	71,051	101,715
—	—	13,447	27,062	43,444	47,049
2,341,896	**2,634,114**	**2,662,808**	**2,637,199**	**3,155,814**	**3,671,199**
261,248	257,250	144,043	108,457	94,448	90,812
2,834,074	**3,176,412**	**3,208,941**	**3,212,103**	**3,711,797**	**4,169,382**

Appendix XVI.—*cont.*

TABLE showing the VALUE of APPAREL and

Countries to which Exported.	1883.	1884.	1885.	1886.
	Value.	Value.	Value.	Value.
FOREIGN COUNTRIES.	£	£	£	£
Germany	30,713	44,775	52,267	59,818
Holland	20,548	27,228	29,985	28,470
Belgium	64,805	69,892	71,436	72,055
France	139,008	238,666	206,451	239,930
Egypt	20,030	20,272	42,291	38,251
United States of America	70,221	100,655	102,246	105,816
South America :				
Chili	17,405	25,071	17,170	12,485
Brazil	25,300	26,852	27,804	43,352
Republic of Colombia	33,407	41,952	54,511	38,571
Argentine Republic	48,216	63,026	43,263	40,932
Other Countries	13,765	30,753	25,368	22,542
Other Foreign Countries	47,970	46,817	124,792	129,851
Total to Foreign Countries	**538,667**	**745,899**	**778,274**	**832,073**
BRITISH POSSESSIONS.				
Channel Islands	11,236	13,017	14,124	8,375
British Possessions in South Africa	549,876	628,368	623,035	548,069
India, Ceylon, Straits Settlements, and British East Indies.	117,465	161,016	167,430	151,406
Australasia :				
West Australia			33,270	39,000
South Australia			230,925	146,415
Victoria	1,924,591	1,895,963	342,258	370,157
New South Wales			883,070	799,712
Queensland			225,427	186,280
Tasmania			47,785	88,684
New Zealand	—	—	389,272	339,017
Other Colonies	—	—	2,303	900
British North America	218,155	225,008	246,203	260,397
British West Indies and British Guiana	120,402	123,229	113,836	106,723
Other British Possessions	20,491	13,170	63,909	51,244
Total to British Possessions	**2,962,219**	**3,060,961**	**3,382,876**	**3,070,138**
To other Countries (not stated whether British or Foreign).	132,918	129,623	—	—
Grand Total Exported from the United Kingdom	**3,633,804**	**3,936,483**	**4,161,150**	**3,902,211**

Appendix XVI.—*cont.*

Slop Clothing EXPORTED, &c.—*continued.*

1887.	1888.	1889.	1890.	1891.	1892.	1893.
Value.	Value.	Value.	Value.	Value.	Value.	Value.
£	£	£	£	£	£	£
74,324	67,226	64,195	60,884	61,680	61,250	55,615
25,521	26,365	30,232	30,003	34,570	27,894	25,679
37,582	29,566	35,754	31,954	35,028	30,659	31,062
224,182	194,710	198,617	224,055	218,175	121,170	59,389
24,758	29,045	39,451	40,706	42,668	45,315	51,893
111,024	117,048	179,225	205,770	138,189	127,086	102,270
11,420	26,934	37,884	23,226	24,049	37,305	29,652
31,465	73,896	49,226	53,670	49,862	32,043	46,761
95,080	36,187	22,048	23,122	20,934	28,292	19,820
55,448	64,377	80,225	29,724	11,673	20,550	18,901
25,284	25,584	23,835	19,280	8,289	13,849	27,822
163,820	188,009	200,858	208,635	222,300	177,627	175,164
855.878	**837,712**	**952,863**	**949,641**	**877,034**	**723,540**	**644,377**
11,483	12,175	16,067	20,910	27,715	31,753	35,268
829,715	941,015	1,315,657	1,328,424	1,119,852	1,263,626	1,250,796
167,298	169,550	129,140	163,841	177,470	170,713	161,856
33,020	58,005	50,386	55,892	52,195	69,138	52,025
144,321	205,988	182,410	211,182	229,074	174,460	144,221
326,070	146,788	137,017	109,058	154,622	136,210	209,619
658,185	805,590	719,482	739,408	947,510	763,063	505,250
194,544	277,372	254,252	195,020	264,085	240,948	160,674
46,680	57,750	61,349	68,309	89,057	74,245	18,554
280,260	271,948	277,520	284,808	305,489	551,151	320,068
1,554	1,308	1,592	792	1,164	1,879	1,747
227,748	294,984	341,349	406,068	576,798	505,584	342,004
110,105	110,783	135,757	189,502	149,944	171,248	263,894
52,562	65,754	70,464	73,376	82,657	79,164	78,959
3,091,428	**3,820,877**	**4,025,650**	**4,086,056**	**4,273,897**	**4,123,551**	**3,615,273**
—	—	—	—	—	—	—
3,947.306	**4,658,589**	**4,978,513**	**5,035,697**	**5,150,931**	**4,847,091**	**4,259,650**

INDEX.

www.ingramcontent.com/pod-product-compliance
Lightning Source LLC
Chambersburg PA
CBHW030323270326
41926CB00010B/1482